Frederick Cornwallis Conybeare

The Apology and Acts of Apollonius

and other monuments of early Christianity

Frederick Cornwallis Conybeare

The Apology and Acts of Apollonius
and other monuments of early Christianity

ISBN/EAN: 9783337402822

Printed in Europe, USA, Canada, Australia, Japan

Cover: Foto ©ninafisch / pixelio.de

More available books at **www.hansebooks.com**

THE

APOLOGY AND ACTS OF APOLLONIUS

AND OTHER

MONUMENTS OF EARLY CHRISTIANITY

EDITED WITH A

GENERAL PREFACE INTRODUCTIONS NOTES ETC.

BY

F. C. CONYBEARE M.A.

Late Fellow of University College Oxford

London
SWAN SONNENSCHEIN & CO.
NEW YORK: MACMILLAN & CO.
1894

To my Friend,

GALOUST TÉR-MEKÊRTCHIAN,

Deacon of the Armenian Church,

in memory of many pleasant hours passed in his monastery of edschmiadzin.

CONTENTS.

	PAGE
GENERAL PREFACE	1

APOLOGY AND ACTS OF APOLLONIUS.
INTRODUCTION	29
TRANSLATION OF TEXT	35

ACTS OF PAUL AND THEKLA.
INTRODUCTION	49
TRANSLATION OF TEXT	61

ACTS OF S. PHOCAS.
INTRODUCTION	89
TRANSLATION OF TEXT	103

ACTS OF S. POLYEUCTES.
INTRODUCTION	123
TRANSLATION OF TEXT	126

ACTS OF SAINT EUGENIA.
INTRODUCTION	147
TRANSLATION OF TEXT	157

ACTS OF S. CODRATIUS.
INTRODUCTION	191
TRANSLATION OF TEXT	193

ACTS OF THEODORE.
INTRODUCTION	217
TRANSLATION OF TEXT	220

ACTS OF S. THALELÆUS.

	PAGE
INTRODUCTION	239
TRANSLATION OF TEXT	243

ACTS OF S. HIZTIBOUZIT.

INTRODUCTION	257
TRANSLATION OF TEXT	261

ACTS OF S. CALLISTRATUS.

INTRODUCTION	273
TRANSLATION OF TEXT	289

ACTS OF S. DEMETRIUS.

INTRODUCTION	337
TRANSLATION OF TEXT	341

ADDENDA 353

INDEX OF NAMES AND SUBJECTS . . 355

MONUMENTS OF EARLY CHRISTIANITY.

GENERAL PREFACE.

THE object of the following translations is to give the reader, in a succession of vivid pictures or glimpses, an insight into the practical working of Christianity during the first three centuries of its history. *Aim of these translations.* While we freely admire the heroism of the martyrs, we must not suppose that the highest temper of the new religion was displayed in these desperate struggles,[1] through which its champions bore witness to the truth, as they deemed it, of their beliefs, and in engaging in which they were, on any view, asserting the rights of individual conscience and private judgment against the overbearing weight of a government despotic in its form, and supported in its assaults by innumerable popular forces and scruples, social, religious, and political.[2] The best fruits of Christ-

---

[1] In the following pages we shall not find any martyr who in the moment of agony prays, Father, forgive them, they know not what they do. The note struck is more frequently one of hatred, defiance, and imprecation.

[2] Cp. *Minucii Felicis Octavius*, cap. 37 : quam pulchrum spectaculum

ianity were of course reaped not in these crises, not in these supreme moments of storm and stress, but in the higher religious conceptions, in the wider charity, in the purer social and family life, in the elimination of obscene or cruel religious rites and amusements, which on the whole went with the abandonment of paganism. But these blessings could not be secured for the multitude, could not be secured at all, unless a stand were made against enactments which made the very name and profession of Christian an offence punishable by any, even the most horrible, forms of death. A martyrdom resembled a battle in general history; freedom from molestation and liberty to enjoy the fruits of peace could not be secured in any other way.

The originals of these translations are to be found in a repertory of select martyrdoms, written in the ancient Armenian tongue, and published at the Armenian monastery of San Lazaro, in Venice, in the year 1874. These originals are in nearly all cases themselves versions of still more ancient Greek or Syriac texts. In some cases Latin versions also of considerable antiquity are preserved, and will be found in the *Annals of Baronius*, or in the vast

Armenian, Syriac, Greek, and Latin texts of Martyrs' Acts.

---

deo, cum Christianus cum dolore congreditur, cum aduersum minas et supplicia et tormenta componitur, cum strepitum mortis et honorem inridens carnifici se inculcat, cum libertatem suam aduersus reges et principes erigit, cum soli deo cuius est cedit, cum triumphator et victor ipsi qui adversum se sententiam dixit insultat.

collection of the Lives of the Saints of all ages, at which the Society of the Jesuits has now been at work for over one hundred years, and which is known as the Bollandist Acts of the Saints. I have not chosen to translate the Armenian form of these documents rather than the Latin or Greek without reason; and my reason is this: that as a rule the ancient Armenian version gives an earlier form of the narrative than either the Latin or Greek or Syriac manuscripts now yield us. For it is one of the first things which the student of early Christian literature has to learn, that its documents were continually being altered and recast to suit every fresh development or change in the dogmatic beliefs, moral conceptions, and discipline of believers, whether orthodox or heretical. What was believed in the first century was not believed in the same way, and was not all that was believed in the second; and what was orthodox in the second century was in many cases heterodox, and in nearly all cases insufficiently explicit in the third and fourth centuries.[1] The value of the Armenian versions lies in this, that they often give us access to a more primitive form of a Christian writing than has survived in Greek or Latin. To take an

The Armenian form as a rule the oldest.

Christian revision of texts in each age.

---

[1] Thus the Armenian Acts of Athanagines retain the colophon of one, Hilarion, who states that in composing the Acts he "on paper made orthodox all that was said" (by the various actors). Athanagines no doubt, like many martyrs of Nicomedia, was an Arian.

example: the Armenian text of the Acts of S. Eugenia represents her as choosing for her model Thekla, the convert of S. Paul. Now Thekla, even as early as the days of Tertullian, became suspect, on account of her having arrogated to herself the right to baptize. Accordingly we find that in the old Latin version, dating probably from the fourth century, every mention of her is carefully expunged from the Acts in question, and Paul and his epistles replace her and her story in such a manner as even to make nonsense of the context. So again into the Epistle of the Smyrneans, written about A.D. 160, and describing the death of Polycarp, there were foisted, as early as the time of Rufinus' Latin translation of it, a series of references to the Holy Catholic Church. Now the latter phrase did not come into vogue until the latter half of the third century, and some critics have in consequence maintained that the letter of the Smyrneans is a forgery of that date. But the difficulty vanishes when we turn to the old Armenian version of the "Church History" of Eusebius, who quotes the letter at length; for there we find, instead of the obnoxious phrase, the simple and primitive expression which we meet with in the Acts, viz., "the Churches" in such and such a region.

But what the third and fourth century editors most delighted to do, was to embellish an earlier document with miracles, if it were free from them; or if it already contained miraculous elements, then

Interpolation of miracles.

to vary and enhance them. Rationalists have impugned the historical character of the New Testament, because it has in it such elements; and even orthodox critics, among Protestants at least, have for the same reason condemned in the most sweeping manner the so-called legends of the saints; so much so that no serious historian has ventured to use them. Both sets of critics are equally unphilosophical. The real miracle would be, if we should find a homely narrative emanating from Galilee in the first century to have originally contained no such elements; and most of the arguments adduced against the value of the Gospels as a contemporary narrative, would prove, *mutatis mutandis*, that S. Bernard's account of the miracles of his friend, S. Malachi, is spurious. In appraising the historical value of an early Christian document, we ought to condemn it, not in case it contain miraculous elements, but in case it be wholly lacking in local colour, in case the sentiments and teachings put into the mouths of the actors and the actions attributed to them be foreign to their age and country, so far as of these we have any reliable knowledge. Here are the true touchstones of truth and genuineness; and we shall be encouraged to apply them, if we find that in a narrative that on the whole stands well these tests, the miraculous elements vary and are different in the different recensions of the

Early documents not to be condemned because they relate miracles.

The true tests of genuineness.

text; so that like the plus and minus quantities of an algebraical formula, they eliminate one another, and in the net result disappear, leaving behind them a solid residuum of graphic and life-like narrative. This is particularly the case with regard to the Acts of Paul and Thekla, as we shall point out in dealing with that history; in the Acts of Thalelæus we meet, though in a less degree, with the same sort of corroboration of their general truth. So is the old adage confirmed: ἐσθλοὶ μὲν γὰρ ἁπλῶς, παντοδαπῶς δὲ κακοί.

Characteristics of early Acts. There are a few characteristics of the Acts of Saints of the first three centuries which deserve to be noticed in a general preface.

1. The most historical element in them often lies where we should the least expect to find it, namely in the dialogues between the judge and the accused. This will be a surprise to those who are familiar with the somewhat different method pursued by ancient historians, who put into the mouths of the actors not what they actually said, even where this was readily accessible, but what they ought in the judgment of the historian to have said. Thus Tacitus, on the occasion of the admission of the inhabitants of Gallia Comata to the ius honorum, puts into the mouth of the Emperor Claudius a speech which we know he did not make, because the actual words he used are preserved in an inscription found at Lyons, the contents of which were taken from

The dialogue most often genuine,

the *Acta Senatus*, or journal of the Senate. The early Christians must be allowed to have started with a higher standard of truth. They considered it of the first importance to register the last acts and words of a saint, and one of their number was frequently deputed to fulfil the task. In addition to their own reports they could draw upon the official reports of the law-courts, though these may not have been always accessible to them before the age of Constantine, when in the archives of many a court the reports of the trials of the third century at least may easily have survived. And in this connection we must remember that Christianity was such a grave offence that the *procès-verbal* of trials would be carefully recorded and preserved by a government so methodical and observant of precedents as was the Roman. From the time of Domitian, if not at a still earlier date, the very name of Christian exposed a person to the penalty of death. If information was laid against a man to the effect that he was a Christian, he was summoned before a magistrate and ordered to sacrifice to some god, often to the genius of the reigning emperor. The usual answer returned was: "I am a Christian, and will not sacrifice to idols and to foul evil spirits." Tortures were then used to compel submission, and if these failed the culprit was sentenced to death.

2. Jesus of Nazareth addressed His teachings to Jews, who needed no inculcation of the truths

of monotheism; and accordingly we find very little denunciation in the Gospels of the folly and sin of idolatry. It is far otherwise with the Epistles of Paul, which are addressed to converts from polytheism. His polemic, when not directed against those who insisted on circumcision and the sabbath, is turned against the worship of images and of many gods, instead of the One who made the heavens and the earth and created man in His own image.

<small>Monotheistic teaching of the Jews and early Christians.</small>

But the protest in Greek literature against idolatry and polytheism did not begin with S. Paul and with Christianity. Leaving out of account the lofty monotheism, coupled with ridicule of the popular religion, which we meet with in the writings of a long line of Greek philosophers, beginning with Xenophanes in the fifth century B.C.; it is enough here to note, that the works of a writer like Philo of Alexandria, who died about A.D. 40, at the advanced age of seventy, are a sustained polemic against the worship of any created being, whether sun or moon or stars, whether man or beast or the work of men's hands. In an almost prophetic passage this writer makes the proud boast that his race were destined to be the teachers of true religion to the whole of the civilized world; and there is an aspect of the Jewish monotheistic missionary effort of the first century, of which we may take Paul or Philo as the coryphæi, which is in striking contrast with the general teaching of the Christian

Church in later ages. Neither Paul nor Philo believed in the ancient Gods, in Apollo and Artemis, and in the rest. These gods were to their minds mere names, figments of the heathen imagination, mythoplasms, as Philo calls them; powerless for good or for evil, just because they were lifeless and spiritless inventions, because they were nothing. Philo was inclined to regard the gods and goddesses as personifications of the elements; so Here or Juno, he tells us, is derived from the word air, and Demeter is a name given to the earth, because the earth is the mother of all. These explanations he borrowed from contemporary Stoics like Cornutus, who were apologising for a worn out mythology. But Philo was not apologising, and merely wished to explain and account for the heathen beliefs as the outcome of an allegorising process akin to poetical metaphor. Between Paul or Philo and the earliest of the Christian Apologists there is however a change of attitude. The old gods were nothing but so much lifeless wood and stone in the estimation of Paul, and therefore he had no objection to his converts eating meats which had been offered to idols. It made no difference in the meats that a senseless form of words had been pronounced over them, and therefore the Christian might partake of them without misgiving. How different is the attitude of Justin Martyr, and of the entire Church for centuries after. We are apt to suppose that conversion to the religion of Christ signified and

Contrast of Paul and Philo with early Christians.

brought with it a disbelief in the gods of paganism. Nothing could be further from the truth. The convert continued to believe in the gods as firmly as before; the only difference was that he now came to regard them, not as benevolent beings, but as malevolent ones. They were the fallen angels, ministers of Satan lying in wait to destroy men, and often for that end taking up their abode in, and disguising their natural foulness under the most beautiful statues. Such was the nemesis which in the decadence of Greek thought overtook the faith and art of Phidias and Scopas. It is ever the same with a new religion. The gods of one age become the devils of the next; and it is to the credit of the northern nations of Europe, that they succeeded in metamorphosing their old gods into elves and fairies, instead of into malevolent demons. Intellectually, then, the early Christians were but a very short remove from the paganism they denounced; and very soon after the age of Paul the eating of meats offered to idols became the worst form of apostasy. It was not the appearance of making a concession to heathenism which made the act so heinous; rather the consecration to idols polluted the food in itself in a mysterious way analogous to, but the inverse of, the consecration of the elements in the Christian Eucharist. It was as it were transubstantiation turned upside down; and undoubtedly the belief in the mystical transformation of the bread and wine into the body

Lingering polytheistic belief of Christian Apologists and saints.

and blood of Christ grew up, quite naturally, with the belief that the evil demons communicated in some hidden way their own evil properties to the meats offered to them. The two beliefs were closely akin, if not both equally remote from the monotheistic rationalism of the Jew Paul. "Evil demons," says Justin Martyr, *Apol.*, 55, "in the remote past disguised themselves and committed adultery with women, and ruined children, and wielded terrors over men, so that those who did not take right account of such things were terrified and were carried away by fear; and not knowing that they were wicked demons, gave them the titles of gods, and gave to each of them the particular name that each of the demons chose to assume." In the same way Augustine in the *De Civitate Dei*, bk. i., ch. 31, tells us that the gods of the ancient Romans were *Noxii Demones*. We are thus prepared to find the Christian saints resorting to exorcism against the gods of the heathen. The Holy Pancrazio, we read, came to Taormena in Sicily, and went into a temple, where they worshipped the god Falkon. The saint stood facing the image and said : "O Falko, deaf and dumb and blind brute, who art thou, and what doest thou here? How many years hath thou lived here, cajoling the creatures of my God, and having offerings made to thee, thou foul and abominable idol of a devil?" And the devil who was dwelling in the idol said ; "Two hundred and sixty years have I lived here, and have received sacrifices and offerings from the city of

Taormena, each year three unblemished children and seventy and three fat and beauteous oxen and swine and many lambs." Then the Holy Pancrazio cried out and said: "I adjure you, foul devils, in the name of our crucified Messiah our God, gather ye all hither and lift the deaf and dumb idol of Falkon from the temple and cast it into the sea, thirty stades distant from the shore, and engulf yourselves along with it in the bottom-most depths." So again in Trebizond, at the end of the the third century, the evil spirit, which dwelt in the idol, cried out at the approach of the Saint Eugenius and said: "Eugenius, why dost thou persecute us, and drive us away from our home; for we are not gods but miserable demons, and we beheld the beauty of these images and were filled with desire and dwelt in them. And now we pray thee, drive us not out from this place, thou holy one of God." But the saint was without mercy, and commanded them to retire into an uninhabited mountain in the Caucasus. The demons thus ousted from their images were Dia, and Apollo, and Artemis.[1]

3. This leads us in natural sequence to another

---

[1] Minucius Felix, the first of the Latin Apologists had the same belief (ch. 27): Isti igitur impuri spiritus [dæmones], ut ostensum magis et philosophis [et a Platone], sub statuis et imaginibus consecratis delitescunt et adflatu suo auctoritatem quasi præsentis numinis consequuntur, dum inseruntur interim uatibus, cum fanis inmorantur, dum nonnumquam extorum fibras animant, auium uolatus gubernant, sortes regunt, oracula efficiunt falsis plurimis inuoluentes pauca uera. A more comprehensive confession by a Christian of his faith in the heathen gods and goddesses cannot be conceived of.

general characteristic of the early Christians, namely, their Iconoclasm. The obvious way of scotching a foul demon was to smash his idols; and we find that an enormous number of martyrs earned their crown in this manner, *Destruction by saints of Ancient works of art.* especially in the third century, when their rapidly increasing numbers rendered them bolder and more ready to make a display of their intolerance. Sometimes the good sense or the worldly prudence of the Church intervened to set limits to so favourite a way of courting martyrdom; and at the Synod of Elvira, c. A.D. 305, a canon, was passed, declaring the practice to be one not met with in the gospel nor recorded of any of the apostles, and denying to those who in future resorted to it the honours of martyrdom. But in spite of this, the most popular of the saints were those who had resorted to such violence and earned their death by it; and as soon as Christianity fairly got the upper hand in the fourth century, the wrecking of temples and the smashing of the idols of the demons became a most popular amusement with which to grace a Christian festival. As we turn over the pages of the martyrologies, we wonder that any ancient statues at all escaped those senseless outbursts of zealotry. In India at the present day we meet with the same sort of zeal in the Mahommedan population. The Hindoos delight to embellish the walls of their temples with scenes drawn from their copious mythology; and a Mahommedan, as he passes by at dusk, seldom neglects the opportunity of poking out the eye of a favourite divinity with the point of his walking-stick.

4. In very many martyrdoms the saint is made to recite his creed; and we find on the whole that the creeds given in Acts of the second century are simpler than those given in third century Acts. Thus in the Acts of Apollonius, Christ is merely said to have been the Word of God, made man in Judea, where He taught all goodness to men, and was crucified. No mention is here made of His resurrection or of His miraculous birth. As Apollonius was familiar with Paul's epistles, the omission of the resurrection from his creed must be accidental. But the absence from such professions of faith of references to the miraculous birth from a virgin is so frequent, that we may infer that it was not universally received among Christians of the second century; as, indeed, we know from Justin Martyr, that it was not. Sometimes we read simply that the Christ was born into the world in an ineffable manner; *e.g.* in the Acts of even so late a saint as Demetrius of Thessalonica. In the third century the references to the Virgin Mary become fairly common, though no early martyr ever invoked her aid. Their prayers were ever addressed to Jesus the Messiah. Towards the end of the third century, and not before, do we meet in genuine Acts with the doctrine of the Trinity in Unity. Before that epoch the saints were content with the simpler formula of God the Father, and of His Son Jesus Christ.

Early forms of Creed in older Acts.

5. It is the fashion in the present day, especially with our court divines, to pretend that the teaching of hell-fire and of eternal torture therein, is no essential or original part of Christianity. If we dip but cursorily into the *Acta Sanctorum* we are forced to come to a very different conclusion. Every saint was sure that apostasy would cause him to be cast after his death into the eternal fires of hell, and it was as a means of escape from the terrible destiny which threatened all men, that Christian baptism recommended itself to most converts. For the belief was not born with Christianity, nor was it distinctively Jewish. A few years before the birth of Christ we have the poet Lucretius denouncing the popular religion for the reason that it affrighted its votaries with such teaching :—

All the saints believed in the eternal fires of hell.

Christianity took over this belief from paganism.

> "Tantum religio potuit suadere malorum.
> . . . .
> Nunc ratio nulla est restandi, nulla facultas
> Æternas quoniam pœnas in morte timendumst."

In Vergil we have the same note :—

> " Felix qui potuit rerum cognoscere causas,
> Atque metus omnes et inexorabile fatum
> Subiecit pedibus, strepitumque Acherontis avari.

The same is the burthen of Plutarch's tract upon superstition. One brief passage is enough—*Moralia*, p. 166, f.: —" Tear not away the superstitious man from his temples; for there is he chastised,

Plutarch's opinion.

'there he meets with his punishment. Why waste words. For all men death is the end of life ; but of superstition 'tis not the end ; for it overleaps the limits and transcends our life, and lengthens out its terrors beyond this world. It attaches to death a dream of immortal evils ; and just when we are ceasing to toil and sorrow here, it pretends that we are beginning with anguish that will never cease. Wide open stand the deep gates of hell that they fable, and there stretches a vista of rivers of fire and stygian cliffs ; and all is canopied with a darkness full of fantasms, of spectres mowing at us with terrible faces, and uttering pitiful cries." The Christians, to their eternal shame, availed themselves eagerly of an infirmity of the human mind which pagan philosophers had deplored. And so we find the first of the Latin fathers, Minucius Felix, contemplating with satisfaction the fate in store for the heathen and their gods (ch. 35): "et tamen admonentur homines doctissimorum libris et carminibus sæpius ambientis ardoris . . . et ideo apud eos etiam rex Iuppiter per torrentes ripas et atrem uoraginem urat religiose ; destinatam enim sibi cum suis cultoribus pœnam præscius perhorrescit. Nec tormentis aut modus ullus aut terminus. Illic sapiens ignis membra urit et reficit, carpit et nutrit. Sicut ignes fulminum corpora tangunt nec absumunt, sicut ignes Ætnæi et Vesuuii et ardentium ubique terrarum flagrant nec erogantur : ita pœnale illud incendium non damnis ardentium pascitur, sed inexesa corporum laceratione nutritur. Eos autem merito torqueri, qui deum nesciunt, ut impios, ut iniustos, nisi profanus nemo deliberat, cum parentem omnium et omnium ¶ dominum non minoris sceleris sit ignorare quam lædere."

Here we have the medieval hell. But we make a mistake, if we think that this awful shadow was not cast across the human mind long before the birth of Christianity. On the contrary, it is a survival from the most primitive stage of our intellectual and moral development. The mysteries of the old Greek and Roman worlds were intended as modes of propitiation and atonement, by which to escape from these all-besetting terrors, and Jesus the Messiah, was the last and the best of the $\lambda v\tau\acute{\eta}\rho\iota o\iota\ \theta\epsilon o\grave{\iota}$, of the redeeming gods. *Jesus the last of the θεοί λυτήριοι of paganism.* In the dread of death and in the belief in the eternal fire of hell, which pervaded men's minds, a few philosophers excepted, Christianity had a *point d'appui*, without availing itself of which it would not have made a single step *Belief in hell fire the fulcrum of early Christianity.* towards the conquest of men's minds. Its ultimate prevalence over other forms of initiation was chiefly due to the superior speculative truth of its monotheistic conception of the world, inherited from the parent Judaism, and rendered intelligible to the masses by the outward and parallel spectacle, which the Roman empire presented to their eyes, of the entire world brought under the sway of a single will. And in this last connection it

C

may be no mere fancy to say that the Christian conception of the relation of the Son to the Father was, if not suggested, at any rate brought home to the ordinary Christian imagination, by the familiar spectacle of the absolute Cæsar adopting another as his son, to sit at his right hand and be co-equal with him in counsel and supreme power.

6. Another point strikes us in reading the Acts of the Saints. It is the extent to which there gathered round the personality of a favourite martyr the stories which had been believed of the demigods and heroes of an earlier age. Thus Callistratus is borne to the shore by dolphins, like Amphion; and saints innumerable began their careers by destroying a dragon, like Perseus, or like Hercules, a voracious lion, or like Theseus, a destructive bull. And the predicates of one ancient god attached themselves to one saint and of another to a second. Thus the mariners of Pontus prayed to Phocas as of old time they had prayed to Poseidon. *"Mutato nomine de te fabula narratur."* A rich harvest awaits any student of folk-lore who approaches the legends of the saints from this point of view.

Older myths gathered round the early saints.

How far early Christians renounced the world.

7. We should err, if we ascribed to the Christians of the first three centuries as a regular and every-day characteristic, that detachment from the interests of this world, that readiness to abandon it, which, nevertheless, they so frequently displayed in seasons of persecution. We

cannot suppose that in ordinary times the Christians of the second and third centuries were more ready to cast off the ties of family and forego the comforts of life than were the unconverted. And probably they interpreted the Gospel precepts, "Let the dead bury the dead," and "Who is My mother? and who are my brethren?" in the same sense in which we interpret them, namely, as advice not so much to neglect the ties with which nature has surrounded us, as to draw closer the ties of charity, which should link us with all about us. Such precepts of course could not otherwise than occur to martyrs, when the ties of blood seemed to stand in the way of the heavenly rewards which they believed to await those who, rather than recant, suffered tortures and death. We shall see, for instance, that Polyeuctes casts these precepts in the teeth of his father-in-law in a manner which seems almost brutal. So Perpetua, the mother of a new-born babe, in the excess of her devotion to the cause, is ready to cast to the winds the instincts of maternity. But in many such cases we must take into account that the bodily feelings of the saint had been racked with tortures before they were brought to utter such sentiments.

None of our documents here translated, with the exception perhaps of the Acts of Thekla, go back to the very first stage of Christianity. In those earliest times the followers of Jesus the Messiah, as it is now commonly admitted by all schools of critics, be-

Asceticism of Jesus and Paul due to belief that the end of world was at hand.

lieved that their Prophet was going to return and begin almost at once the millennium or kingdom of heaven upon earth. The kingdom was at hand, and no man knew when the heavenly Bridegroom might appear with His angels. The most pressing necessity was therefore to repent. Call there was none to marry and beget children, or to take thought for the morrow and lay up the riches that spoil. How hardly should they that had riches enter into the kingdom of heaven. Jesus said, "Verily I say unto you, there is no man that hath left house, or brethren, or sisters, or children, or lands for My sake, and for the gospel's sake, but he shall receive a hundredfold, now in this time, houses and brethren, and sisters and mothers, and children and lands, with persecutions; and in the age to come eternal life."[1] Nor it would seem were there wanting those who already, in the age contemporary with Christ, and, indeed, long before, had responded to such a summons as this, though from the lips of other unknown prophets. Witness the Therapeutæ, of whom Philo has left a description at the very beginning of the Christian era, attesting moreover that they were spread all over the inhabited world. These men and women, he says, give up their goods, and flee without looking back, leaving their brethren, their children, their wives, their parents, their throng of relatives and of

The same is also met with in Philo's Therapeutæ.

---

[1] See especially Matt. xvi., 27, 28; and xix. 27-29.

faithful friends, their native lands in which they were bred and born. And why? In order that they might retire into the desert, and there living, men and women together, yet in perfect chastity, devote themselves to prayer and praise, to watching and fasting, and perpetual contemplation of God, and of His powers and goodness. In remote regions generations passed away before the Christians could resign their dream, and give up the old hope that the kingdom of God upon earth was really at hand. As late as the beginning of the second century we have such allusions as the following (*Neu entdeckte vierte Buch des Daniel Commentars von Hippolytus.* Dr. Ed. Bratke. Bonn, 1891, p. 15, l. 9):—

The millennial belief still survived in Syria in the 2nd century,

"For I will narrate what happened not long ago in Syria. A certain bishop ($προεστώς$) of the Church, being too little versed in the divine scriptures, and because he also neglected to follow the voice of the Lord, went astray and led others astray also. . . . He persuaded many of the brethren with their wives and children to go out into the wilderness to meet the Christ; and they went wandering in the mountains and wastes, there losing their way; and the end was that all but a few were apprehended as robbers, and would have been executed by the hegemôn, had it not been that his wife was a believer, and that in response to her entreaties he put a stop to proceedings, to prevent a persecution arising because of them.

What folly was it and want of sound instruction that induced them to seek the Christ in the wilderness; just as in the time of Elijah the prophet, the sons of the prophets looked among the mountains for Elijah, who had been taken up into heaven, for the space of three days!

"And in the same way there was another in Pontus, who was, like the former, president (προε-στώς) of the Church, a prudent man *also in Pontus.* and lowly-minded; yet as he failed to read, mark, and understand the scriptures in sound manner, he was more given to trust to the visions which he himself saw than to them. For he fell first into one, and then a second, and then a third dream, and at last began to proclaim to the brethren that he knew this and that as a prophet knows, and that this and that was about to come to pass. And they listened to his preaching, to the effect that the day of the Lord is imminent (2 Thess. ii. 2), and with weepings and lamentations they prayed to the Lord night and day, having before their eyes the approaching day of judgment. And he brought the brethren to such a pitch of fear and trembling, that they abandoned their lands and fields, letting them become waste, and sold, the most of them, their possessions. But he told them thus: Unless it happen as I have told you, then believe ye not any more in the scriptures, but let each of you do as he pleases. So they went on expecting the coming event, and when nothing that he told them came about, he was himself put to shame as having lied; but the scriptures turned out to be true after all; while the brethren were found to be cast on a rock of offence. So that after that the virgins married, and the men went their way to till their fields. But those who had recklessly sold their properties, were found afterwards asking to have them back again. This is what happens to silly and light-headed people, who instead of attending strictly to the scriptures, prefer to obey the traditions of men and their own vagaries and their own dreams and mythologies and old wives' tales."

Yet it was certainly the genuine teaching of Jesus which misled these poor people. "Ye err," He had said to those who asked Him to which of her seven husbands a woman would in the resurrection belong, "because ye know not the scriptures nor the power of God. For in the resurrection they neither marry nor are given in marriage, but are as angels of God in heaven." So Matthew xxii. 29; but in Luke the precept that none but the unmarried can inherit the kingdom of heaven is stated without reserve; for in answer to the same question we read that Jesus said: "The children of this age marry and are given in marriage; but *they that are deemed worthy to attain to that age and to the resurrection from the dead neither marry nor are given in marriage.* For they can no longer die. For they are equal to angels, and are sons of God, being sons of the resurrection." That is to say,

Jesus' repudiation of marriage as incompatible with resurrection and the kingdom of God.

the question, to which husband the woman would belong was quite beside the point, seeing that any marriage whatever was an absolute bar to entrance into that new age and life, which He (Jesus) was about to inaugurate "before *this* generation shall pass away." Similar is the teaching ascribed to S. Paul in the Acts of Paul and Thekla, especially in chap. xii. In the same spirit Jesus refers (Matt. xix. 12) to "the eunuchs who had made themselves eunuchs because of the kingdom of heaven." For these men had by their self-mutilation raised themselves above all temptation to marry.[1] St. Paul was thus true to the teaching of Jesus when he dissuaded Thekla and others from marriage. In the kingdom of Christ "there can be no male and

<small>The same spirit observable in Paul.</small>

---

[1] So in *Clem. Rom.*, Ep. ii. 12, we read that the Lord on being asked when His kingdom should come, answered, When the two shall be one, and that which is without as that which is within, and the male with the female neither male nor female. Justin Martyr, the father of Christian apologists, quotes the precept given by Jesus in Matthew xix. 12 with particular approval in his Apology, I. chap. xv. ; and in chap. xxix. of the same treatise he relates how a Christian, libellum obtulit Alexandriæ Felici præfecto rogans ut medico licentiam daret testes ipsi resecandi. The prefect refused permission. During the life-time of Jesus we hear of the same precept being followed by Alexandrian Jews or proselytes. Thus Philo writes (*Quod detur Pot. Insid.*, i. 224), ἐξευνευχισθῆναί γε μὴν ἄμεινον ἢ πρὸς συνουσίας ἀκνόμους λυττᾶν. It is curious that modern commentators on the N.T. overlook passages so illustrative of Matthew xix. 12. To the Aryan races, like the Greeks and Romans, the practice of eunuchism was somewhat abhorrent, and so soon as the Christian church became in the main a church of the Gentiles, it hastened to discountenance a practice, which however its founder seems to have regarded with approval, and which may even have constituted one of the *flagitia* alleged against the early Christians. (See Origen Comm. on Matt. xix. 12, and Clem. Alexand. Ed. Syllb., p. 229n, 468c, 451A.)

female" (Gal. iii. 38). Marriage was to his mind a second best, just so much distraction from the business of the Lord, whether for man or for woman (1 Cor. vii. 34). "Art thou loosed from a wife? then seek not one." However it was better to marry than to burn, and if a man found that he could not restrain himself and live on platonic terms with his virgin, then he did best to marry her (1 Cor. vii. 36).[1]

The precept not to marry, like the companion precept to possess no riches, was thus originally meant to prepare men for the kingdom of heaven which was at hand. But as the years rolled by, the expectation of the second coming and of the thousand years reign of Christ on earth, grew dim and receded into the background of the Christian mind. And it is an effort to us, as we read to-day the apocalyptic passages of the New Testament, to realise that they were written in view of a millennium which was to come even during the lifetime of the hearers of Jesus.

But although the old apocalyptic dream thus faded away, the belief in virginity as the true state of the elect has survived in some churches even to the present day. With the early fathers virginity was a never-ending, never-failing topic for edificatory hymns Belief in superior holiness of virgins survived in the Church.

---

[1] From this passage we incidentally learn that those platonic marriages between Christians were already common in Paul's day, which Cyprian of Carthage was obliged to interdict on pain of excommunication, because of the frequent abuses to which they give rise.

and discourses. It was also a fertile source of martyrdoms, and many were the maidens who, being betrothed and their nuptials arranged, took a sudden resolution to remain virgins; and in such cases the outraged, but ungallant, bridegroom often consoled himself by accusing his mistress of Christianity. In the Acts of S. Peter, which are certainly very old, though of course their attribution to Linus is false, we read that that apostle by his preaching persuaded many women old and young, rich and poor, to take vows of virginity.[1] In the fourth century when the Church conquered the world or the world the Church, a compromise was effected; and those who wished to practise the tenets of primitive Christian poverty and purity took shelter from the now all-absorbing world within the walls of nunneries and monasteries.

A few words are necessary in conclusion as to the method I have pursued in editing these translations. Where there exist other ancient texts besides the Armenian translated, I have added in footnotes the chief varieties of text which they furnish; in order to give the reader an idea of the development which a text has at various times undergone. In the case of the

Method pursued in these translations.

---

[1] *Martyrium beati Petri*, cap. i. : "Unde factum est ut beati Petri sermonibus magnus pudicitiæ apud multas diversæ ætatis ac potestatis seu nobilitatis fœminas amor exarserit, ita ut pleræque etiam Romanorum matronæ a commixtione uirilis thori seruare munda corda simul et corpora, quantum ex ipsis erat, diligerent." These Acts are an admirable commentary on the story of Paul and Thekla.

Apology of Apollonius which I have been so fortunate as to detect in the Armenian martyrology, I have added many notes illustrative of the text. I have also prefixed to each piece an introduction discussing its authenticity and any other questions of interest which arise in connection with it.

In the martyrology, printed at Venice in 1874, there still remains enough of interest to make a second volume as large as this. I have chiefly translated those pieces which are new and hitherto unknown, *e.g.* the Acts of Apollonius, A.D. 185, of Quadratus or Codratius, c. A.D. 250, of Hiztibouzit, a converted magus; or those which in the Armenian assume such a shape, that the question of their spuriousness needs to be re-argued. Of the latter class the Acts of Phocas, of Eugenia, and of Thekla are the most important. The first of these turns out to be a partly genuine monument of the Bithynian persecution, in which Pliny was concerned. The second has been strangely confirmed by recent discoveries in the Roman catacombs. The third adds a new and genuine chapter to the history of S. Paul.

THE APOLOGY AND ACTS OF APOLLONIUS.

OUR first example is drawn from the reign of Commodus. By this time, as Eusebius informs us, the new faith had made many converts, not only among the poor of Rome, but among the rich and noble. We have the statement of Eusebius that Apollonius was renowned for his culture and philosophy; it is also probable that he was a man of exalted and even senatorial rank. This alone would explain the circumstance that Perennis, before whom he was brought to trial, asked him to defend himself before the Senate. The date of his martyrdom is known from the fourth century catalogue of martyrs by Liberius, also from the Roman and other calendars, to have been 185 A.D.

Evidence of Eusebius.

The tone of the martyr's defence then delivered, is full of solemn force and simplicity, and gives the reader a loftier idea of the Christianity of the time than the florid special pleading of Tertullian, whose Apology for Christianity is later only by a few years. If the philosopher on the throne, Marcus Aurelius, had been a Christian and had been summoned to give an account of his religion, he would, we feel, have given just such a one as this.

Tone of this Apology Stoical.

By way of preface it is best to give a translation of the 21st chapter of the fifth book of the history of the Church by Eusebius, which has hitherto[1] contained all that was known of this martyr. It is as follows:—

---

[1] That is to say by European scholars. It is significant of the general and undeserved disregard of Armenian literature, that these Acts although

"And about the same period of the reign of Comodus,[1] our affairs took a change in the direction of clemency; and by God's grace peace came over the Churches of the entire world. This was the time when the saving word led the souls of all men, of every race, to the reverent worship of the God of all things. So that by this time numbers of those who in Rome were most distinguished for their wealth and family came and received for their own the salvation which was prepared for every house and every race. Now this was more than the demon who hates what is good and is envious by his very nature could endure. So he stripped himself again for the contest, and contrived a variety of fresh plots against us. And in Rome accordingly he brought before the tribunal Apollonius, a man who among the believers of that day was renowned for his culture and philosophy; and to accuse this man he incited one of his own servants who are suited thereunto. But the unhappy man went into the suit in an ill-starred way, for, according to the regulation of the Emperor, it was not permitted that those who informed against such as Apollonius should live. And he had his legs broken, for the Judge Perennius pronounced such a sentence upon

Text of Eusebius, Hist. Eccl., v. 21.

---

printed by the Mechitarists of Venice as long ago as 1874, were neither noticed nor translated into any European tongue, until I printed this English rendering of them in the *Guardian* of 18th June, 1893. Yet during the last ten years the notice of Apollonius in Eusebius' history has been discussed and rediscussed, and the loss of the Acts themselves lamented by Görres and Neumann in Germany, Aubé in France, and many others. Upon my drawing his attention to them, Prof. Harnack of Berlin immediately contributed a learned monograph upon them to the Royal Prussian Academy (*Sitzung der Phil. Hist. Classe vom 27 Juli*, 1893). He writes of them thus : " Es ist in der That die vornehmste Apologie des Christenthum, die wir aus dem Alterthum besitzen. Ein edler Sinn, muthig aber nicht trotzig, spricht aus ihr. Die Antworten zeichnen sich durch Festigkeit und Würde, Freimuth und Ruhr aus; sie überraschen an einigen Stellen durch ihre Schlagfertigkeit." I take this opportunity of acknowlodging my indebtedness to Prof. Harnack's prompt monograph, from which he has allowed me to borrow in my notes much material.

[1] The name Commodus is spelt in the same way in the Armenian *Acta*. Commodus reigned A.D. 180–92.

him. But the martyr so dear to God, after that the judge had besought him much and earnestly, and asked him to give an account of himself before the Senate, delivered a most reasonable defence before all of the faith for which he was being martyred,[1] and then was beheaded, and so reached his consummation, in accordance, it seems, with the decree of the Senate, for there is an ancient law which prevails among them, that those who have once come before the court and will not change their resolution, shall not be excused on any ground. In the compilation which we have made of old martyrdoms you may learn what was said by him before the judge and the answers which he gave to the questions of Perennius; and the whole defence which he made to the Senate; this whoever wishes may know from beginning to end."

Hieronymus does not appear to have had any other knowledge of Apollonius than is given in the passage of Eusebius just quoted; for in his catalogue of Christian writers he gives us (c. 42) the following notice: "Apollonius, Romanæ urbis senator sub Commodo principe a servo proditus quod Christianus esset, impetrato ut rationem fidei suæ redderet, insigne volumen composuit, quod in senatu legit; et nihilo minus sententia senatus pro Christo capite truncatur, veteri apud eos obtinente lege, absque negatione non dimitti Christianos, qui semel ad eorum iudicium pertracti essent." In the above the words "insigne volumen" are, as Prof. Harnack points out, due to the characteristic exaggeration of Hieronymus, and the words "impetrato ut" to mere inability to construe the Greek of Eusebius which lay before him. In point of fact the Apology which the Armenian Church has preserved to us is very brief, and it was Perennis the prefect who begged Apollonius to defend himself before the Senate, not Apollonius who begged to be allowed to do so. Another statement in the above extract of Hieronymus which goes beyond the account of Eusebius is also merely due

Evidence of Jerome.

Inaccuracy and want of Greek scholarship in Jerome's account.

---

[1] Or "the faith to which he was witnessing."

to hasty and inaccurate translation of the Greek. It is that Apollonius was betrayed by one of his own servants. What Eusebius said was that one of the devil's servants who are always ready for such jobs,' betrayed Apollonius. No fourth-form boy could have made more errors in translating these twenty lines of Eusebius than does Hieronymus.

Eusebius makes the remarkable statement that the informer was immediately afterwards condemned by Perennis to have his legs broken in accordance with an imperial edict. This statement has already moved the suspicion of several writers;[1] nor is it likely that an informer would be punished for giving information which led to condemnation and beheadal of the accused. The Armenian Acts give no hint of such a circumstance, though it may have been contained in them in their complete form. Harnack is of opinion that it was stated in them that the informer had his legs broken, and that Eusebius out of his own conjecture ascribed this action to an imaginary edict of Marcus Aurelius, which he had just before given in his history (bk. v., ch. 5, § 6). This imaginary edict threatened informers against Christians with death in consequence of the so-called miracle of the Thundering Legion. The entire statement may have arisen out of the fact that in all their histories of martyrdoms the early Christians liked to learn that those who had brought suffering on the martyrs suffered retribution even in this life.

Addition made to the Acts by Eusebius.

Trustworthiness of these Acts.

This leads up to the question whether these Acts of Apollonius are trustworthy and authentic. Of this there cannot be any doubt, and for these reasons:—

1. Their tone is thoroughly that of the second century. They are simple and forcible, and there are no miraculous additions. As Harnack remarks: "They bear the stamp of life and genuineness."

2. Tertullian must have read them, if he really imitates them in his Apology which he wrote A.D. 197. Prof. Harnack

---

[1] *E.g.* C. F. Neumann.

The Apology and Acts of Apollonius. 33

thinks that Tertullian has so imitated §§ 19, 38, 41 of Apollonius.

3. In any case the shorthand notes of Apollonius' trial were accessible to the fellow-religionists of the condemned, and these were doubtless used by the writer of these Acts.

4. Eusebius reckoned these Acts to be genuine, and on that account gave them a place in his collection of old martyrdoms, a work which is now, sad to say, lost to us. This in itself is strong evidence in favour of them. For in other cases where Eusebius mentions particular Acta to be genuine, and where time has preserved to us the documents so mentioned, we never find his judgment astray.

The close resemblance between § 4 and a passage in the Acts of Polycarp, proves at the best that the second century redactor of the Acts of Apollonius had seen those of Polycarp. But the answer is so often met with in Acta, that we may safely infer that it was the stereotyped reply which Christians were taught to give to magistrates who pressed them to recant.

<small>Resemblance to Acts of Polycarp.</small>

The simplicity of the Creed which Apollonius formulates has already been dwelt upon in our general preface. It is fresh evidence of the early date of these Acts. We may almost infer that the martyr had not heard of the legend of the birth of Christ from a virgin. And if he knew of the resurrection he does not think it necessary to allude to it. What attracted him in Christianity was clearly its superior morality, its teachings of truthfulness, mercy, purity of life, of lofty monotheism far removed from the idolatrous cults around him.

<small>Simple Creed of Apollonius.</small>

Taken in conjunction with the passage in the History of Eusebius, the procedure which seems to have been followed in the case of Apollonius calls for a good deal of remark. But on so technical a matter I am content to refer the reader to the monograph of Prof. A. Harnack, to which I have already referred; and will proceed at once to give a translation of the Armenian Acts themselves. In printing

<small>Procedure followed in trial of Apollonius.</small>

them I have observed the division into sections which Harnack has made in his German edition, to which I owe those of my footnotes which are subscribed A. H.

THE MARTYRDOM OF THE HOLY APOLLONIUS, ASCETIC.

CHRIST, Who giveth all things, prepareth a crown of righteousness for those who are well-minded and stand firm by the faith in God; for the chosen ones of God are called to this righteousness, in order that, having fought the good fight with fortitude, they may attain the promises which God, Who lies not,[1] hath promised to those who love Him and believe in Him with their whole soul. One of these also was the blessed martyr and goodly champion[2] of Christ, Apollonius. He had lived a good and ascetic life in the great Rome,[3] and, desirous of the earnest[4] of his heavenly call, he was numbered among the holy martyrs of Christ. The blessed one bore witness before the Senate and Terentius the Prefect,[5] and gave his answers with great boldness, whose memorials[6] are as follows :—

---

[1] The Arm. = ἀψευδής. A. H. notes that this introduction is composed of passages from the Pastoral Epistles, see 2 Tim. iv. 7, 8; 1 Tim. vi. 17; Tit. i. 2. With ἀψευδής comp. the Acts of Polycarp 14, 2 : ὁ ἀψευδὴς καὶ ἀληθινὸς θεός.

[2] ἀθλητής probably stood in the Greek original.

[3] The expression "in the great Rome" shows that this introduction was not written in Rome. A. H.

[4] The Arm. here = καὶ σπουδάσας ἀρραβῶνα τὴν ἄνω κλῆσιν (? τῆς ἄνω κλήσεως). Comp. Eph. i. 14; Phil. iii. 14.

[5] The Arm. literally = χιλιάρχης. The Text of Eusebius has Perennius, who was prefect of the Prætorian guard in the reign of Commodus. Perennis was the real name. Terentius is an obvious corruption of Perennius, either in an early Greek text or in the Armenian itself.

[6] Or *Acts*.

1. Terentius, the Prefect, commanded that he should be brought before the Senate, and said to him—"O Apollonius, wherefore dost thou resist the invincible laws and decree of the Emperors, and dost refuse to sacrifice to the gods?" 2. Apollonius said—"Because I am a Christian; therefore, I fear God Who made heaven and earth, and sacrifice not to empty idols."

3. The Prefect said—"But thou oughtest to repent of this mind of thine because of the edicts of the Emperors, and take oath by the good for-

---

§ 1. The Acts cannot have begun in this way; for not only do we not learn how the accusation came to be made, though Eusebius must have known in order to write as he does, but the personal details are also lacking. —The expression "commanded" agrees with the words of Eusebius translated above from the *H. E.*, v. 21, § 4 : πολλὰ λιπαρῶς ἱκετεύσαντος τοῦ δικαστοῦ καὶ λόγον αὐτὸν ἐπὶ τῆς συγκλήτου βουλῆς αἰτήσαντος.—Unfortunately no reason is assigned for the accused being brought before the senate; neither is Apollonius called a senator. The hearing of the case as here related takes place before the Prefect *and the Senate.*—There was no general edict prior to the reign of Decius compelling every Christian to sacrifice. All that is here referred to is the rule allowed by Trajan and then repeatedly insisted upon, especially by M. Aurelius, that every Christian when accused should sacrifice; see the Acta Carpi et Papyli, 4 : ἔγνωσται σοι πάντως τὰ προστάγματα τῶν Αὐγούστων περὶ τοῦ δεῖν ὑμᾶς σέβειν τοὺς θεοὺς τοὺς τὰ πάντα διοικοῦντας· ὅθεν συμβουλεύω ὑμῖν προσελθεῖν καὶ θῦσαι (cf. *Texte u. Unters. z. altchristl. Litt.-Gesch.*, III. s. 454 f.). Acts of Polyc. 8 : τί γὰρ κακόν ἐστιν εἰπεῖν, Κύριος Καῖσαρ, καὶ ἐπιθῦσαι, etc. A. H.

§ 3. For the name Comodus see Eusebius. For the fact narrated compare Tertull. Apol. 28 ff. and in particular the Acts of Polycarp, 9: ὁ ἀνθύπατος . . . ἔπειθεν ἀρνεῖσθαι λέγων· αἰδέσθητί σου τὴν ἡλικίαν, καὶ ἕτερα τούτοις ἀκόλουθα, ὡς ἔθος αὐτοῖς λέγειν· ὄμοσον τὴν καίσαρος τύχην, μετανόησον, cf. § 10. In Acta Scillit. (p. 112 ed. Robinson) the proconsul Saturninus says : "et nos religiosi sumus, et simplex est religio nostra et iuramus per genium domini nostri imperatoris, et pro salute eius supplicamus, quod et uos quoque facere debetis." A. H. Compare also Minucii Felicis Octavius, cap. 29 : Sic eorum numen inuocant, ad imagines supplicant, genium id est dæmonem rei implorant ; et est eis tutius per Iovis genium peierare quam regis.

The Apology and Acts of Apollonius. 37

tune of the autocrat Commodus." 4. Apollonius replied—" Hear with understanding this my answer. He who repents of just and good works, in truth such a man is godless and without hope ; but he who repents of lawless deeds and of evil thoughts, and returns not again to them, such a one is a lover of God, and hath regard to the hope. 5. And I now am firmly resolved in this my mind to keep the beautiful and glorious command of God, which He taught by my Lord Christ, Who knoweth the thoughts of men, and beholdeth whatsoever is done in secret or in the open. 6. It is best to swear not at all, but in all

---

§ 4. Comp. Acts of Polyc. ii. : ἀμετάθετος ἡμῖν ἡ ἀπὸ τῶν κρειττόνων ἐπὶ τὰ χείρω μετάνοια· καλὸν δὲ μετατίθεσθαι ἀπὸ τῶν χαλεπῶν ἐπὶ τὰ δίκαια. Armenian Acts of Eustratius (vol. i. p. 441 of the Venice Martyrology) : The duke said : " O Eustratius, unless you repent and turn back from your superstitious folly, expect not to be saved from my hands by reason of the pernicious counsels you have espoused." The holy Eustratius answered : "O Lysias, they ought to repent who drift from things that are good into badness, but not they who spurning evil deeds and designs follow after the truth. Even as I from the beginning have followed after the just laws of my true God."

§ 5. καλὸν καὶ ἔνδοξον. For use of ἔνδοξον see I. Clem. 9, 19, 23, 34, 43, 45, 58. A. H.

§ 6. Harnack prefers a rendering which is equally compatible with the Armenian : Ich will wahrhaftig schwören bei dem wahren Gott, obschon wir auch den Kaiser lieben und für seine Majestät Gebete darbringen. He remarks thus : We may notice the circumspection of the accused ; he recognises that the oath is necessary in this bad world ; but only the oath by God is allowable. He exemplifies the prohibition of swearing from Matt. v. 34 ff. ; Jacob v. 12 ; Justin, Apol. i. 16. περὶ δὲ τοῦ μὴ ὀμνύναι ὅλως τἀληθῆ δὲ λέγειν ἀεί, οὕτως παρεκελεύσατο κ.τ.λ. To which I may add the following references. Josephus, *Wars of the Jews*, bk. ii. ch. 8, Whiston's translation : " They (the Essenes) are eminent for fidelity and are the ministers of peace. Whatsoever they say also is firmer than an oath. But swearing is avoided by them ; and they esteem it worse than perjury. For they say, that he who cannot be believed without swearing by God, is already condemned." ὀργῆς ταμίαι δίκαιοι, θυμοῦ καθεκτικοί

things to live in peace and truth; for a great oath is the truth, and for this reason is it a bad and an ill thing to swear by Christ; but because of falsehood is there disbelief, and because of disbelief there is swearing. I am willing to swear in truth by the true God that we, too, love the Emperor, and offer up prayers for his Majesty."

7. The Prefect said—" Come, then, and sacrifice to Apollo, and to the other gods, and to the Emperor's image." 8. Apollonius said—" As to

---

πιστέως προστάται, εἰρήνης ὑπουργοί. Καὶ πᾶν μὲν τὸ ῥηθὲν ὑπ' αὐτῶν ἰσχυρότερον ὅρκου, τὸ δὲ ὀμνύειν περιίστανται χεῖρόν τι τῆς ἐπιορκίας ὑπολαμβάνοντες. ἤδη γὰρ κατεγνῶσθαι φασὶ τὸ ἀπιστούμενον δίχα θεοῦ. The ordinance not to swear was older than Jesus of Nazareth, for in Philo de x oraculis 2, 194, we read: κάλλιστον δὴ καὶ βιωφελέστατον καὶ ἁρμόττον λογικῇ φύσει τὸ ἀνώμοτον, οὕτως ἀληθεύειν ἐφ' ἑκάστου δεδιδαγμένῃ, ὡς τοὺς λόγους ὅρκους εἶναι νομίζεσθαι. Δεύτερος δέ φασι πλοῦς τὸ εὐορκεῖν· ἤδη γὰρ ὀμνὺς εἰς ἀπιστίαν ὑπονοεῖται. This is exactly the thought of Apollonius. And the following passage of Philo has a superficial resemblance to the very words of the Gospel. Ἄξιον ἐπαινεῖν καὶ τοὺς, ὁπότε βιασθεῖεν ὀμνύναι, τῷ μέλλειν καὶ βραδύνειν καὶ ἀποκνεῖν ἐμποιοῦντας δέος οὐ μόνον τοῖς ὁρῶσιν, ἀλλὰ καὶ τοῖς προκαλουμένοις εἰς τὸν ὅρκον· εἰώθασι γὰρ ἀναφθεγξάμενοι τοσοῦτον μόνον "νὴ τόν" ἢ "μά τον," μηδὲν παραλαβόντες, ἐμφάσει τῆς ἀποκοπῆς, τρανοῦν ὅρκον οὐ γενόμενον (de spec. Legibus, 2, 271).

§ 7. Since Apollo is here the first of the gods to be mentioned and indeed the only one mentioned by name, it is probable that the session of the Senate was held in Palatio and actually ἐν τῷ Ἀπολλωνίῳ, see Mommsen, Röm. Staatsrecht, III. 2 (1888), s. 929, n. 3; Preller-Jordan, Röm. Mythologie, 1³ s. 147 ff. 307 ff.—As regards the Emperor's image see Plinii Ep. ad Traianum (96): " . . . et imagini Tuæ, quam propter hoc iusseram cum simulacris numinum adferri, ture ac uino supplicarent," etc. See also Acta Carpi : θύσαί σε δεῖ· οὕτως γὰρ ἐκέλευσεν ὁ αὐτοκράτωρ. A. H.

§ 8. "Bloodless Sacrifice," see Justin, Dial. c. Tryph. 117, 118, 41, also under § 44. A. H. Compare also Minucii Fel. Oct. cap. 32: hostias et uictimas deo offeram, quas in usum mihi protulit, ut reiciam ei suum munus? ingratum est, cum sit litabilis hostia bonus animus et pura mens et sincera conscientia. Igitur qui innocentiam colit, deo supplicat, qui iustitiam, deo libat, qui fraudibus abstinet, propitiat deum, qui hominem periculo subripit, (deo) opimam uictimam cædit.

The Apology and Acts of Apollonius. 39

my change of mind, and as to the oath, I have given thee answer ; but as to sacrifices, I and all Christians offer a bloodless sacrifice to God, Lord of heaven and earth, and of the sea, and of every living being, in behalf of the spiritual and rational images who have been appointed by the providence of God to rule over the earth. 9. Wherefore, according to the command of the God-given precept, we make our prayers to Him Who dwells in Heaven, Who is the only God, that they may justly rule upon this earth, knowing for certain that he (*i.e.* Commodus) also is established Emperor, through none other, but only through the one King, God, Who holds every one in His hand." 10. The Prefect said—"Surely thou wast not summoned hither to talk philosophy. I will give thee one day's respite, that thou mayest consider thine interest and advise thyself concerning thy life." And he ordered him to be taken to prison.

11. And after three days he commanded him

---

§ 9. "Divine precept" : Apollonius refers to 1 Tim. ii. 1 f. ; Compare the prayer at the close of the 1st Ep. of Clement. A. H.—Perhaps the sense of the original was "that they (*i.e.* the spiritual and rational images of God) may be justly ruled " ; for the passive and active forms are commonly confused in Armenian MSS.—"that he also, etc." The pronoun here refers back to the Emperor mentioned in § 7.

§ 10. Monotheism was favourably regarded as a philosophy, but when it went with refusal to sacrifice it was deemed to be obstinate folly. See Harnack's note on Acta Carpi, 9. In § 23 the Prefect wonders at the "philosophy" of Apollonius ; in § 31 he politely rejects his teaching as unintelligible.

§ 11. The "three days" must be an error ; for not only in § 10, but also §§ 43, 44 but a single day (night) is spoken of. A. H.—I have rendered "hast thou formed for thyself," or "given to thyself." The literal sense of the Arm. is "have I given to thee ; " but, if we assume

to be brought forward, and said to him—"What counsel hast thou formed for thyself?" 12. Apollonius answered—"To remain firm in my religion, as I told thee before." 13. The Prefect said—"Because of the decree of the Senate I advise thee to repent and to sacrifice to the gods to whom all the earth gives homage and sacrifices; for it is far better for thee to live among us than to die a miserable death. Methinks thou art not unacquainted with the decree of the Senate." 14. Apollonius said—"I know the command of the Omnipotent God, and I remain firm in my religion; and I do no homage to idols made with hands, which have been fashioned of gold and silver and wood, and which neither see nor hear; because they are the work of men's hands, and they know not the true service of God. 15. But I have learnt to adore the heavenly God, and to do homage to Him alone, Who breathed the breath of life into all men and continually dispenses life

---

an infinitesimal corruption in the text, the sense becomes that which the context demands, and which I accordingly print in the text.

§ 13. The sententia or resolution of the Senate is twice referred to; here it suddenly takes the place of a reference to the Emperor's edict. A. H.

It is a trite fact that Commodus was greatly influenced by his Christian mistress to be lenient to Christians. Perhaps on that account he left as much as he could of the responsibility of the dealing with them to the Senate, who may have been in this matter more conservative and less lenient than the Emperor.

§ 14. See § 19. Ps. cxv. 135. Habak. ii. 19. Jes. xliv. 9 ff. A. H.— These words and similar came instinctively to the lips of every early martyr.—"And they know." Here "they" must refer to "men" just before. I translate the Arm. as it stands.

§ 15. See Acts xvii. 24: αὐτὸς διδοὺς πᾶσι ζωὴν καὶ πνοὴν καὶ τὰ πάντα.

The Apology and Acts of Apollonius. 41

unto all. 16. And I will not again debase myself and cast myself down into the pit. For it is a great shame to do homage to vile things, and it is a servile action to adore what is vain. And men sin in adoring such things. Foolish were those who invented them, and yet more senseless they that adore them and honour them. 17. The Egyptians do homage to an onion in their folly. 18. The Athenians unto this very day make and adore the head of an ox in copper, which they call the good fortune of Athens. And this they have even set up in a conspicuous place near to the statue of Zeus and Heracles, in order that they may pray to them. 19. And yet what more is this than dried clay or a baked potsherd?

---

§ 16. The worship of idols is self-degradation (see § 20); cp. the question in Tatian's Orat. 19: σὺ τῶν ζώων καὶ φυτῶν ἐλάττων ὑπάρχεις; —"I will not again debase," or "I will not any more debase." The following upon § 15, "I have learned," proves that Apollonius was a convert who had been brought up as a Pagan. Philo thus always speaks of the Jews as not simply having learned, but as having learned from birth to abhor polytheistic error, e.g., D.V.C., vol. ii. 481, οἱ Μωυσέως γνώριμοι μεμαθηκότες ἐκ πρώτης ἡλικίας ἐρᾶν ἀληθείας.

§ 18. Hr. Michaelis of Strassburg, communicates to A. H. a note upon the Good Fortune of Athens (lit. of Athenians). "I know of no direct testimony to such a brazen ox-head. By the 'good fortune' must here be meant either a τύχη Ἀθηναίων (τύχη τῆς πόλεως, Athen. Mitth. 1883, p. 288, set up in the Piræus towards the middle of the second century after Chr.), or an ἀγαθὴ τύχη or if the gender permits an ἀγαθὸς Δαίμων. On the other hand I know of a combined cult of Zeus and Heracles, CIA. II., 616, line 21 ff. ἐπαινέσας δὲ καὶ τοὺς ἐπιμελητὰς καὶ τοὺς ἱεροποιοὺς τῷ Σωτῆρι καὶ τῷ Ἡρακλεῖ καὶ τοῖς Σωτῆρσιν, etc." It seems as if Apollonius had himself witnessed in Athens the cult which he describes. A. H. Comp. Minucii Fel. Oct. cap. 28 §§ 7-9, and especially the words: item boum capita et capita ueruecum et immolatis et colitis, de capro etiam et homine mixtos deos et leonum et canum multu deos dedicatis.

§ 19. Comp. Tert. Ap. 14: Socrates in contumeliam deorum quercum et hircum et canem deierabat. A. H.

Eyes have they, and see not; ears have they, and hear not: hands they have, but draw not things to themselves; feet have they, and walk not; for the mere form bestoweth not real substance; and I think that Socrates also was making ridicule of the Athenians when he swore by the poplar tree, and by the dog, and by dry wood. 20. In the first place, men sin against themselves by worshipping them. 21. In the second place, they are guilty of impiety towards God, because they do not know the truth. The Egyptians, again, have

---

§ 21. For the cult of the dove cp. Philo, Sermo II. de Provid. Mangey ed. ii. 646. Clem. Al. Coh. ad Gentes, p. 25, is the only other passage in Christian apologists where I have met any notice of its cult. Perhaps Christians were charitable to the cult, because they had themselves inherited from the Pagans the belief that this particular bird was in an especial manner the messenger and indeed the visual embodiment of the Divine Spirit (see Matt. iii. 16, Luke iii. 32). The comparison of the holy Spirit or Reason of God to the φιλέρημος τρύγων, "the desert-loving pigeon" is found in Philo Judæus, vol. ii., p. 491, and elsewhere. The Talmudists so compared the Spirit of God which moved upon the face of the waters to a dove (Gen. i. 2). From Philo the comparison passed to Clement of Rome, the friend of St. Paul (see Fragm. 8). Perhaps through Clement or his school it made its way into the Gospels and has become in Luke's Gospel not a mere comparison and metaphor, but a material confusion of one thing with another. See also Carm. Sibyl., vii. 83, where God sends down upon Jesus at the Jordan ὄρνιν ἀπαγγελτῆρα λόγων. The gospel story then is compounded out of two pre-existent elements: 1. The comparison of the Spirit of God to a τρύγων, which we have in Philo and in the Talmud. 2. The belief that birds, especially doves, were messengers of the gods, which was the basis of ancient augury, and still survives among us, *e.g.*, in our superstitions as to ravens, magpies, etc.

§ 21. For the Egyptian cult of a mortar cp. Minuc. Fel. Oct., cap. 23: et deus aereus uel argenteus de immundo uasculo, ut accepimus factum Aegyptio regi, conflatur tunditur malleis et in incudibus figuratur; et lapideus deus caeditur, etc. Theophilus of Antioch declaims in the same style against the Egyptian superstitions. Philo of Alexandria is the source of all the later and Christian rationalistic invective against the Egyptian cults; comp. for example in Mangey's edition the following passages: 2. 193, 2. 570, 1. 374, 2. 76, 2. 472.

given the name of God to the onion, and to a wooden mortar, and to the fruits of the field, which we feed upon, and which enter the belly, and pass out into the sweepings; these things have they adored; aye, and they do homage to a fish, and to the dove, and to the dog, and to a stone, and a wolf; and they worship every one of them, the fictions of their own minds. 22. In the third place, men sin whenever they pay homage to men and to angels and to demons, naming them gods."

23. The Prefect answered—"You have philosophised enough, and have filled us with admiration; but dost thou not know this, O Apollonius, that it is the decree of the Senate that no one shall be named a Christian anywhere at all?" 24. Apollonius answered—"Aye, but it is not possible for a human decree of the Senate to prevail over the decree of God. For so far as men frivolously hate those who benefit them and slay them, just in this wise in many ways men stand aloof from God. 25. But know thou this, that God has appointed death, and after death judgment upon all, over kings and poor men,

---

§ 22. This passage is indirectly aimed against the worship of the Emperor.

§ 23. There are here two readings in the Arm. MSS. The one = ne omnino christianus ubicunque appareat. The other = ne omnino christianus ubicunque nominetur. The latter is the true reading, for it was penal to call oneself even by the mere *name* of Christian. But this rule was made by the emperors already in the first century and not by the Senate. Cp. Justin. Ap. i. 4. τὸ ὄνομα ὡς ἔλεγχον λαμβάνετε.

§ 24. Between the first and second propositions of this § it seems as if we must assume a lacuna of some length. A. H.

rulers and slaves and freemen, and philosophers and ignorant men. 26. But there is a distinction of death (from death); for this reason the disciples of Christ do daily die, torturing their desires, and mortifying them according to the Divine Scriptures. For we have no part at all in dissolute desires, nor do we allow impure sights, nor a lewd glance, nor an ear that listens to evil, lest our souls be wounded thereby. 27. But since we live such a fair life, and exercise such good resolutions, we think it no hardship to die for the true God; for whatsoever we are, we are because of God, and for Him we endure tortures, that we may not die miserably the everlasting death. 28. And moreover we do not resent having our goods taken from us, because we know that, whether we live or whether we die, we are the Lord's. Fever, or jaundice, or

---

§ 26. Cp. Minucii Fel. Oct. 30: nobis homicidium nec uidere fas nec audire. Idem, cap. 32 : At nos pudorem non facie, sed mente præstamus : unius matrimonii uinculo libenter inhæremus, cupiditate procreandi aut unam scimus aut nullam. Conuiuia non tantum pudica colimus sed et sobria . . . plerique inuiolate corporis uirginitate perpetua fruuntur potius quam gloriantur; tantum denique abest incesti cupido, ut nonnullis rubori sit etiam pudica coniunctio.

§ 26. The Arm. = ἀλλ' ἀφορισμός ἐστιν τοῦ θανάτου. I owe to A. H. a perception of the true sense, which is that there is more than one kind of death, viz.: spiritual as well as bodily death.—By the Divine Scriptures Apollonius here refers to Gal. v. 24 (vi. 14; Rom. vi. 6); the Pauline Epistles are therefore to him divine writings, see §§ 9, 39.

§ 28. For loss of property cp. Heb. x. 34: τὴν ἁρπαγὴν τῶν ὑπαρχόντων ὑμῶν μετὰ χαρᾶς προσεδέξασθε. Perhaps the lost introduction to these Acts referred to confiscation of the goods of Apollonius. Cp. Athenag., Suppl. 1 and the enactment of Marcus Aurelius in regard to forfeiture of goods even after death in case of high treason (majestas); Cod. Just. 9, 8, 6. What follows is word for word from Rom. xiv. 8. A. H.

any other disease can slay a man. I may expect to die from one or the other of these." 29. The Prefect said—"Art thou bent upon death?" 30. Apollonius answered—"It is my desire to live in Christ, but I have no fear of death, because of any love of life ; for there is not anything that is more estimable than the life eternal, which is the source of deathlessness for the soul that hath lived here a noble life." 31. The Prefect said—"I do not understand thy meaning." 32. Apollonius said—"And what can I do for thee? for the Word of God illumines the heart, as the light gives sight to our eyes."

33. A certain philosopher who was at hand said—"O Apollonius, thou dost insult thyself, for thou art gone exceedingly astray, although though dost even think to speak profound truths." 34. Apollonius said—"I have learnt to pray and not to insult; but thy dissembling bears witness to the blindness of thy heart, for the truth appears to be an insult only to the senseless. 35. The magistrate said—"Tell me plainly what thou didst mean." 36. Apollonius answered—"The Word

---

§ 30 "Source." The Arm. = mother. For a similar and almost contemporary use of μητήρ see Galen περὶ ψυχῆς παθῶν, 53 : καίτοι τούτων ἁπασῶν οὐκ ἂν ὀκνήσαιμι φάναι μητέρα πλεονεξίαν. I have met with the same use in later Acta.—A. H. remarks on the distinction made by Apollonius between ζωὴ αἰώνιος and ἀθανασία ; the former is general and causative, the entire future world, the latter like ἀφθαρσία is a gift therefrom to the individual soul. Comp. II. Clem. ad Cor. 20, 5 : ἀρχηγὸν τῆς ἀφθαρσίας, δι' οὗ καὶ ἐφανέρωσεν ἡμῖν τὴν ἀλήθειαν καὶ τὴν ἐπουράνιον ζωήν.

§ 32. The Arm. = nam uidens cordis est uerbum Dei, sicut perspicax oculorum lumen. Might the sense be, that the word reaches the seeing heart as light the seeing eye?

of God, the Saviour of souls and of bodies, became man in Judæa and fulfilled all righteousness, and was filled gloriously with Divine wisdom, and taught a pure religion, such as beseemed the sons of men, and to put to silence the beginning of sins. 37. For He taught us to pacify anger, to moderate desire, to abate and diminish appetite, to put away sorrow, to take part in pity, to increase love, to cast away vain-glory, to abstain from taking vengeance, not to be vindictive, to despise death, not indeed from lawlessness, but as bearing with the lawless; to obey the laws of God, to reverence rulers, to worship God, to intrust the Spirit to immortal God, to look forward to judgment after death, to expect rewards after the resurrection to be given by God to those who have lived in piety. 38. Teaching all this by word and deed, along with great firmness, and glorified by all for the benefits which He conferred on them, He was slain at last, as were also before Him philosophers and just men. For the just are seen to be a cause of offence to the unjust. 39. As also the Divine Scripture saith:

---

§ 37. "To reverence rulers." See 1 Pet. ii. 17; τὸν θεὸν φοβεῖσθε, τὸν βασιλέα τιμᾶτε. A. H.—The sense of the passage which I render: "to intrust the spirit, etc.," is not quite clear. The rendering "to believe [or intrust] the spirit immortal in God" is rather the sense of the original as it stands. A minute rearrangement of the letters in the Armenian text would give the sense: "To intrust the soul to immortal God." This last is certainly the true sense. Comp. Luke xxiii. 46: "Father into Thy hands I commit my spirit."

§ 38. A. H. Compares Tertul. Apol. 14: "Propterea damnatus est Socrates, quia deos destruebat, plane olim, *i.e.* semper ueritas odio est." And Acta Pionii, 17.

The Apology and Acts of Apollonius. 47

We will bind the just man, because he was a cause of offence to us; 40. but also one of the Greek philosophers said: The just man shall be tortured, he shall be spat upon, and last of all he shall be crucified. 41. Just as the Athenians passed an unjust sentence of death, and charged him falsely, because they yielded to the mob, so also our Saviour was at last sentenced to death by the lawless: by the lawless who were filled with envy and malice against Him, 42. as also against the prophets who were before Him, who spake beforehand concerning Him thus: He shall come and shall do good unto all and shall persuade all men by His goodness even to worship God the Father and Maker of all, in Whom also we believe, rendering homage, because we learned from Him pure commandments, which we knew not, and, therefore, we are no longer in error, but, having lived a good life, we await the hope to come."

43. The magistrate said—"I thought that thou wast changed in the night from that mind of thine." 44. Apollonius said—"And I expected that thy thoughts would be changed in the night and the eyes of thy spirit be opened by my answer: and

---

§ 39. The reference is to Isaiah iii. 13. § 40. The reference is to Plato, *Rep.* II. p. 361 seq. A. H. notes that this passage is not quoted elsewhere in the older Christian literature.

§ 42. A free summary of prophetic teaching. A. H.—"The hope to come" = τὴν μέλλουσαν ἐλπίδα.

§ 44. Comp. the passage quoted from Minucius Felix in illustration of § 8, especially the words "qui hominem periculo subripit, deo opimam uictimam cædit."

that thy heart would bear fruit, and that thou wouldst worship God, the Creator of all, and unto Him continually offer thy prayers by means of compassion; for compassion shown to men by men is a bloodless sacrifice and holy unto God."

45. The magistrate said—"I would fain let thee go, but I cannot, because of the decree of the Senate; yet with benevolence I pronounce sentence on thee"; and he ordered him to be beheaded with a sword. 46. Apollonius said—"I thank my God for thy sentence." 47. And the executioners straightway led him away and beheaded him, while he continued to glorify the Father and Son and Holy Spirit; to Whom be glory for ever. Amen."

---

§ 45. "With benevolence." The Arm. = φιλανθρώπως. The magistrate might have sentenced Apollonius to be thrown to the wild beasts, or to other equally shocking forms of death.

ACTS OF PAUL AND THEKLA.

INTRODUCTION.

AMONG the many apocrypha or uncanonical histories which grew up during the first three centuries of Christianity about the apostles and their immediate followers, there is not one that is so full of human nature as the so-called Acts of Paul and Thekla. In this document we read how Paul came to Iconium, and there preached in the house of one Onesimus. A rich maiden named Thekla overheard him from a window of her house and at once resolved to follow his teaching and devote herself to a life of perpetual virginity. Her mother, who had betrothed her to a rich young man named Thamyris, was vexed thereat, and at her instance Paul was by the authorities scourged and cast out of the town. Thekla follows him to Antioch, and as she enters that city a certain Alexander who was giving a show of wild beasts to the inhabitants, meets her and tries to kiss her. She resists, tears his garments and pulls the sacrificial wreath off his head. For this act of sacrilege she is in accordance with Roman provincial law condemned to be thrown to the wild beasts. At this point she is befriended by a certain Queen Tryphæna, who eventually adopts her.

Acts of Thekla full of human nature.

The Acts of Paul and Thekla have not hitherto received much credence from serious historians, and Conybeare and Howson in their life of S. Paul confine their mention of it to a footnote, which begins thus: "It would have been a mischievous confusion of history and legend to have introduced S. Thekla of Iconium into the text. But her story has so prominent a place in all Roman Catholic histories, that it cannot be alto-

Their authenticity.

gether omitted." And an outline of the story follows in their note.¹ But recent archæological and geographical researches, especially those of Professor W. M. Ramsay, have gone far to establish the historical character of the narrative. First came the discovery in Asia Minor of coins bearing the name of Queen Tryphæna, coins which indicate that she would have been a woman of about sixty in the year 50 A.D., which was the date of Paul's first visit to Iconium. Link by link the evidence has been added to, till Professor Ramsay is able to give us the following account of her: "Queen Tryphæna was daughter of Polemon, king of part of Lycaonia and Cilicia, and also of Pontus. She married Cotys, king of Thrace, and became mother of three kings. . . . In A.D. 50 she was nearly sixty. This suits the Acta perfectly well. . . . Tryphæna was cousin once removed of the Emperor Claudius. The apocryph refers to this very relationship to the Cæsar." Claudius died in A.D. 54, and was succeeded by Nero, who had scant respect either for the memory or the relations of his predecessor. And Professor Ramsay justly observes, that after the accession of Nero, no Roman official in a far-off province would have paid any attention to Tryphæna's kinship with the

Established by the researches of Mommsen and Ramsay.

---

[1] Conybeare and Howson base their rejection of the tale in particular on the statement that Onesiphorus went out along the royal road to Lystra, to meet Paul coming from Antioch. Their objection was just in the then stage of topographical knowledge and with only the Greek text before them; but this very statement of the route taken by Onesiphorus, especially in the clearer form in which the Armenian and Syriac give it, is, now that Professor Ramsay has shown how the roads ran in the year A.D. 50, a clinching proof of the authenticity of these Acts. The old military road of Augustus ran from Antioch of Pisidia to Lystra direct, and threw off half-way a footpath to Iconium, which lay off it many miles to the east. This was so in S. Paul's day. But at a later time a new road was made from Antioch to Lystra passing *through* Iconium. Thus Onesiphorus, in order to meet Paul, would follow the footpath to its junction with the royal road which led to Lystra. It is remarkable how what was in a less perfect stage of knowledge both of text and geography an insurmountable objection to these Acts, has turned out to be a prime proof of their genuineness.

Acts of Paul and Thekla. 51

deceased Claudius, and that the very memory of that kinship would have speedily passed away from men's minds, even as the very name of the queen was lost. "Our knowledge of the dynasty rests almost wholly on the evidence of inscriptions and coins ; in literature there occurs hardly any reference to it. It left no mark on the history of the world, and had no place in the memory of posterity." He justly concludes that the basis of the apocryph must be a document almost contemporary with Paul, written before the recollection of Tryphæna, of her kinship with Claudius, and of the consequent action of the local Roman official had had time to die out.

But this is not the only sign of contemporary origin to be found in the story. Professor Ramsay, who has studied the ancient roads of this part of Asia Minor not in books only, but on the spot, avers that the story reflects a condition and direction of the high-roads in the neighbourhood of Iconium which existed in the year 50 A.D., but which ceased to exist before the end of the century. "Onesiphorus went out from Iconium till he came to the point, a few miles south of Misthia, where the path diverged from the built Roman road that led from Antioch to Lystra." Here Professor Ramsay with insight gathered on the spot, dwells on the divergence of the path to Iconium from the royal or built highway which ran to Lystra.

Modern geographical proof of their truth.

In the Greek text of the story, which alone Professor Ramsay had before him when he wrote the above words, it is merely related that Onesiphorus went along the royal road to Lystra. But in the more ancient text, of which I shall presently give a translation, it is expressly said that he went out as far as the *junction of the path with the royal road which came (or ran) to Lystra*. Here is an admirable and undesigned coincidence with Professor Ramsay's account of the movements of Onesiphorus, and also with the lie and arrangement of the roads, which from ancient milestones found in the neighbourhood he conjectures to have existed in the year 50, before the lines of communication were altered.

For many other touches of local colour, and of truth to the

then condition of Iconium and the surrounding country which are exhibited by the tale, we must refer the reader to the pages of Professor Ramsay's book on *The Christian Church in the Roman Empire from* A.D. 70–170. His clear and interesting statement of them need not be repeated here, where it is my aim rather to point out how certain anachronisms on which he lays his finger in the story, shrewdly surmising them to be second century additions and interpolations, for the most part vanish when we turn to a form of the story earlier by far than that which the Greek manuscripts give us, to the form, namely, in which the tale is told in an ancient Armenian version which has come down to us.

The difficulties inherent in the Greek and Latin texts absent from Syriac and Armenian versions.

Let us enumerate these anachronisms and points of difficulty. They are the following :—

Enumeration of them.

1. Iconium was not a Roman colony in the year 50 A.D., nor did it become one till a century later. It could therefore not have been governed by a pro-consul of the name Castelius or of any other name. There would have been at Iconium in the days of Paul no higher official before whom Paul could be brought than a local judge or dikast, assisted perhaps by a council; and this judge would not have the power of inflicting the penalty of death.

The pro-consul Castelius.

2. The charge of being a Christian could not have been brought as early as the year 50 A.D. The charge of being a magician, however, and of interfering with others, especially with women, is, says Professor Ramsay, "characteristic of that early period, and points to an origin not later than A.D. 80." Readers of Philostratus will remember that it was the very charge brought a few years later in the same regions against Apollonius of Tyana.

The charge of Christianity.

3. In the Greek MSS. we read that Paul with Onesiphorus was going from Iconium to Daphne. Now Daphne was the

site of a famous heathen grove and temple close to Antioch in Syria. Consequently the writer of these words considered that the Antioch of the story was the Syrian Antioch, distant at least 300 miles from Iconium, and not the Antioch of Pisidia, distant only 80. "In the versions preserved to us, Antioch of Syria has been substituted for Antioch of Pisidia through the misunderstanding on the part of an enlarger and editor, who is much older than Basil of Seleucia (5th century)."[1] This Basil wrote a poem in Greek on the martyrdom of Thekla.

Mention of Daphne.

4. Alexander is entitled the Syriarch. This title he can only have borne if it was in Antioch of Syria that the events narrated took place. In the other Antioch of Pisidia the corresponding title would have been Galatarch.

And of a Syriarch.

5. The name Falconilla, says Ramsay, is an anachronism in these regions so early as the year 50 A.D.; it did not come into vogue before the year 130 A.D.

The name Falconilla.

6. The Queen Tryphæna is made to say: There is no one to help me; neither child, for she is dead, nor kinsman, for I am a widow. Says Professor Ramsay: "The real queen had at this period three sons living as kings, and powerful relatives. In the long process of alteration through which the work has passed, a little additional colouring was liable to be added to the cry of the widow."

Queen Tryphæna's kindred.

7. The words of the governor's act, says Ramsay, setting Thekla free, have not been left uninterpolated by later taste; at least the epithet God-fearing, *Theosebes*, is due to a later age and to the desire of making the governor bear witness to the truth.

8. Onesiphorus, we read, went out to meet Paul with his children, with Silas and Zeno and his wife Lectra. Ramsay objects especially to the name Lectra, as unlikely.

The name Lectra.

---

[1] Ramsay, p. 381.

9. Thekla found Paul at Myra; but Myra is a sea-port in Lycia, distant from Iconium in a straight line some 200 miles over impassable mountains. On the other hand the context indicates that the place where Paul was found was not far from Antioch. Otherwise how could Thekla have heard so soon of Paul's whereabouts, and how could Tryphæna have at once sent clothing and gold? Moreover, Paul only touched at Myra some years afterwards on his third missionary journey; but the tale indicates that this was Paul's first visit to Iconium, and that he was a stranger there. It follows that the entire episode, if it be historical, belongs to Paul's first journey, and not to his third. At the same time Myra is a port to which a traveller overland from Antioch of Pisidia might take ship; while it is inconceivable that anyone going from the Syrian Antioch should arrive there, except by a long sea-voyage. Professor Ramsay concludes that "the Myra episode was inserted before the confusion with the Syrian Antioch had been caused by one who connected the tale with Paul's third journey." His reasoning apparently was that the action could not be conceived as taking place at Paul's first visit to Iconium, for he disappears from the scene of action so quickly; whereas, according to the Acts of the Apostles Paul remained in the country, and soon returned to Iconium after his first expulsion or flight from it.

Mention of Myra.

The above are the chief points in the Greek narrative, which are difficult to reconcile with the hypothesis that in these Acts of Paul and Thekla we have at bottom a document written well before the end of the first century. Professor Ramsay urges that hypothesis, and argues that these points of inconsistency with so early a date, are due to the hand of an interpolator who lived soon after A.D. 130. It will go far to confirm Professor Ramsay's hypothesis, besides proving his remarkable sagacity as a critic, if an earlier text of the Acta can be produced from which all these points of difficulty are absent. Now in the ancient Armenian language there exists a version of these Acta, which was made from a still

All the above difficulties vanish in the Armenian version.

Acts of Paul and Thekla. 55

earlier Syriac version at the beginning of the fifth century; from this older text we find that, with a single exception, all the matters conjectured by Professor Ramsay to be interpolations of the second century vanish.

1. Paul is brought at Iconium before a local dikast, and mention is made of a council or gerûsia. There is no hint of a Roman pro-consul named Castelius.

2. The second difficulty is not quite removed by the Armenian text, yet it is minimised. For in the Greek text Demas and Hermogenes are made to say at the banquet: "Bring him before the governor Castelios on the charge of persuading the multitude to embrace the new teaching of the Christians, and he will speedily destroy him." But the Armenian has: "This man teaches a new and outlandish doctrine in the name of Christ, and forthwith when one gives ear to it, it destroys him." I think the original text has here, by a very slight change, been made to imply that Christianity was an offence for which a man might be sentenced to death by a Roman governor, as was the case at a later time.

3. The Armenian has no mention of Daphne, and so leaves it to be inferred that the Antioch mentioned was not the Syrian, but the Pisidian Antioch.

4. In the Armenian Alexander is not called a Syriarch.

5. The name Falconilla is absent from the Armenian.

6. Instead of being made to say that she has no kindred or children to help her, Tryphæna says that no one of her noble family is ready to assist her. These words imply that she had at the time highly-placed relatives, and the reference was no doubt to her royal sons, as to whom Ramsay suggests, that they had quarrelled with their mother for dynastic reasons. Thus this point, instead of invalidating the story, turns out to be confirmatory of it.

7. From the Armenian form of the governor's act releasing Thekla the epithet God-fearing is absent. He simply says: "The God has delivered Thekla and given her to you." There is no reason to suppose that he knew anything of Thekla's religion, or was in these words referring to the God of the

Jews. He probably believed that Thekla was, like many other young Phrygian girls, vowed to the service of the local deity, and thought that that deity had intervened to save her. Thekla herself, it will be remembered, had declared herself to be a slave or hand-maid of the God (in Greek, θεοδούλος). Meaning no doubt that she was the slave of the true God about whom Paul had taught her, though Alexander would of course have interpreted her words in the conventional sense.

8. In the Armenian Onesiphorus goes out from Iconium with his household and Zeno and his wife. The names Silas and Lectra are not mentioned.

9. For Myra in Lycia the Armenian gives a name Meru or Mero, and says nothing about Lycia. The Syriac version also, of which the Armenian is a very early translation, has the name Merv, and says nothing of the place being in Lycia, nor is "in Lycia" added in all the Greek MSS. Possibly Myra is here a corruption of Merus, the name of a city some miles from Antioch in a north-westerly direction. Perhaps there was some place answering to the name Merv still nearer to Antioch; from which place Thekla sent out to seek for Paul, and whence also the gifts of money and clothes were sent by Tryphæna. The agreement between the Armenian and the Syriac in spelling the name Merv is notable, because many of the other names in the tale are misspelt in the Armenian, a fact intelligible enough, if we remember that the vowels were not added in Syriac MSS. Thus Thamyris is spelt Themeros in the Armenian, and Tryphæna becomes Triphonia, and Thekla Thekl. It is only the names like Iconium and Alexander, names familiar to the Armenian translator, which are rightly spelt.

There still remain however in the story, even as the Armenian form presents it, episodes which must be apocryphal. Such is the story of Thekla's being

The burning of Thekla an interpolation, but in the Armenian and Syriac.

sentenced to be burned. It was doubtless not less annoying in Iconium, in the first century than it would be in Oxford in the nineteenth, that a street preacher who came proclaiming the immediate advent

Acts of Paul and Thekla. 57

of the millennium should turn the heads of the rich young ladies, for whom their mothers had just arranged good matches, and persuade them that the only right thing for them was to devote themselves to perpetual virginity. But even if by such teaching Paul did something to merit the being scourged and expelled from Iconium, yet Thekla certainly did not merit to be burned alive, because she was deceived by it. Nor is it in keeping with the attitude of her mother, and of Thamyris; for this was one rather of embarrassed affection than of harsh hatred. We know moreover that it was not part of the original account, for there exists a Greek homily as old as 300 A.D., dealing with the story of Thekla, and not only making no mention of this episode, but replacing it by a different one.[1]

We may thus without hesitation cut out this unlikely episode, and consider that Thekla's references thereto in her later utterances are also the interpolations of a later reviser of the tale. In that case we should not expect these references to be added quite uniformly in all the texts; and this is actually the case, for we find that in the Greek, Thekla, when relating in chap. xlii. to Paul and Onesiphorus all that she has undergone, mentions the burning. In the next chapter (xliii.), in talking to her mother she says nothing about it; but in the Armenian it is in chap. xliii., in talking to her mother that she refers to it, whereas in chap. xlii. she does not mention it. This is good proof that these references were added to the tale at a later time, when the episode of the burning was introduced. Were they part of the original text, they would come in the same part of it. A similar want of uniformity among the texts, some giving and some omitting allusions to the burning, is seen in chaps. xxiii., xxiv., xxxi.

There is no room within the limits of the present paper to consider the doctrinal value of the Acts of Paul and Thekla. It is enough to point out that the claim of Thekla, though a woman, to baptise, far from being minimised in the older Armenian text, *Thekla's claim to baptise.*

---

[1] See the note at end of this introduction.

is in it presented more strongly and pointedly than in the Greek. It is the same with regard to the teaching of virginity.

The inculcation of virginity by the Acts. It is therefore certain that this teaching was part of the original first century document, instead of being, as Ramsay is inclined to think, a Montanist addition of the second century. ‡ The teaching of the Acta with regard to marriage and virginity is consonant with that which Paul addresses to the Corinthians in his first epistle to them, chap. vii. 25 foll. : "Concerning virgins (*i.e.* chaste men) I have no command from the Lord, but I give my judgment. . . . I think then that by reason of the present necessity, that it is good for a man so to be. Art thou bound to a wife? Seek not to be loosed. Art thou loosed from a wife? Seek not a wife. . . . But this I say, brethren, the time is short, that henceforth they who have wives be as if they had them not ; and they that weep as though they wept not, and they that rejoice as though they rejoiced not, and they that buy as though they kept not their property, and they that use the world as if they had no use for it. For the outward show of this world is passing away. But I would have you free from earthly cares. The cares of the unmarried man are fixed upon the Lord, and he strives to please the Lord. But the cares of the husband are fixed upon worldly things, striving to please his wife. The wife also has this difference from the virgin ; the cares of the virgin are fixed upon the Lord, that she may be holy both in body and spirit. . . . Thus he who gives his daughter in marriage does well, but he who gives her not in marriage does better."

Such was of necessity the teaching of one who believed, as Paul no doubt believed, that the Messiah would shortly reappear on earth, and then and there begin his thousand years reign in Jerusalem, establishing a kingdom in which there was to be no marrying or giving in marriage, and in which, if we may believe the Gospel of Luke, only the unmarried would be deemed worthy to share.

The Armenian version seems to have kept a touch of local colour in its description of Paul's refuge after the expulsion

Acts of Paul and Thekla.

from Iconium. Paul was fasting, himself and Onesiphorus and his wife and sons, in a certain house of a young man, *of which the opened door looks in the direction of the road of Iconium.* This touch is absent even from the Syriac version.

The mention of a sepulchre as Paul's place of refuge not in the Armenian.

In the following notes I have only added in full the variants of the Syriac text as translated by the late Professor Wright. These variants well illustrate the growth of the tale. The Greek and Latin texts are accessible to any one in the editions of Grabe, Thilo or Lipsius, and I have not encumbered my notes with all their variants, but have given only the more important ones they contain. (The Armenian is a literal version of the Syriac text, but free from certain interpolations already present in Syriac MSS. of the fifth century.) The Syriac again is free from interpolations present in the old Latin version ; and this again is a purer text than the Greek, which more than any other betrays the accretions and changes of various ages. Lipsius is therefore quite wrong in attaching so little value to the Syriac texts, which as purified by the Armenian must henceforth be taken as the basis of the true text. Except for the interpolation of the burning of Thekla, the Armenian may very nearly represent the original form of the text as it stood in the first century.

The Syriac and Armenian forms give the oldest text of these Acts.

Lipsius' error on this point vitiates his text.

The martyrdom of Thekla is frequently referred to in the earliest Acts of the Martyrs. Her story it is which inspires Eugenia in the reign of Commodus. The exordium of the Acts of Polyeuctes refers to Thekla and Perpetua, and there were certainly many virgin martyrs who drew their first inspiration from the same source. The earlier martyrdoms contain many indications that the History of Thekla was one of the earliest Christian books generally diffused. Thus, S. Eugenia calls it "a divine book about God" (Acts, ch. iii.), and, "the holy book" (*ibidem*). S. Eugenius, a martyr of

Influence of these Acts on later Martyrs.

Trebizond under Diocletian, couples Thekla in his prayers with David and Daniel. In connection with the Armenian version it is interesting to note that in the Armenian convent of Edschmiadzin, in the province of Ararat, there is built into the wall of the conventual church an old Greek bas-relief of Paul and Thekla which must belong to the fifth century at latest.

NOTE.—Pseudo-Chrysostomi op. Ed. Migne, vol. 2, p. 746. Εἰς τὴν ἁγίαν πρωτομάρτυρα καὶ ἀπόστολον Θέκλαν ἐγκώμιον. Parentes multis eam uerbosisque commonitionibus ad coniugium incitabant. . . . Uiderat quippe sponsi (*i.e.* Christi) pulchritudinem, et ab eius contuitu non avellebatur: instabat mater, quae ad nuptias impellebat. . . . accedebat procus nuptiali eam colloquio titillans . . . confluebant adulationibus captantes propinqui . . . supplicabant serui cum lacrymis . . . terrebant iudices poenis; at omnes illa magno animo proculcans clamabat, Principes non sunt timori bonis operibus, sed malis (Rom. xiii. 3). Cum uero statuas uirginitatis etiam in uiis erigi martyri oporteret, talis quaedam puellae est exorta tentatio. Liberata iudicio, Pauli praedam sectabatur, et rumorem sequuta ducem, uiis quae ad Paulum ferebant, sese est ausa committere. Porro diabolus puellam obseruabat, et cum iter agentem obseruasset, hostem immittit in puellam procum, uirginitatis tanquam in deserto praedonem. Cumque iam iter perficeret, generosa uirgini admissarius a tergo procus et acer indagator captam eam esse iam inclamabat; difficiles undique angustiae urgebant; robustus erat, qui bellum inferebat; infirma, cui bellum inferebatur. Ubinam aliquod illi a perfugio illo perfugium. Tum uero in caelum conuersa uirgo ad eum, qui omnibus ubique ipsum inuocantibus adest, cum lamentis clamabat, Domine Deus meus, in te speraui (Ps. vii. 2). The Latin version here quoted is that of Fronto Ducaeus. I have given the title of the fragment as it is read in the Greek. In the horologion of the Greeks Thekla is similarly entitled ἰσαπόστολος.

ACTS OF PAUL AND THEKLA.

1. Paul was coming on his way up to the city of Iconium after his persecution, and *there* accompanied him on the road Demas and Hermogenes, copper-smiths and brasiers; and these were full of a spirit of mutiny, though in their words they honoured Paul and addressed him as one whom they loved. But Paul was looking unto[1] the grace of the pity of Christ, and was walking with them without any dissembling, and loved them alike. And he so loved them that he continued to relate to them the teaching of the Lord of all, and the explanation and the birth and resurrection, as of one he loved, and was refreshing their souls with the greatness of Christ, and was for ever recounting to them how he (or *it*) was manifested to himself. 2. Now a certain blessed man, of the name of Onesiphorus, heard that Paul is on his way to the city of Iconium, and went out to meet him, taking with him his household and Zenonia his wife;[2] they went to meet Paul and welcome him. For Titus had told them and had given them the characteristics of

---

[1] The Arm. *hajzer*=was asking, must be a corruption of *hajer*=was looking.

[2] The Arm. text B has: "his household, and Zenon and his wife."

Paul's appearance; because he—Onesiphorus—did not know Paul in the flesh, but only in the spirit. 3. So he went forth and stood at the cross-ways of the high-road which ran to the city of Lystra,[1] and there halted and waited for him. And he was looking at those who came and went, bearing in mind the characteristics which Titus had given him; when he saw Paul coming along, a man of moderate stature, with curly[2] hair, . . . scanty, crooked legs, with blue eyes, and large knit brows, long nose, and he was full of the grace and pity of the Lord, sometimes having the appearance of a man, but sometimes looking like an angel.[3]

4. When Paul saw Onesiphorus, he was very glad. Quoth unto him Onesiphorus, "Hail to thee Paul, apostle of the blessed one"; and unto him Paul, "Hail to thee and to all thy house, Onesiphorus." But Demas and Hermogenes were full of ire and bit their lips with resentment and said to Paul, "Were not we also of the blessed one, that thou

---

The Syriac has: "went out with the sons of Simon and with Zenon and with his wife to meet Paul." Lipsius reads: "went out with his children Simmias and Zenon and with his wife Lectra."

[1] Syriac: "Stood where the roads meet, on the highway which goes to Lystra." Greek: "he began to walk along the royal road which runs to Lystra."

[2] Or "crisp."

[3] Syriac thus describes Paul: "A man of middling size, and his hair was scanty, and his legs were a little crooked, and his knees were projecting (or far apart); and he had large eyes, and his eyebrows met, and his nose was somewhat long; and he was full of grace and mercy; at one time he seemed like a man and at another he seemed like an angel." The Greek and Latin texts do not vary materially. No text but the Armenian adds the trait "blue eyes."

Acts of Paul and Thekla. 63.

didst never give such greeting to us?" Paul made answer and said to them, "For I see not in you the fruit of well-doing." Quoth unto them Onesiphorus, "Obey me (B. If thou be aught. C. If ye be aught),[1] come into my house,. ye also, and rest." 5. And when Paul had come into the house of Onesiphorus and there was great rejoicing therein, they fell on their knees and then rose up and brake bread.

Paul came forward and began to preach the word of the Lord concerning the truth of souls [2] and the resurrection of the dead, and spake thus: "Blessed are the pure in heart, for they shall see God. Blessed are they that keep themselves chaste, because they shall be called the temple of God. Blessed are they that mortify their bodies and souls, because unto them speaketh God. Blessed are they who despise the world, for they shall be pleasing to God. Blessing unto them who shall have wives, as if they had them not; for they shall inherit the earth. 6. Blessed they who shall have the fear of God in their hearts, because they shall be called angels. Blessed they who tremble at the words of God, which they hear, for the Lord shall call them. Blessed be they who have received the wisdom of Jesus Christ, because they shall be called sons of God. Blessed be they who keep the baptism, for they

---

[1] B and C represent 2nd and 3rd Armenian MSS. of the Acta. The Greek gives the words: "For I see not," etc., to Onesiphorus, and omits the ensuing words: "Quoth unto them Onesiphorus."

[2] Syriac: "the controuling of the flesh."

shall rest[1] in Father, Son, and Holy Spirit.[2] Blessed they who shall receive the law of Christ, because they shall be for a great light. Blessed those who for the love of Christ shall leave the flesh, for they shall inherit immortal life,[3] and shall stand eternally on the right hand of the Son of God. Blessed are the merciful, for they shall find mercy from the Father, and in the day of judgment they shall receive the kingdom. Blessing to the souls and bodies of virgins, for they shall be pleasing to God, and shall not lose the reward of their chastity: for the working of the Father's words[4] shall be found in them, and they shall inherit life in the day of the Son of God, and rest eternal shall be theirs."

7. And while Paul was discoursing all these great things of God in the house of Onesiphorus in a great assembly, a maiden named Thekla, the daughter of Thekla,[5] who was betrothed to a man whose name was Thamyris,[6] went and sat at a

---

[1] Syriac: "rest in," which is probably the true sense of the Armenian.

[2] All Syriac MSS. omit "and H. S." So Greek.

[3] The Greek has: "because they shall judge the angels." The Latin runs: "quoniam angelis æquabuntur." The next clause seems to have originally run: "καὶ ἐν δεξίᾳ τοῦ πατρὸς (or τοῦ θεοῦ) σταθήσονται." But as it was later on recognised to be the privilege of Jesus alone to stand on the right hand of God, there were substituted the words καὶ ἐν δ. τοῦ Χριστοῦ (or τοῦ υἱοῦ τοῦ θεοῦ) εὐλογηθήσονται. Lipsius absurdly reads τοῦ πατρὸς εὐλογηθήσονται, neither one thing nor the other.

[4] Greek = "For the word (ὁ λόγος) of the Father shall be to them a work (ἔργον) of salvation unto the day of His Son, and they shall have rest for ever and ever."

[5] Syriac: "Theocleia." So Greek and Latin texts.

[6] The Armenian spells: Themeros, a mistake natural in a translation from unpointed Syriac.

window which was close to their roof, and there listened to the discourse of Paul which he spake concerning chastity. Nor did she leave the window ever by day or by night, but listened to the prayers of Paul and wondered at his faith; the more so, because she saw many women going in unto Paul, to listen to the precepts and commands of God which he taught. And it was a matter of regret and longing to her, that she saw not his face, but heard only his bare words. 8. And she never for a moment departed from the window where she sat. Then her mother sent for Thamyris to whom she had betrothed her as wife. When Thamyris heard that his mother-in-law summoned him, he came at once, and he thought that she would give him Thekla to take her to wife. Thamyris made answer and said, "Where is Thekla, my wife (or betrothed), that I may see her?" The mother-in-law answered Thamyris and said: "I have somewhat to tell thee, Thamyris. Thekla who was betrothed to thee, lo, for three days and three nights she quits not a window, she eats not nor drinks nor rises thence; but she strains her eyes to gaze upon a strange man, and hearkens to his words as if they were pleasing, though they are illusive and vain and disgusting. And I am surprised that a wise maiden should thus run after such wicked and delusive talk. 9. I tell thee, Thamyris, that yonder man has undone the city of the Iconians, and he deceives Thekla, who was betrothed to thee. And many other women and young people have gone in unto him, and he teaches them to worship one God and to live in chastity. And Thekla is bound by him, as a spider on a web, and has given herself up to longing and to disastrous works of destruction; and she never raises her eyes from the window nor forsakes it; nor does she eat or drink, but the virgin is quite absorbed. But do thou, Thamyris, go in and talk with her, for she is betrothed to thee to be thy wife.

10. And Thamyris went in to her who was betrothed to him in marriage, because for one thing he loved Thekla, and in the second place he was afraid of her solemn longing. He made answer and said to her, "Art thou not betrothed to me? What is this that thou doest, and what is this evil destruction that possesses thee? Return to me and be ashamed before me." And her mother also spoke and said, "Why dost thou look down and refuse to answer, nay, and art like unto one that is mad?" When the household saw her, they all began to weep, and Thamyris wept, for that his wife held aloof from him; and her mother for that her daughter separated herself from her; and the handmaids that they were separated from their mistress. And there was great sorrow and grief in the house. But Thekla cared not for all that, but bent down her ear to hear the words of Paul.

11. Then Thamyris was full of wrath and he ran out into the street and marked the men who came from or went in unto Paul. And suddenly

Acts of Paul and Thekla. 67

he saw two men who disputed one with the other. Then Thamyris came upon them and said to them: "What are ye, or what is come unto you, or what are the words about which ye dispute? Who is yonder man who is in there with you, who ensnares the souls of young men and maidens, and who gives the commandment that there be no marriages at all?[1] I am willing to give you much money, if ye will tell me who and whence is the man, because we are leaders of the city." 12. But Demas and Hermogenes, when they saw him, came to him and said: "Yonder man of whom thou speakest, we know not who and whence he is; but this we know, that he separates the young men from the virgins and the virgins from the young men, and declares that you cannot rise from the dead[2] unless you maintain yourself in chastity." 13. Thamyris made answer and said to them: "Come, my friends, and rest with me." So they went home with him to supper readily, and Thamyris made them a great repast and prepared for them many good dishes. For Thamyris loved Thekla, and wished to take her as his wife on the day appointed by his mother-in-law. And Thamyris said to them as they lay on the couch: "Tell me, my dear friends, what is the teaching which this man teacheth, that I may know it. For there are not a few who condemn

---

[1] The Greek has: ἵνα γάμοι μὴ γίνωνται ἀλλὰ οὕτως μένωσιν. The Syriac and Armenian show no sign of their Greek original having been here adapted to the language of Paul's epistles.
[2] Compare on this passage the general preface.

the same, and I am very grieved for my wife, because she has given herself up to a strange man and foreign, and behold, I am separated from her." 14. Demas and Hermogenes answered and said to him: "Thou Thamyris, go and inform the judge[1] about him, and thou shalt say thus: This man teaches a new and outlandish doctrine in the name of Christ, and forthwith when he hears it, it (*or* he) destroys him. But thou shalt take thy wife, and we teach thee the resurrection of the dead which he teaches."

15. When Thamyris heard this, being filled with spite and rancour, he rose early at dawn and went to the house of Onesiphorus, himself with the senators,[2] with many men bearing rods, and provided as well with a large armed force. He answered and said to Paul, "Thou destroyest the city of the Iconians, and Thekla who was betrothed to me thou hast ensnared with thy teaching, so that she will not be mine to wife. Come therefore let us go before the judge."[3] And all

---

[1] The Syriac = "Thamyris, bring him before Castelus the Hegemon, and say, 'This fellow teaches the new doctrine and is a Christian, and lo, straightway he will destroy him, and thou shalt take Thekla thy betrothed (to wife), and we will teach,'" etc. The Greek text has: "Bring him before the Hegemon, Castelius, and say, he persuades the multitude to accept the new teaching of Christians, and so he will destroy him, and thou wilt have thy wife Thekla; and we will teach thee as to the resurrection which he declares there to be, that it has already happened in the children whom we have [and we arise having recognised the true God]. Some Latin MSS. omit the name Castelius here as also below.

[2] The Arm. = μετὰ τῶν γερόντων, which must be right, as Iconium would have had a local senate. The Greek has μετὰ ἀρχόντων καὶ δημοσίων. The Syriac MSS. differ one from another: one reads, "With the chief men"; another: "With the priests."

[3] Syriac: "Come to Castelus the Hegemon." So also the Greek.

Acts of Paul and Thekla.

the city cried: "Drag out the wizard, for he has corrupted and destroyed our women with outlandish teaching." And all the armed men took charge of Paul. 16. When Paul was come with those who held him and stood before the judge, Thamyris lifted up his voice and said to the judge:—"This man, we know not who and whence he is, but he suffers not virgins to belong to their husbands; let him then say before thee wherefore he teaches such teaching." But Demas and Hermogenes, the copper-smiths, who were full of malice, came forward to him,[1] and said: "Say that he is a Christian, and behold forthwith he[2] destroyeth him." When the judge heard the words of Thamyris and of all the men who held Paul, he said to him: "Tell me, Paul, who and whence thou art and what thou teachest? For there are not a few who speak evil of thee and accuse thee."

17. Then Paul lifted up his voice, and said: "I will unfold that which I teach; hear, O judge. I teach one God, who returneth not evil for the evil which men do; God, who desireth not anything, except that the sons of man should live, sent me in order that I might save them from destruction and purge them of their uncleanness and from all deadly desires, unto the end that they sin no more. For this end hath God sent me, that

---

[1] The Greek and Latin omit the words, "The copper-smiths . . . to him."

[2] The Greek has, "Thou destroyest him," or: "Thou shalt destroy him."

in Him of whom I preach the good tidings may be the hope of all men. Who was greatly desirous to save His people from error, that they should sin no more and not walk in licentiousness ; but that there may be in them awe and fear by means of the faith in God, that they may know the love and fear of the truth. Therefore that which God revealed unto me, that I teach. What do I owe unto these men ?"[1]

When the judge heard these words, he commanded that Paul be bound again, and kept in prison, until there be a good opportunity to hear him. 18. But Thekla on the same night took her bracelet and gave it to the door-keeper of his house; and he opened to her the door; and then she went on to the gaoler who kept Paul, and gave to him a golden mirror, in order that she might go in unto Paul. And he took from her the mirror and let her in. So she went and sat at the feet of Paul and heard the great things of God. But Paul was in no wise sad, but was full of assurance and openly rejoiced the hearts of all who were with him with the commandments of

---

[1] The Greek has, "And Paul lifted up his voice, saying, ' If I this day answer what I teach, hear, O proconsul. God living, God of requitals (ἐκδικήσεων), God who is jealous, God wanting in nothing, desiring the salvation of men, sent me, to draw them away from destruction and impurity and from all pleasure and death, that they sin no more. Wherefore God sent His own Son, whose good tidings I preach, and teach men to have their hope in Him, who alone suffered with the erring world, in order that men be no longer under judgment, but have faith and fear of God and knowledge of holiness and love of truth. If then I teach the things revealed to me by God, what wrong do I do, O proconsul?' "
The dogmatic teaching of the Greek text seems more developed.

Acts of Paul and Thekla.   71

God. And Thekla with great joy kissed the feet and the chains which bound the feet and hands of Paul.

19. But when her household sought Thekla and found her not, they thought that she had perished, and they went and sought her in the highways. But there came a comrade of the door-keeper's, who gave information about him and said, "I saw Thekla give her bracelet to the door-keeper and pass by." And when they tortured the door-keeper, he avowed it under compulsion, and said : "Yea, she came and said, 'I am going to the stranger who is bound in the prison.'" So they went and found her as the door-keeper told them ; they came and found her sitting at the feet of Paul, and saw several other people as well, who were listening to the great things of Christ.[1] And Thamyris went out along with several men who were with him, full of anger, and they told the judge all that had taken place.

20. Then the judge bade them bring Paul before him, and the young men ran and loosed Paul and dragged him forth from the prison, But Thekla threw herself on the ground and wept bitterly on the spot where Paul had sat in bonds and taught her the Commands of God. Then the judge again ordered Thekla to be brought before him ; and Thamyris ran, and many men with him, and took Thekla and dragged her in. When the judge saw her, he was very grieved about

---

[1] Syriac, "Of God," or : "Of the Most High."

her;[1] but Thekla right gladly stood up before him and was in no ways cast down. Then on a sudden all the armed men cried out and said: "Destroy this wizard." But the judge said nothing to Paul. And then the judge sat down on his throne and called Thekla. And the judge said to her: "Wherefore art thou not for (or to) thy husband according to the laws of the Iconians?" But Thekla simply stood there, just as she was, and riveted her eyes upon Paul and gave no answer whatever to the judge. Her mother raised a loud and shrill scream, and said, "Destroy the senseless one in the theatre, that all women may look at her and forbear to learn this evil teaching." 21. When the judge heard this, he was very distressed about her; but he ordered Paul to be scourged and cast out of the city. And he gave sentence that they should burn Thekla with fire in the middle of the theatre. The judge rose up to go to the theatre and all the host with him, to see Thekla burned in the fire. And, as a sheep wandering among the hills in search of the shepherd, even so Thekla sought for Paul. And as she looked round on all the men there, she saw the Lord Jesus Christ sitting full opposite her (Syriac, "beside her") in the likeness of Paul. Thekla made answer and said: "Paul came and sat in front of me, as if I could not endure,[2] in the vision which has ap-

---

[1] The Greek omits this clause.
[2] This is the literal sense of the Armenian, of which the text here seems

Acts of Paul and Thekla. 73

peared to me." And while she kept her eyes fixed upon him, the Lord rose up and went into heaven.

22. But the young men and the women brought wood and laid it in the theatre to burn Thekla, and they brought her naked into the theatre. When the judge saw this he began to weep and raised a lamentation, and wondered at the power ✗ which was in her. They piled up the wood and undid it, and the youths compelled her to go up on to the fire as it blazed up. And Thekla immediately went up atop of the fire.[1] Then the flames of the blazing fire rose and gathered round her, yet not one tress of her hair caught light, because the Spirit of God had pity on her, and a roaring sound went forth from heaven, and a cloud of wet was over her, and hail and heavy rain was poured forth from heaven. And many men who listened and saw were destroyed; and the fire was quenched and Thekla was saved.

23. But Paul was fasting, along with Onesiphorus and his wife and sons in a house[2] of

---

faulty. The Syriac="As if I were not able to bear whatever may come upon me." For a similar incident, cp. Euseb., *H. E.*, v. 1, 206, where Blandina having been exposed on the cross, διὰ τῆς εὐτόνου προσευχῆς πολλὴν προθυμίαν τοῖς ἀγωνιζομένοις ἐνεποίει, βλεπόντων αὐτῶν ἐν τῷ ἀγῶνι καὶ τοῖς ἔξωθεν ὀφθαλμοῖς διὰ τῆς ἀδελφῆς τὸν ὑπὲρ αὐτῶν ἐσταυρωμένον, ἵνα πείσῃ κ.τ.λ. *Cp.* "Translatio Philippi" in M. R. James' *Apocr. Anecd.*, p. 161, 16, ὡς καὶ τὸν Ἰησοῦν φαίνεσθαι αὐτοῖς ἐν σχήματι τοῦ Φιλίππου. The parallel in John xx. 15 will occur to everyone.

[1] The Syriac adds: "She stretched out her hands in the form of a cross." So the Greek and Latin Texts. Just below the Greek runs, that God had pity on her, and made a subterranean noise, etc.

[2] The Syriac has: "In a sepulchre which was open by the roadside of the

a young man, of which the opened door looks in the direction of the road of (or *to*) the city of Iconium. When they had been there many days a-fasting, the children say to Paul, "We are hungry." And they would have had nothing to give in payment; for Onesiphorus had abandoned his house and means of living, and had gone forth along with his friend Paul. Then Paul took off his tunic and gave it to the youth, and said, "Go, my child, and buy bread as much as it fetches." The youth went to buy bread and there saw Thekla their neighbour. He wondered, and said : "Thekla, whither goest thou?" She says to him: "I am going after Paul, because I have been saved from the fire.[1] And the youth said, "Come, I will lead you to him; for he is distraught, and sighs and grieves, and it is now six days that he fasts and prays of God for thee." 24. Thekla went with him to the house of the young man,[2] and came to Paul and found him on his knees in prayer, beseeching and saying, "Our Father which art in heaven,[3] I pray thee that the fire may not touch Thekla, but rather quench it from her, for she is Thine." And Thekla stood behind him, and she opened her mouth and said : "Father, which madest heaven and earth, and

---

Iconians." The Greek MSS. have ἐν μνημείῳ ἀνοικτῷ (some ἐν μν. καινῷ or κενῷ) ἐν ὁδῷ ᾗ ἀπὸ 'Ικονίου εἰς Δάφνην πορεύονται. The old Latin and Syriac omit the words εἰς Δάφνην.

[1] One Greek MS. (Lipsius' F) omits the words ἐκ πυρὸς σωθεῖσα.
[2] Syriac : "To the sepulchre." So the Greek and Latin.
[3] The Greek MSS. have Πάτερ Χριστοῦ or similar expressions.

Acts of Paul and Thekla. 75

Thou art the Father of saints,[1] I thank Thee that Thou hast had pity upon me and hast saved me in order that I may behold Paul." Paul rose up and saw her, and answered and said : " God, who knowest the hearts of all, Father of our Lord Jesus Christ, I thank Thee that Thou hast saved her, for whom I supplicated Thee, from the fire,[2] and hast granted to me, and to those with me, to behold her ; in Thy hands is it to rescue from all afflictions those who glorify Thy name for ever.

25. And Paul rejoiced exceedingly along with those who were with him.[3] And the lad brought five loaves of bread, with vegetables and salt besides, and water ; and they rejoiced in their deeds and were made strong in the grace of the pity of Christ. And said Thekla to Paul : " I will cut short my hair and will follow after thee, whithersoever thou goest." Said Paul : "'Tis a hard struggle, and thou art beautiful ; perhaps another temptation may beset thee, even a greater than the first, and thou wilt not be able to bear it." Said Thekla to Paul : " Give me only the seal of

---

[1] Syriac : "Of the Holy (One)." The Greek is yet more developed : ὁ τοῦ παιδὸς τοῦ ἀγαπητοῦ σου Ἰησοῦ Χριστοῦ πατήρ. So the Latin.

[2] Here the reference to the fire has not made its way into the Greek and old Latin : εὐλογῶ σε ὅτι ὁ ἠρώτησα ἐτάχυνάς μοι καὶ εἰσήκουσάς μου. They also omit the words of Paul which ensue in the Armenian and Syriac.

[3] The Greek="And there was within in the tomb much love" (ἀγάπη πολλή. Latin : gaudium magnum). Just below the Greek and Latin texts omit the words : "and salt besides." It was a primitive Eucharist which they celebrated with bread, water, vegetables and salt. See Harnack's tract on the use of water in the primitive Eucharist, and compare Philo, *De Vita Contemplativa*, ii. 484, where hyssop is the vegetable partaken of with leavened bread and salt and water.

Christ and temptation cometh not nigh me." Said Paul to Thekla: "Be patient, and thou shalt receive that which thou seekest."[1] 26. And Paul sent away Onesiphorus along with his household, and they went to their home. But Paul took Thekla by the hand and the men who were with her, and they went and came to the city of Antioch. And as they were entering in, one of the chief men of the city of Antioch, Alexander by name,[2] who had done many deeds in Antioch, as soon as he saw Thekla, loved her at sight, and began to flatter Paul and cajole him with promises of much silver and gold. Said Paul: "I know not the woman of whom thou speakest, and she is nothing of mine at all." For Alexander was violent, and came and constrained Thekla, and put his arms round her in the middle of the market-place. But she would not brook his action, but cried out and sought for Paul with much lamentation, and said: "Hurt not one who is a stranger, insult not the handmaids of God. I am daughter of leading citizens of the city of Iconium, and because I would not be wife to Thamyris my husband, they cast me out of my city. And straightway she attacked Alexander and rent his raiment, and tore off the golden crown of the figure of Cæsar,[3] which he had on his head, and dashed it to the ground,

---

[1] Syriac: "Receive the waters (of baptism)." So the Greek text of Lipsius, though some MSS. have τὴν θωρίαν τοῦ (or Χριστοῦ). The Latin has: Signum salutis *or* lauacrum regenerationis.

[2] Greek: Συριάρχης (or Σύρος) τις 'Αλέξανδρος.

[3] The Greek and Latin texts simply say "the crown" τὸν στέφανον without describing it further. See note at the end of these Acts (p. 88).

Acts of Paul and Thekla. 77

and left him naked, destitute and full of shame. 27. Now Alexander loved her at sight, but since she had put him to shame by the way she had treated him, he straightway gave information to the judge, to the effect that Thekla did thus and thus to me, and she denies not that which she did; but do thou judge her and order that she be thrown to the wild beasts. And[1] Alexander himself it was, who was giving the show of wild beasts to the city. And when all the citizens heard, they were astonished and they raised a cry before the judgment seat, saying: "Unjust is your judgment with which you condemn Thekla."[1] And Thekla came and stood before the judge and adjured him and said: "This favour grant me, that until they cast me to the beasts I may preserve my chastity." And the judge, when he heard these words, said to Thekla: "Go, preserve it where thou wilt." And there was there a certain lady of a royal[2] house and rich, Tryphæna by name, whose daughter had died, and she took her to herself to her house, and she was consoled at the sight of Thekla.

28. When the wild beasts had come into the theatre, they came to fetch Thekla from the house of Tryphæna, and took her to the theatre, and stripped her, but put around her a linen loin-cloth, and set her there naked. And they let loose

---

[1.1] The Greek omits these words. The Latin and Syriac retain.

[2] The Greek and Latin have simply: "A certain rich woman, Tryphæna." On the faith of the Syriac, Lipsius adds βασίλισσα in his Greek text.

upon her a lioness; and the lady Tryphæna was at the door of the theatre and wept piteously. The lioness came and began to lick Thekla; and the judge and all his armed men wondered at the power which God gave her. They wrote on boards and showed to all men who sat there this writing: "Read (*or* ye called), Thekla the sacrilegious violator of the gods, who dashed the imperial crown from the head of Alexander, who wished to treat her impurely." And all the men along with all their children cried out and said: "We appeal to God against the iniquity that is being committed in the city." And again they sent against her other wild beasts; and these did not touch her. Then the audience rose and left the wild beasts; and immediately there came the lady Tryphæna and took Thekla, because her own daughter,[1] who was dead came in a dream by night and addressed her mother and said: "Mother mine, take this Thekla, persecuted and stranger that she is, to thyself in my place, that she may pray for me, in order that I may be worthy to pass into the place of the holy and just." 29. And when Tryphæna had taken Thekla to herself, she was full of concern about her; for one thing, because they would take her on the morrow and cast her to the wild beasts, and next because her daughter[1] who was dead had filled her with pity for her. And the lady said: "Lo, this second

---

[1] Lipsius in his text adds the name Falconilla, which however is not in all the Greek and Latin MSS.

time affliction and sorrow befalleth my house; but do thou supplicate and pray for my daughter that she may live; for thus I beheld in my dream." And at the same time Thekla rose suddenly and raised her voice clearly and aloud, and said: "God who art in heaven, Father of the Most High,[1] grant to the lady Tryphæna according to her wishes, that her daughter, may live for ever and ever." When the lady heard this, she sat down, plunged in grief, and wept piteously and said: "Alas, that thy fair beauty should again be devoured by the wild beasts!"

30. And at the break of dawn Alexander came in haste to carry off Thekla, for it was he who was giving the show of wild beasts in the theatre of the city. He made answer and said: "Behold, the judge is seated, and all the armed men hurry; give here at once Thekla that we may destroy her by throwing her to the wild beasts." And Tryphæna brake forth into shrill laments; and from the voice of her sorrow Alexander fled, and said that he was frightened. The lady made answer and said: "We appeal to God. This second time doth affliction and sorrow come upon my house, and there is not any one to help me, for my daughter liveth not, who is dead; and no member of my noble house cometh to my assistance, and I am a widow woman.[2] But do thou, Thekla,

---

[1] In the Greek Thekla is made to attest the divinity of Christ: ὁ θεός μου, ὁ υἱὸς τοῦ ὑψίστου ὁ ἐν τῷ οὐρανῷ.

[2] The Greek has: καὶ οὐδεὶς ὁ βοηθῶν οὔτε τέκνον, ἀπέθανεν γάρ, οὔτε συγγενής, χήρα γάρ εἰμι. So the Latin texts.

go; and may thy God render thee assistance."

31. Again the judge sent other men to bring Thekla, but the lady would not give Thekla into their hands, but held her fast by the hand and kept her. And she went and led her firmly by herself, saying: "My darling daughter[1] I escorted to the tomb; and thee, Thekla, I escort and lead to be the ravine of the wild beasts." And Thekla broke into loud and bitter lamentations, and was beside herself with grief, and groaned before God and said: "O Lord, my God, in whom I trusted, and who deliveredst me from the fire,[2] give recompense to the good Tryphæna, who took pity upon me Thy handmaiden, and preserved my chastity."

32. And forthwith there was a violent dissension among the multitude, and a breaking forth of loud cries, because the beasts were spurred on and provoked. And half were for letting the wild beasts loose upon her, and many men and women raised a clamour and called her a sacrilegious violator of the temples, and of the gods. But the other half said: "Woe to the city for the iniquity which ye do; destroy us all, O judge. Bitter is the spectacle which we behold, and unjust is the judgment with which Thekla is judged."

33. And young men came and tore Thekla from the hands of the lady Tryphæna, and led her into the theatre to throw her to the wild

---

[1] The Greek and Latin MSS. add the name Falconilla.
[2] One Latin MS. (Lipsius' *d*) omits this reference to the fire.

Acts of Paul and Thekla.

beasts; and they took and stood her in the middle of the arena. They stripped off her garments and put on her a linen loin-cloth, and she stood forth naked as she was, and said: "O Lord God, Father of our Lord Jesus Christ, Thou art the help of the persecuted; Thou art the protector of the poor; turn and look upon thy handmaiden who standeth naked and covered with shame, before all this great host. My Lord and my God, remember Thy handmaiden in this season."[1] Then they brought and let loose upon her a leopard that was very wicked, and after that they brought a lioness and loosed it on her. But Thekla stood there, and kept her arms stretched out in the likeness of one crucified on a tree,[2] and the lioness ran and rushed upon her, but when it reached her it came and crouched at her feet. Then the leopard came up and wished to leap upon her, but the lioness lay before her and forthwith tore it asunder. Then they brought a bear that was very strong, and it ran to throw itself upon Thekla. But the lioness which crouched at her feet rose and took the bear and immediately rent it. And then they loosed yet another lion which was trained to attack men, and which belonged to Alexander himself, and this lion too they set onto Thekla; but the lioness which sat at her feet met the lion and they fought with one another, and after a while they killed one

---

[1] The Greek and Latin texts omit this prayer.
[2] Syriac: in the form of a cross.

another. Then all the more did the women, who sat there and looked on, lament, saying that the lioness which helped Thekla was dead. 34. And again they let loose upon her yet other wild animals, and when Thekla saw how many were the wild beasts, she stretched out her hands and stood in prayer. And when she had finished praying she turned round and saw behind her a pool full of water, and she said: "Lo, now is the time for baptism." She lifted up her voice and said, In the name of Jesus Christ, behold this day am I baptised for (or *on*) the last day. When the women who sat there beheld this, they broke into laments and said: "Throw not thyself into yon water, for evil are the wild beasts that are therein." And the judge when he beheld her wept at the thought that the beasts in the water should devour such beauty and grace. But Thekla straightway plunged into the water and went down; and the beasts when they saw her, as it were a flash of fire, were destroyed and remained on the top of the water; and there was round about her, and she was overshadowed by, a luminous cloud, so that it did not plainly appear that Thekla was naked. 35. When the women who sat in the theatre, saw that they were loosing yet other wild beasts upon Thekla, that were more evil than the former ones, they began to scream and say: "We appeal to God, what do we behold in the city!" Then women came and began to throw spices over Thekla; some of them threw fruit of nard, and some of them marjoram, and others balsam[1] and many other fragrant spices they scattered in the arena. But they brought and let loose on her many other wild beasts; and the beasts came and sat round her, before and behind, and dozed, and not one of them did harm to Thekla. Again Alexander ran and said to the judge: "I have two strong and fierce bulls, let us bring them and bind between them her that is thrown to the wild beasts; perhaps they will become angry and destroy her. And the judge said to Alexander: "Go and do as seemeth good to thee." And he sent and had the bulls brought. And they led Thekla and put her between the brutes and took and threw her on her face, and tied her feet tight between the two bulls. And they brought spits and heated them by placing them in the live fire, and when they were kindled they applied them to the sensitive parts of the bulls, to infuriate them, that in their fury they might destroy her; and the bulls were maddened with the pain of the brands. But the flame of the fire caught the bonds with which the feet of Thekla were bound; and Thekla leapt up in front of the bulls, as if no harm had happened to her, and as if she had not been bound at all by the feet. 36. And the Lady Tryphæna was at the door of the theatre, and gave a sudden scream and fell in a swoon; for she thought that Thekla was dead. When the slaves saw that she screamed and fell in a faint, they

---

[1] This word is not in the lexicons. Another MS has aparusums. Syriac: tarphuse. I owe the rendering balsam to Prof. Margoliouth.

began to cry out and tear their garments and say: "Woe to us, our mistress is dead." And all the city trembled. Then Alexander was overcome with fear, he ran and came to the judge and said: "Have pity on me and the city, and release her that is condemned to the wild beasts; let her go quite free, that the whole city may not be destroyed." Peradventure the Cæsar may hear of this which we do, and will destroy the city, for the Lady Tryphæna who tarried at the gate of the theatre is the Cæsar's kinswoman, and is dead.

37. Then the judge said, "Bring hither Thekla"; and the young men ran to fetch Thekla from among the wild beasts, and set her before the judge. And he said to her: "Who art thou, and how is it that the animals attack thee not?" And she said: "I am the handmaiden of God; and He who is with me, He is the son of the living God; in whom I have hoped, because through Him it is that the beasts attack me not. For He is the term of salvation, and the protector of all who are persecuted, and the hope and life of the hopeless. But I say unto thee, O Judge, and to all who are before thee, that he who believeth in God, of whom ye behold the great things which He has wrought unto His handmaiden, he shall live for ever, and he who believeth not in Him, shall die the death everlasting. 38. When the judge heard this from the mouth of Thekla, he bade her bring her clothes. Said the judge to her: "Take away her loin-cloth and put before her her raiment

which she gave thee." Thekla made answer and said to the judge : " He that clothed me with power in the midst of the beasts, the same clotheth thee[1] with life in the day of judgment." And Thekla took off the loin-cloth, and took and put on her clothes, And the judge read a proclamation before all the host and said : " God hath delivered Thekla and given her to you."[2] And the women who sat there in the theatre raised a loud cry, and with loud voices began to give glory to God, and said : "Great is the God of Thekla,[3] who hath given her life and saved her among the wild beasts." And at the sound of the voices of the women who cried out the whole city was shaken. 39. And instantly they ran and gave the news to the Lady Tryphæna, and she running came and found her and took her in her arms and kissed her, and said : " My daughter Thekla, now I believe that my darling daughter is alive.[4] But come to my house, Thekla, and I will assign to thee all that is mine."

And Thekla went with her and entered into her house, and rested there eight days, and taught the Lady Tryphæna all the commands of God. And the Lady Tryphæna believed and many of her handmaidens, and there was there great rejoic-

---

[1] Syriac: "Will clothe me." Where Wright notes : "We should naturally expect *will clothe thee*, ἐνδύσει σε.
[2] Syriac: "Thekla, who is God's, and Thekla who is righteous, I have released and given unto you."
[3] Syriac : " God is one, and the God of Thekla is one."
[4] In the Greek : νῦν πιστεύω ὅτι νεκροὶ ἐγείρονται· νῦν πιστεύω ὅτι τὸ τέκνον μου ζῇ. But the MSS of Lipsius ABF omit the first clause.

ing. 40. But Thekla, for that she loved Paul, sent to seek him in all directions; and when they found him, they told her and said: "Lo, he is in the city of Merou."[1] And she rose and left the house of the Lady Tryphæna, and she put on male attire and took with her many men and handmaidens of the lady; and she came and entered the city of Merou. And there Thekla found Paul, sitting and teaching the commands of God. Thekla came and stood before him; and when Paul saw her and the men who were with her, he wondered, and thought at once that yet some other temptation had come upon her. Thekla made answer and said to him: "I have received baptism, for he who commanded thee to preach, the same commanded me also to baptize." 41. And forthwith Paul arose and took her and all the men who were with her and led them to the house of Hermes. Paul sat down and Thekla and the other men also who were with her; and Thekla related to him all that God had done unto her. And Paul wondered exceedingly at the power which was given to her. And all who were there, and heard what God had done to her, were much confirmed in the truth, and they all with one accord glorified and blessed God, who worketh wonders for all who believe in Him and keep His commandments. They prayed and besought God for the Lady Tryphæna, who had taken pity upon His handmaid and preserved her

---

[1] In the Syriac: "*Merv.*"

Acts of Paul and Thekla. 87

in chastity. Said Thekla: "I go to the city of Iconium." And Paul said: " Go, teach there the commands and words of God." And when the Lady Tryphæna heard that Thekla was on her way to the city of Iconium, she took much raiment and gold and sent it to Thekla; and she took the raiment and some of the gold, and sent it to Paul for the service of ministering to widows.
42. And Thekla went and entered the house of Onesiphorus, and fell on her face on the spot where Paul sat, and taught the commands of God; and she wept and said: "Our God, God of this house in which there dawned on me light from Christ Jesus,[1] who helped me in prison and rescued me among the wild beasts before the judge,[2] and gave me baptism for ever and ever, that I may come unto the blessedness, which is preserved for me and for those who keep the commandments of Christ.[3] For He is one, God on high, who sitteth on the throne of the cherubim. For unto Him is glory for ever and ever, Amen.

43. After all these wonders which God wrought unto her, she found in the city of Iconium that Thamyris her husband (Syr. *betrothed*) was dead, [but her mother Theocleia was alive].[4] Saith Thekla to her: " Mother mine, if thou canst

---

[1] The Syriac adds: " The son of God." So also some, but not all the Greek and Latin MSS.
[2] The Greek has: βοηθὸς ἐπὶ ἡγεμόνων, βοηθὸς ἐν πυρί. But two MSS. of Lipsius CK omit the last clause.
[3] The Syriac has: ''Commandments of God."
[4] I have added the words bracketed from the Syriac. They must have dropped out of the Armenian.

believe, there is one God on high, my Lord, who is in heaven. But if thou lovest gold and silver and riches which are corruptible, lo, it is given to thee henceforth. If thou wilt believe that there is one God in heaven, and that beside Him there is no other God, thou canst live and keep whatsoever I tell thee; for behold I stand before thee, who was rescued from the fire[1] and from the evil wild beasts and from the presence of the judge. For the same my God and Lord hath holpen me, who gave me power to endure." All this testimony she bore unto her mother and she departed from the city of Iconium, and went to Seleucia, and there she illuminated many men with the word of God, and slept in a quiet place of rest.

The book of the blessed Thekla is finished. Glory to God All-mighty and to His anointed, and to the Holy Spirit, who gave power to the translator and writer. May the same God fulfil His pity in both worlds, for ever and ever. Amen.[2]

---

[1] The Greek and Latin texts omit this clause and the next.

[2] This last paragraph is not in the Greek and Latin texts, and is due to the Armenian translator.

See Note on p. 76.—Mr. G. McN. Rushforth has explained to me the nature of the crown which Alexander as Galatarch was wearing. It was a gold wreath, bearing in front a medallion of the reigning Augustus. The portrait bust in the Vatican Museum, No. 280, miscalled of the aged Augustus, carries exactly such a wreath as these Armenian Acts describe, and is probably a portrait of some provincial president of the Cæsar-worship under the Antonines (see Bernoulli, *Röm. Ikonog.*, ii. 30, and Lightfoot, *Apost. Fathers*, vol. iii. 405 seq.). In tearing such a crown oft the head of the Galatarch, Thekla directly assailed the *numen* of the reigning emperor. There could be no graver offence. These provincial dignitaries were at a later time known as *coronati* simply. These acts are the only ancient writing in which a description of the crown is given.

THE ACTS OF S. PHOCAS.

INTRODUCTION.

THE Greek text of the Acts of Phocas is to be found in the *Acta Sanctorum*, in July, vol. iii. p. 642 foll. In my translation, however, I have followed the Armenian form, which is plainly older than the Greek. For example, the Greek text omits the dedication of the Acts to the faithful who are dwelling in Pontus, Bithynia, Paphlagonia, Galatia, Cappadocia, and Armenia, and it also exaggerates the 500 confessors of Pontus and Bithynia into 50,000, and pretends that they are all present in the court of law. So in chap. xvi. the one lamp of the Armenian becomes ten thousand. *The Greek Text of these Acts.*

The Bollandist editor rejected these Acts as spurious, mainly because they do not accord with what he knew of the history of Trajan's reign. Africanus, he argues, who was Consul in A.D. 112, was not in Pontus during his year of office; nor did Trajan die in the year 112, but in 117. The Acts however do not necessarily imply this. *These Acts rejected by the Bollandists too hastily.* Africanus, who was Consul in 112, may have been administering Bithynia as legate in 117; and though the last section relating the death of Trajan is clearly added in order to satisfy the craving of the Christian reader, who liked to be assured that the persecutor suffered for his sins even in this life, yet we do not know so much of the life of Trajan as to be able to deny point-blank that he was in Asia Minor at the time, and even in Pontus. That in the same paragraph in which the Bollandist editor condemns these Acts, he also condemns the Acts of Thekla as the scum of forgeries, is a warning to us, not to be too ready in our denial of the genuineness of the piece. The following points in the narrative make, I think, for its genuineness; not indeed as it stands, but as it may have stood before mythical accretions formed around it in the third and fourth centuries

1. The fact that the martyrdom is ascribed to the reign of Trajan. On this point it is well to quote the late Bishop Lightfoot's remarks, in the second volume of his *Apostolic Fathers* (second edition), p. 18:

Signs of their authenticity.

"Amidst many spurious and questionable stories of persecutions alleged to have taken place during the reign of Trajan, only three are reported on authority which can be trusted. Of these three, two are concerned with the fate of individual Christians —of Simeon at Jerusalem, and of Ignatius at Antioch; the third only, the Bithynian persecution, of which I have been speaking—was in any sense general. For this last alone, so far as our authentic information goes, Trajan was personally responsible. . . . It was as a statesman and a patriot that he conceived himself obliged to suppress Christianity." And just before, p. 17: "It is generally supposed that the historian of the early Church, in order to arrive at the truth with regard to the extent of the persecutions, has only to make deductions for the exaggerations of Christian writers. In other words it is assumed that the Christians forget nothing, but exaggerate everything. This assumption however is shown to be altogether false by the history of the manner in which the record of this Bithynian persecution has been preserved. With the possible exception of the Neronian outbreak, it was the most severe of all the persecutions, of which we have any knowledge, during the first and second centuries; *yet no record of it whatever was preserved in any Christian sources.* Tertullian derived his knowledge of it from the correspondence of Pliny and Trajan; Eusebius from Tertullian; later Christian writers from Tertullian and Eusebius, one or both. The correspondence of a heathen writer is thus the sole ultimate chronicle of this important chapter in the sufferings of the early Church. What happened in this case is not unlikely to have happened many times. Again and again the Christians may have undergone

1. Ascription to reign of Trajan.

The Acts of S. Phocas.

cruel persecutions in distant provinces, without preserving any special record of what was too common an occurrence with them."

But in spite of the facts here emphasised, Trajan was not regarded by the Church, in later times, as having been a persecuting emperor. As Lightfoot says, *l. c.*, p. 2: "To the Fathers who wrote during the latter half of the second century, as to Christian writers of subsequent ages generally, Trajan appears as anything rather than a relentless persecutor." And in his notes he adds pertinent passages to this effect from the writings of Melito, of Tertullian, Lactantius, and Eusebius. If then the word was passed round among the Christians, so widely as may be inferred from this list, that Trajan was a friend of the Church, it is in the last degree unlikely that a forger would have sat down in the third century, and have penned the Acts of Phocas, in which Trajan is held up to odium as a relentless persecutor. In the subsequent course of his note, therefore, Lightfoot does not show his usual sound judgment, when he writes thus : "The usual authors who represent Trajan in an unfavourable light are chiefly martyrologists and legendmongers, to whom this dark shadow was necessary to give effect to the picture." The truth is that no writer would be more careful than a martyrologist to adjust his fictions to the current conceptions of the Church ; no one less likely than he, to lay the scene of his inventions in a reign, which by a general consensus of Christian opinion was free from the stain of persecution. Such a consensus there was in favour of Trajan, and so strong was it that in later centuries Trajan only just escaped canonisation by the Pope Gregory the First. It is inconceivable that the death of Phocas would be so directly attributed to him as in these Acts it is, unless the writer of them had had something to go upon.

<small>Error of Bishop Lightfoot on this point.</small>

2. If then this martyrdom took place in the province of Bithynia-Pontus, under Trajan, are there any points in the narrative which are confirmed by the solitary notice of this persecution, which Pliny's letter has preserved to us? And can we, too, be sure that these Acts were penned independently of

that letter, and by a writer who had no knowledge of it? These two questions may conveniently be answered together. In the exordium of the Acts, chap. 3, we read that: "In the times when Trajan was emperor many Christians were snatched away from the flock, to sacrifice to vain idols; at which time they made search for the blessed saint." For Phocas, so we read in chap. 9, was both learned and famous; so much so that the governor, Africanus, was sorry and full of pity for him, that he should throw away his life. His fame had already reached even the Emperor's ears (chap. 4). In chap. 3 we learn very precisely how many persons in the joint province had suffered for the faith: "Dost thou not know," says the governor to the saint, "that here and in the other province there are over 500 men whom thou seducest into not sacrificing to the gods?" Now, what forger, writing either with or without a knowledge of Pliny's letter, would have been content with so meagre an estimate of the numbers of the Christians affected by the Bithynian persecution? Pliny wrote to Trajan thus: "Ideo dilata cognitione ad consulendum te decucurri. Visa est enim mihi res digna consultatione, maxime propter periclitantium numerum. Multi enim omnis ætatis, omnis ordinis, utriusque sexus etiam, vocantur in periculum et vocabuntur. Neque civitates tantum sed vicos etiam atque agros superstitionis istius contagio pervagata est; quæ videtur sisti et corrigi posse. Certe satis constat prope iam desolata templa cœpisse celebrari et sacra sollemnia diu intermissa repeti pastumque venire victimarum, cuius adhuc rarissimus emptor inveniebatur. Ex quo facile est opinari quæ turba hominum emendari possit, si sit pœnitentiæ locus." It is certain that a mere compiler of spurious martyrdoms, whose only aim was to edify the faithful of a later age, and who had Pliny's letter in his hands, would not have been content with 500 confessors in two provinces. He would have magnified the turba hominum into at least 50,000, as some old Greek copyist of these Acts has actually done; for in the Greek text we find this passage of the Acts altogether rewritten, thus:

2. Small number of Confessors in the Persecution of Trajan, according to these Acts.

The Acts of S. Phocas.

"Dost thou know that more than 50,000 men stand here (*i.e.* in the court), and that thou art stirring up and turning away the provinces from sacrificing?" It is true, but irrelevant, to answer that Eusebius declares the persecutions of Trajan's reign to have been partial and local; for he, as Lightfoot remarks, is studiously exculpating the memory of Trajan himself; whereas the writer of these Acts is as studiously assailing it. Were the latter a forger, he would have had every reason to exaggerate the number of the Christians who had refused to sacrifice. That he does not do so, but gives a number so much smaller than Pliny's own account would lead us to expect, is the strongest possible proof that in these Acts we have a genuine memorial of this little known persecution.

3. We have also herein a proof that the writer of them was ignorant of Pliny's letter; had he known of them, he could not have been content with only 500 confessors. He did not, like the writers of the Roman Acts of Ignatius, and of the Acts of Sharbil, preserved in Syriac, write with the help of that letter. And this very ignorance also argues their antiquity. For Pliny's letter was known, it would appear, to Melito[1] as early as 170; by the end of the second century Tertullian alludes to it; Eusebius about 300 A.D., and after him Lactantius and Sulpicius continued to give it vogue. It was so well known that the later legendmongers, just referred to, mentioned it, even though they were inimical to Trajan's memory. If the knowledge of this letter was so widely and so early diffused, both in the East and the West, how shall we account for the fact that the writer of these Acts not only betrays no knowledge of it, but could not conceivably have written as he does, if he had known of it? Would a third or fourth century romancer have neglected a source of information open and notorious to everyone, and bearing directly on the place and time in which he was pitching, so to speak, the scene of his narrative? Would he not have seized upon Pliny's phrases: "Turba hominum . . . omnis ætatis, omnis ordinis, utriusque sexus etiam . . .

3. The writer of these Acts ignorant of Pliny's letter to Trajan.

[1] This is doubtful, but see Lightfoot, *Ap. Fath.*, vol. i., p. 2, note 3.

periclitantium numerum . . . prope iam desolata templa," and have made the most of them? There is but one conclusion possible, namely, that he wrote before Pliny's letter became known to Christendom. But in that case he can hardly have written later than the middle of the second century.

4. Pliny writes: "Fuerunt alii similis amentiæ quos, quia cives Romani erant, adnotavi in urbem remittendos." In the same way Phocas is sent on to be tried directly by the Emperor. Tradition relates the same of Ignatius. We do not however know that Phocas was a Roman citizen, and Ignatius was sent to Rome in order to supply a spectacle, and not to be tried. But the Acts of Phocas anyhow report the martyr to have been a famous and a learned man, the fame of whom, as a Bishop, had already reached the ears of the Emperor. He may very well have been a Roman citizen also; for the diffusion of citizenship must have gone with the Hellenism which, as Mommsen says (*The Roman Provinces*, vol. ii. p. 331): "took a mighty upward impulse in Bithynia, under the imperial period, and the tough Thracian stamp of the natives gave a good foundation for it." According to Mommsen the same progress occurred in Pontus; and Sinope, of which city Phocas was in life the Bishop, and after death the Patron Saint, obtained from the dictator Cæsar the rights of a Roman colony, and beyond doubt also Italian settlers. This renders it extremely probable that Phocas was a Roman citizen.

Other indicia ueritatis in these Acts.

5. Trajan says in his rescript to Pliny, that the accused are to be spared if they deny that they are Christians, and prove the same "supplicando dis nostris." So the last word of Phocas is the avowal that he is a Christian and that he will not sacrifice. This was no doubt the stereotyped answer of all confessors, and as such was introduced into innumerable forged Acts of the fourth and succeeding centuries. By itself therefore such an answer would not prove these Acts to be genuine. But it should be noted that these Acts of Phocas agree in tone with other genuine Acts of the second century. For instance, the magistrate says to the Saint, when he is first brought into court: "Is this the Phocas who denies the existence of the

gods, and reckons not the autocrat Trajan to be a god." So when Polycarp was brought before him, "the Proconsul enquired whether he were the man. And on his confessing that he was, he tried to persuade him to a denial, saying, "Have respect to thine age, and other things in accordance therewith," as it is their wont to say; "swear by the genius of Cæsar; repent and say, 'away with the atheists!'" Again Phocas, in the same way as Polycarp, is anxious to instruct the magistrate in the truths of his religion. "Hear thou plainly," says Polycarp, "I am a Christian. But if thou wouldst learn the doctrine of Christianity, assign a day and give me a hearing." Again Phocas says to Trajan (chap. 11): "We ought to obey the government, not unto impiety, but unto true religion." So Polycarp says: "We have been taught to render, as is meet, to princes and authorities appointed by God, such honour as does us no harm."

Resemblance to Acts of Polycarp.

6. There is yet another point of resemblance with the Acts of Polycarp, which may be noticed. The governor says to Phocas: "How is it that the Christians demean themselves towards thee as towards a God?" And Phocas answers, "that he the unworthy Bishop is honoured not as God, but only as a man of God and as shepherd of the spiritual flock." Similarly we learn that Polycarp, when about to ascend the pyre, endeavoured to take off his shoes, though not in the habit of doing this before; because all the faithful at all times vied eagerly who should soonest touch his flesh. And after his death the heathen besought the magistrate, at the instance of the Jews, not to give up the body of Polycarp, lest the Christians should abandon the Crucified One, and begin to worship this man.

7. In the Acts of Polycarp it is only the faithful who see the signs and wonders. "When," we read, (Letter of the Smyrnæans, chap. 15) "Polycarp had offered up the Amen and finished his prayer, the firemen lighted the fire. And, a mighty flame flashing forth, we to whom it was given to see, saw a marvel, yea, and we were preserved in order that we might relate what happened to the rest." There is a close re-

semblance between this passage and chap. 10 of the Acts of Phocas, so close that we can hardly conceive of the two narratives having been written independently. In chap. 14 however, where the voice from heaven bids Phocas be of good cheer, Trajan hears it also and is terrified; and this is in strong contrast with chap. 9 of the Letter of the Smyrnæans, where a similar voice is only heard by such of the faithful as were present. In the Acts of Polycarp, moreover, no such miracle as an earthquake with the prostration of the magistrate is related. It looks as if this incident had been imported into the Acts of Phocas as a reminiscence of the great earthquake at Antioch in A.D. 115, when the Consul Pedo was killed in his palace and the Emperor Trajan only escaped by leaping through the window. An earthquake, however, was an incident which almost every writer of Acts of Martyrdom allowed himself to import into narratives in other respects quite trustworthy. And in this connection we must remember that the populations of Asia are more familiar with the terrors of earthquakes than are we who inhabit Western Europe; they pray daily in their litanies to be delivered from them, whereas we do nothing of the sort. An earthquake therefore was a very small tax on the credulity of the readers of ancient martyrdoms, and they hardly expected the Almighty to vouchsafe any smaller sign of His interest in the cause at stake.

8. Phocas is baked alive, and when the Emperor enters the death-chamber he finds the body of the martyr fragrant as nard, or, according to the Armenian, as a rose; like precious myrrh, the Greek adds. The same is related of the bodies of Polycarp and of the martyrs of Lyons, in Acts which are above suspicion.

9. The exordium of the Acts of Phocas closely resembles that of the Letter of the Smyrnæans. Just as the latter is

Exordium of these Acts. addressed to the brethren dwelling in Philomelium and in Asia, so the Acts of Phocas are in the form of a letter addressed to the brethren who are dwelling in Pontus and Bithynia, in Paphlagonia and Mysia, in Galatia, Cappadocia and in Armenia. The resemblance of this dedication to the dedication of the

The Acts of S. Phocas.

First Epistle of Peter is also very noticeable, and cannot be accidental. Yet it is not a case of mere imitation, for the Acts of Phocas add Paphlagonia, Mysia and Armenia, to the list of provinces enumerated by Peter, but omit Asia from it. The intention evidently was to notify the facts of the death of Phocas to the Churches of all the provinces that lay along the north coast of Asia Minor, from the Troad all the way to Trebizond. The survival of this dedication in the Armenian form of these Acts is very weighty evidence in favour of their genuineness; the more so, because the Greek form omits it. A forger of Acts would hardly have added such a dedication to his forgery. Nor in the third century was it any longer the fashion to compose Acts in the form of a letter to certain specified Christian communities. For the Church had by that time reached such a sense of its unity all over the Empire, such a degree of self-consciousness, that the sufferings and death of a martyr had become a matter to be communicated to the entire Christian world, and was no longer held to be of interest to a certain region only. The omission of these regional limitations from the Greek text is in itself emphatic and clear testimony to the way in which at a later time and under the influence of a later stage of church feeling and custom a martyrologist would write. Nor is it in the Acts of Phocas alone that we meet with traces of this more developed self-consciousness on the part of the Church. In the very Letter of the Smyrnæans an early hand has interpolated the phrase Catholic Church no less than four times. The interpolation was extended to Eusebius' citations at such an early time as to figure in the Latin version of Rufinus, made as early as 400 A.D., and also in the earliest MSS. of the older Syriac version. The Armenian version alone, made from a very early copy of the Syriac, is free from the interpolation. So far as I know, the Acts of Phocas and the Acts of Polycarp are the only Acts composed in the form of a letter to particular Churches.

Resembles First Ep. of Peter and also the Letter of the Smyrnæans.

It is a proof of genuineness.

If we could fix a precise date at which the divisions of the

98   *Monuments of Early Christianity.*

Roman provinces corresponded to the enumeration in the dedication, that date would possibly mark the time when these Acts were drawn up. It is enough here, without going into so technical a discussion, to indicate sources which should be consulted by any one desirous of forming a judgment. In Prof. W. M. Ramsay's *Historical Geography*, pp. 195 and 252 ff.,[1] will be found some pertinent passages, lists of the constituent regions of the province of Galatia so drawn up as to show the official divisions of the Roman province at various

Its probable date.

---

[1] The following are some of the passages from Prof. W. M. Ramsay's *Geog. of Asia Minor*.

p. 195. Ptolemy assigns to Galatia the whole coast of Paphlagonia, including Abononteichos and Sinope.   Pliny proves, ad Tr. 90-92, that Amisos and Sinope were attached to Bithynia-Pontus in A.D. 111-3.

In Trajan's reign Cappadocia, Pontus Galaticus and Cappadocicus were separated from Galatia and made a distinct province. C. I. L. iii. Suppl. No. 6819.

Perhaps Galatia was at the same time widened to include the Paphlagonian coast.

p. 252. In 70 A D. Cappadocia was placed under a consular legatus Augusti, and at some time not later than 78 it was united with the province of Galatia. This arrangement lasted until the time of Trajan ; but in the later years of that emperor the vast province had been divided, Galatia was entrusted to a prætorian legatus (as before 78), while Cappadocia was governed by a consular legatus.

The divisions of the Roman province of Galatia were at different epochs as follows :—

The inscr. of Sospes 63-78 A.D. (C. I. L. iii. Suppl. 6818) enumerates Galatia, Pisidia, Phrygia, Lycaonia, Isauria, Paphlagonia, Pontus Galaticus, Pontus Polemoniacus.

In the period 78-100 the combined province in Galatia, Cappadocia, Pontus, Pisidia, Paphlagonia, Lycaonia, Armenia Minor. (C. I. L. iii. 312, 318).

A.D. 100-140 or 150. An unknown governor of Galatia in second half of Trajan enumerates the countries governed by him as Galatia (Phrygia), Pisidia, Lycaonia, Paphlagonia.

A further change is under Antoninus Pius. The C. I. L. Suppl. 6813, enumerates only Galatia, Pisidia, Paphlagonia. Phrygia is omitted, because so little of it was included. Lycaonia at this date was given to Cilicia, which now had three eparchiæ, Cilicia, Lycaonia and Isauria.

About end of 3rd cent. Galatia was divided afresh into Paphlagonia, Galatia, Pisidia.

epochs. The divisions under Trajan seem to me to accord sufficiently well with the enumeration in our Acts. There is however really no reason why the writers of these Acts should have employed the official designations. It is in any case difficult to believe that a forger of the end of the third or beginning of the fourth century, would have added geographical limits to the range of his forgery.

10. There are other points of contact in these Acts with genuine Acts of the second century. "Methinks," says Africanus to the saint, "thou art more of a philosopher than Aristotle." Phocas answers: "I claim not to philosophise, but I wish to be a Christian." Compare this with the Acts of Apollonius, § 33. Perhaps we are to understand from the words of Phocas in chap. 9: "I have forfeited all worldly wealth and riches and possessions in order to possess the single pearl," that he had been deprived of his property. Compare Apollonius, § 28, with Harnack's note.

11. There are very many other points worth noticing about these Acts, not all of them however proofs of their antiquity, though none of them inconsistent therewith. There is the very primitive imagery of the saint's prayer in chap. 15. All his metaphors are those which we meet with in the earliest catacombs; *e.g.* there is the flock and the shepherd, the vineyard, the ark and its pilot. Phocas held the doctrine of the creative Word, and his creed is of a simple and primitive type. "Take in thy hands," he says to Africanus, "the divinely inspired writings; and know the Creator of thyself and of thy emperor. Then wilt thou know that there is God the Father and His Son Jesus Christ, crucified and buried, risen and ascended into heaven, and sitting on the right hand of God." Here there is no reason to suppose that by the scriptures is meant the written Gospel. For in a parallel statement of his creed Paul appeals in the same words to the scriptures, 1 Cor. xv. 3: "For I delivered unto you first of all that which also I received, how that Christ died for our sins, according to the scriptures; and that He was buried;

and that He hath been raised on the third day according to the scriptures." Here Paul cannot be referring to the New Testament, which was not yet written. Phocas was well read in the Epistles of Paul, and the author of these Acts knew the First Epistle of Peter. We are therefore justified in interpreting the expression Divine Scriptures used by him to mean the Old Testament. It is likely enough that there was a written Gospel as early as the year 115 A.D.; but it is impossible that it should be referred to in such a manner at so early a date. The Epistles of Paul however may have been reckoned as divine scriptures earlier than one supposes in the second century.[1] But I cannot myself believe that they were so classed as early as the reign of Trajan. It is certain that Ignatius, often as he quoted them and great as was his respect for Paul, never called them inspired writings. That appellation he reserves for the Old Testament. Phocas appeals to the divine scriptures in attestation of exactly the same tenets in behalf of which Paul appeals to them.

Phocas a student of Paul's Epistles.

12. There are passages where these Acts recall the Ignatian Epistles. I have already referred to the words in which Phocas disclaims the imputation made by Africanus, that the Christians regard him as a god. "Not as a god," he replies, "but as a man of God. For I am very inferior to the apostles of our Lord Jesus Christ. Wherefore they honour me, the unworthy bishop whom thou seest before thee, not as a god, but as the shepherd of the spiritual flock. . . . All the schoolmen of the whole world would not be found worthy to reply to a single one of the disciples of the Lord." This is the language almost of the sub-apostolic age, when the works of the apostles was still fresh in men's minds. In a similar way Ignatius refuses to rank himself with the apostles, Rom. 4: "I do not enjoin you, as Peter and Paul did. They were apostles; I am a convict; they were free, but I am a slave to

Resemblances to the Epistles of Ignatius.

---

[1] Cp. Acta Mart. Scilit. αἱ καθ' ἡμᾶς βίβλοι καὶ αἱ πρὸς ἐπὶ τούτοις ἐπιστολαὶ Παύλου τοῦ ὁσίου ἀνδρός. Here Paul's Epp. are distinguished from the sacred writings.

this very hour." So Trall. 3 : "But I did not think myself competent for this, that being a convict I should order you as though I were an apostle." So Ephes. 21 : "I who am the very last of the faithful," and Magnes. 14 : "the Church which is in Syria, whereof I am not worthy to be called a member."

13. Perhaps we ought to reckon as a mark of the antiquity of these Acts the statement that the converted soldiers, when they were baptised, fulfilled all the law, chap. 16. This reminds one of the sayings of Jesus when John hesitated to baptise Him : "Suffer it now ; for thus it becometh us to fulfil all righteousness."

14. Africanus is the governor before whom Phocas is brought. It is not specified in what province the persecution was taking place; but we may infer from the first and last chapters of these Acts that the tradition which locates the scene of the martyr's trial at Sinope is correct. Sinope was in the province of Pontus, which was governed about the years 111–113 by Pliny the younger with the official title of Legatus Pro-prætore Consulari Potestate. Pliny had been Consul Suffectus in the year 100. In the consular lists we find that Africanus was Consul Ordinarius in A.D. 112. It would not be inconsistent with the principles of the Roman provincial administration that he should have been the Imperial Legatus between the years 112 and 117. In such a case he would have succeeded Pliny. It weighs nothing against these Acts that there is no other record of Africanus having governed Bithynia Pontus; for there is not one out of a hundred such appointments of which we know the details. The reference in chap. 3 of these Acts to Trajan, as having conquered in all his wars, points to the end of Trajan's reign as the time of Africanus' governorship; for it was not till the year 114 that the senate conferred on Trajan the title of Optimus on account of his victories, and in the following year he took the fresh title of Parthicus. According to chap. 19 of the Acts the death of the Emperor followed closely on that of the martyr. And this is perhaps the grain of truth contained in this part of the narrative. But these

Probable date of Africanus' tenure of prov. Pontica.

many traits of probability must not blind us to the large admixture of pure legend which these Acts undoubtedly contain.

Yet these Acts contain legendary elements,
A great part of the interview between Phocas and Trajan has a spurious ring, especially the alarm of the Emperor at the sound of the heavenly voice. The words moreover describing the Emperor's death are a mere tag from the Gospel. I therefore incline to the belief that we have in these Acts an early narrative of the saint's death overlaid with the usual mythical accretions. Such accretions are palpable in the Greek form, if we compare it with the Armenian. As we have seen above, the 500 confessors in two provinces are turned into 50,000 all in one place; one lamp lit in the prison, becomes 10,000, all lit miraculously; the dedication is omitted, and in chap. 17 a fresh miracle is added, as if the Armenian did not contain enough. We cannot suppose that the process of accretion which is so palpable in the Greek has not already begun in the Armenian. Perhaps a lucky chance may yet reveal in some library an old Latin form of these Acts which will aid us still further in clearing away the accretions of legend. Meanwhile it is not too much to say that the Armenian version has in the case of these Acts set us upon the track of a genuine monument of a period of persecution of which the only other extant notice is the Letter of Pliny.

And have been interpolated even in the Armenian form.

There is one last point to which Mr. Hardy draws my attention, the statement, namely, in ch. 3 of these Acts, that "the enemies of God made diligent search" for Phocas. This at first sight seems to be inconsistent with Trajan's words to Pliny that the Christians *conquirendi non sunt*. If, however, we could suppose that Africanus preceded Pliny in Bithynia-Pontus, it would be rather a confirmation than not of these Acts; for Trajan's words imply that until he wrote the Christians were being hunted down. Such a consideration makes it doubly certain that the story of the Emperor's death in ch. xix. is a later and legendary accretion.

SAINT PHOCAS.

I. MANY a time since the coming of the Saviour Jesus Christ, the pitiful and humane, and wise and powerful, our Healer, and Shepherd, and Teacher, and Lord, and God, Christians have received the glorious and ineffable, the holy and spotless mystery, and have sealed it by sufferings long and extreme, by fasting and persecution and flight, by banishment and endurance, through degradation and glory, through torture and salvation. And many a time have the apostles, holy and spotless and equal to the angels, been tortured because of the name[1] and of the glorified mystery, and have given us a type of the suffering of Christ, and of their own irreproachable and inflexible faith. Wherefore, O brethren, who are dwelling in Pontus and Bithynia, in Paphlagonia and in Mysia, in Galatia and in Cappadocia and in Armenia,[2] it has seemed necessary also to us that we should, all of us and everywhere, signify in this writing unto you, the undefiled and beautiful and glorious piety of the blessed martyrs and the memorials of the same, in order that we may become imitators of their good fight, and make ourselves emulous of them. II. For we shall remember the sufferings which

---

[1] The Greek omits "because of the name."
[2] Greek omits from "wherefore" down to "Armenia."

they underwent by fire, and thirst, and cross, and wild beasts, and by suffocation in pools of water, and by carding, and by all sorts of tortures, and by divers torments. For we too are taught to press forward to the goal, and it is our hope to be made partakers in great good things by our Lord Jesus Christ, to whom glory for ever and ever. Amen.

And above all others was the blessed Phocas, conspicuous for bravery and endurance; for not only did he face fire and torture, but while he was of this world he ever lived[1] in the fair and spotless religion, having continually before his eyes the Saviour Jesus Christ. (For if it were possible to compose concerning him in these memorials so long a history, it could not fail to strike great dismay into our readers.[2])

Well, then, the devoutness of the holy Phocas was such as this. All through his youth among us here he was not beguiled by the grievous and destructive serpent, but holy and spotless (as)[3] the dove of the Lord, he bore the yoke meekly from childhood, and was full of piety, and was conspicuous to all. But of those who lacked the means of livelihood he was the help and succour; to the rich he was ready with reproof, and exhorted them to what is of good report and for the welfare of others; and in a word he was unto all everything that is good and holy. (But no one among men could relate, as it deserves to be related, his last

---

[1] Τὴν ἀρετὴν ἐπολιτεύσατο.
[2] The Greek omits this sentence.
[3] The Arm. omit the word "as."

struggle and triumph.) However, unto you that are worshippers of the true God, we will report the little we can. III. In the times when Trajan was Emperor, many of the Christians were snatched away from the flock, to sacrifice to vain idols; and then were they seeking for this blessed saint as for a gem of much value, which, having lost, the possessor calls his friends and his kindred together, that they may search and find it. In like manner the enemies of God made diligent search for the shepherd, for he was a just and holy and true shepherd of the spiritual flock of the Lord. And having taken the blessed saint, they brought him into court.

Africanus the Eparch said: "Is this the Phocas who denies the existence of the gods, and reckons not the autocrat Trajan a god? Come, tell me, then, have not all wars been won by the might of his hand? Who then but he can be God?" But Phocas remained silent. Africanus said: "What sayest thou to that? Dost thou give no answer, or knowest thou not before whom thou hast come?" Phocas said: "If thou speakest about my God who is in heaven, well and good; but if thou sayest of a man that he is God, then expect not at all to hear aught from me." Africanus said: "Are then the autocrats not gods?" Phocas said: "Is this not enough for Trajan that he is called Emperor, but dost thou also give him the incomparable name?" IV. Africanus said: "How is it that the Christians demean themselves towards thee as towards a god? Phocas said: "God forbid that any one should even entertain such a thought; for men that are imbrued in blood and assailable by death, and liable to sin, and who must give an account of their lives, and of the deeds they have done here, and of their religion, and who are brought under the judgment of the unseen God, how can they be competent to bear such an awful name?" Africanus said: " How is it that the rumour of thee hath reached even the Autocrat?"

Phocas said: "Yea, of me not as a god, but as a man of God. For I am very inferior to the apostles of the religion of our Lord Jesus Christ.[1] Wherefore they honour me, the unworthy bishop whom thou seest before thee, not as a god, as thou thinkest, but as the shepherd of the spiritual flock[2] of the Lord. But dost thou thyself, because thou hast been entrusted with authority by the Lord, therefore assume the name of god?" Africanus said: "There should be many schoolmen here, that they might be able to argue with thee." Phocas said: "Although thou shouldst assemble all the schoolmen of the whole world, they would not be found worthy to reply to a single one of the disciples of the Lord." V. Africanus said: "Hast thou such regard for the teaching of the Crucified One?" Phocas said: "Herein behold even more His matchless wisdom; for unless He were above and beyond all wisdom, nay, more, unless all wise men derived from Him, it would not have been

---

[1] ὅθεν οὐκ ἀπαυτομολῶ τῆς τῶν ἀποστόλων τοῦ θεοῦ εὐαρεστίας.
[2] ποιμένα λογικῆς ἀγελῆς.

written, 'Who giveth wisdom to the wise,'[1] and again, 'Who taketh the wise in the depth of their wisdom';[2] and again, 'I will destroy the wisdom of the wise, and I will make a reproach of the skill of the learned.'[3] Dost thou understand that which I speak?" Africanus said: "I was not sent to talk with thee concerning laws and problems, but concerning obedience to the edicts of the Emperors."

Phocas said: "I speak of the one unseen God, and persuade thee not. Wilt thou, then, who speakest about a man[4] like to myself, who is to-day and to-morrow dies, and is blessed if he die well and not ill, wilt thou be able to persuade me?" Africanus said: "Cast from thee this intricate and decorated discourse, and instruct thyself in the lore of thy true life, lest thou compel me to persuade thee with many tortures." VI. Phocas said: "When invited to so noble a feast, I decline it not, the more so as the hour is far advanced." Africanus said: "Yea, all the more because of thy philosophising, for because of that do I pity thee." Phocas said: "If thou hadst pity on me, then while I stand before thee, thou wouldst at once do whatsoever thou art going to do. But that thou mayest know that unless I die, I cannot live."[5] Africanus said: "Murderers

---

[1] ὁ διδοὺς σοφίαν τοῖς σοφοῖς.
[2] ὁ δρασσόμενος τοὺς σοφοὺς ἐν τῇ πανουργίᾳ αὐτῶν (1 Cor. 3, 19).
[3] ἀπολῶ τὴν σοφίαν τῶν σοφῶν καὶ τὴν σύνεσιν τῶν συνετῶν ἀθετήσω (1 Cor. 1, 19).
[4] The Greek adds the words, "lawless and."
[5] The Greek omits from "yea, all the more," down to "I cannot live."

and wizards are not worthy to look on the sun, yet they supplicate for their lives; but thou, whose much wisdom, according to the saying, hath made thee mad, art so bold and obstinate that thou wishest to die. By the sun, methinks thou art more of a philosopher than Aristotle."

Phocas said: "I deign not to philosophise; but I wish to be a lover of Christ, since I know Him to be my God and my King. For Aristotle taught a philosophy which is vain and ensnaring; but Christ taught the conversation of God and true religion,[1] and wisdom, and fortitude, and hath bestowed immortality on those who believe in one God." Africanus said: "Thou hast demonstrated thy emptiness of mind and folly in paying so much regard to one crucified."

Phocas said: "What is it that is a stumbling-block to thee? For it is written, 'A stumbling-block to Jews and folly to Gentiles; but to us believing, Christ the power of God and wisdom of God.'" VII. Africanus said: "What, God crucified?"[2] Phocas said: "But there are gods, male and female, and made out of stone, by the work of hands. But none that are ungodly and of the flesh can discover the path of Christ." Africanus said: "Cure thyself of thy madness; awake and look on the heavens, the sun, and moon, and morning star, and the multitude of the other stars, that thou wouldst abandon and die." Phocas said: "Thou beholdest the circle of the earth, and the

---

[1] θεολογίαν καὶ πολιτείαν ἐνάρετον, in the Greek.
[2] In the Greek, ἐστὶν οὖν θεὸς ἐσταυρωμένος;

blazing torch of the sun, and the round globe of the moon, and the positions of the stars; but their Creator, God, thou beholdest not, neither comprehendest Him. For neither did the sun create the moon, nor the moon the stars; but all this appearance and show was made by the Word of God."[1] Africanus said: "Then, on the other hand, thou declarest the heaven and all that is therein to have been made by another, denying that we ought to serve them, and compliest not?"[2]

Phocas said: "God forbid that I should call the elements God." Africanus said: "Show to me thy God, and I will win over the autocrat."

Phocas said: "Did I not tell thee before concerning the unseen God? For God who sits above the heavens, how can he appear unto man? But if thou wouldst know God, yield to me, and I will teach thee. Thou beholdest then the heavens, the sun and the moon, the stars and welkin. But it is not when they will that they shine, but when they receive the command so to do, 'Tis not because the clouds are gathered into one throng, when and as they will, that they are filled with water; 'tis when they are mustered by the command of the Lord. There comes the summer, not when it wills, but when He thinks good. The sea is at peace or tempest-troubled, not when it so wills, but when it receives the decree from the Lord. Man is healed, not when he wills, but when his Creator bids it. Thou huntest the wild beasts,

---

[1] ἐν λόγῳ θεοῦ καὶ Χριστοῦ γεγέννηται.
[2] φάσκεις, καὶ μηδὲ αὐτοῖς ὑπήκειν.

not when thou wilt, but when they are delivered into thy hand. The Emperor is victorious over the nations, not when he wills it, but when the Lord succours and defends him. The Emperor rules, not when he wills, but when the Lord gives him power to rule.[1] VIII. This God we ought to know and glorify; and worship Him who said, ' I slay and I make to live.' "[2]

Africanus said: But who is supreme over all this, the God crucified of whom thou spakest?"

Phocas said: " How hast thou heard of his sufferings and yet considerest not the might of His resurrection? How camest thou to acknowledge the Crucified One? for this is much for thee. But if thou wouldst know,[3] then take into thy hands the divinely inspired writings[4] and know thy Creator and thy Autocrat.[5] And then wilt thou know that there is God the Father,[6] and His Son Jesus Christ, crucified and buried,[7] risen,[8] and ascended into heaven, and sitting on the right hand of God."[9] Africanus said: " I have heard enough of thy teaching, and methinks Demosthenes might teach as much.[10] So now obey me

---

[1] This last speech of Phocas is somewhat shorter in the Greek.
[2] The Greek has "I will slay and will make to live," ἐγὼ ἀποκτενῶ καὶ ζῆν ποιήσω.
[3] In Greek: If thou wouldst believe.   [4] θεοπνεύστους γραφὰς.
[5] Gk. = the Creator of thyself and of thy autocrat.
[6] Gk. = who is God the Father.
[7] Gk. ἐσταυρωμένος μὲν κατὰ τὸ ἀνθρώπινον, " crucified as regards His humanity," and omits the words " and buried."
[8] Gk. ἀναστὰς δὲ τῇ τῆς θεότητος αὐτοῦ δυνάμει.
[9] Gk. ἐν δεξίᾳ τοῦ πατρὸς καθεζόμενος.
[10] Gk. πολλήν σου περίοδον ἀκήκοας λόγων, ὡς τάχα μηδὲ τὸν Δημοσθένην τοσαῦτα ἀπηγγελκέναι.

and sacrifice, lest thou force me to consume thee with torture and fire. For art thou not aware that there are more than five hundred[1] men here and in the other province, whom thou inveiglest into not sacrificing to the gods." IX. Phocas said : "And how much better will it be, as thou hast said, for me to die than for all the world to perish because of my impiety. But 'tis with joy that I approach the funeral pyre, lest the whole flock be direfully wounded and scattered. For such are the commandments which I have received from the Lord Jesus Christ." Africanus said :[2] "And I am very sorry for thee, and am full of pity for a man so learned and so famous ; but thou endeavourest to oppose me and raise an angry debate." Phocas said : "For all thy sorrow thou art about to destroy me. For I despise all thy threatened tortures, nay, I even spit upon them. Therefore do whatsoever thou art minded to do; for my language or my thoughts thou shalt not control. For the loving care of my Lord is with me, and a confession of faith more profound than tens of thousands of thy Demosthenes."[3] Africanus said : "If thou wast deranged, I would say that thou wast raving ; and

---

[1] ὅτι πλείω πεντακισμύριοι ἄνδρες ἵστανται ἐνταῦθα καὶ τὰς ἐπαρχίας ἀνατρέπεις μὴ θύειν.

[2] But the Greek continues with : "If thou wast advanced in age (προβεβηκώς), I should say that thou twaddlest ; and if thou wast poor, I should suspect thee on that point, and so forth." These words are given later on to Africanus in the Armenian, who, for προβεβηκώς, advanced in age, read παραβεβηκώς = deranged. The passage which intervenes ([2]) to ([3]) is absent in the Greek.

if thou wast poor, I should say that on that account thou wast willing to die." Phocas said: "I have forfeited, all worldly wealth and riches and possessions, if only to possess a single pearl, which neither thou nor the autocrat can ravish from me. But if it please thee to torture me because I sacrifice not to abominations, lo, here I am; torture me as thou must." Africanus said: "We sacrifice to the holy and spotless gods, and thou callest them abominations." Phocas said: "Not only abominable, but presumptuous and cheating and adulterous and temple-robbing; yea, and devils and lifeless. And not only they, but all who speak of any other god but the one God who is over all and almighty. To whom as Creator be glory and honour through our Lord Jesus Christ, for ever and ever."

X. And when the multitude of brethren who stood there had said "Amen," there was suddenly a noise like the voice of many waters, and a great earthquake, so that Africanus fell down with fright, and was laid half dead on the floor, speechless, as well as all the guards who stood around him. Among whom we saw, we to whom the Lord wished to manifest it.[1] For a bright light shot from heaven ten times brighter than the sun; and two angels appeared on steeds of fire. And fear and trembling fell upon us. But they were embraced by the blessed Phocas[2] and then re-

---

[1] ἐν οἷς ἴδομεν, οἷς ὁ κύριος ἐβουλήθη δεῖξαι.
[2] αὐτοὶ δὲ προσειπόντες τῷ μακαρίῳ Φωκᾷ, and in the Gk. it is "three angels of fire on horseback" who appear.

The Acts of S. Phocas.

ascended to heaven. And after half an hour, Terentina, wife of Africanus, ran up all dishevelled, and with her five sons and all her attendants fell down before the blessed Phocas, and earnestly entreated him to restore to her her husband, undertaking that she would believe with all her household, which she actually did. Then the blessed Phocas called together [1] all the congregation [2] of the church and offered up prayers for his salvation. But he, having escaped in so marvellous a way, went and told Trajan of the incomparable might of Christ and of the great hope of the Christians.[3] XI. And Trajan called Phocas and said to him: "Thou art Phocas." And he said: "I am." Trajan said: "And thou knowest not my absolute power. Why dost thou not obey our commands? In whom art thou exalted,[4] or what God dost thou worship? However, methinks such rhetors [5] as thyself stand in no want of advice. But put thyself into a fitting mood and be not recalcitrant. For though thou mayest not be in thy right mind [6] thou canst know who is Trajan and who is he whom thou worshippest." Phocas said: "Is it meet to speak and defend oneself, O Emperor, before thee and even so run in the race

---

[1] But the Gk. = which the blessed Phocas actually did, for having called together, etc.

[2] τὸν κλῆρον = the clergy.

[3] Gk. = But he thus rescued by a miracle went off to lay before the king the wonderful power of the Lord and hope of the Christians.

[4] τίνι πεποιθώς;

[5] Gk. = Such age as is thine wants no counsellor, but should give itself good counsel and not disobey (παρακούειν).

[6] εἰ μὴ γὰρ ἑαυτοῦ γένῃ καὶ τῆς ὑπολήψεώς σου, γνώσῃ, τίς ἐστι.

I

which impends?" Trajan said: "Yea, it is necessary for thee to speak and in particular to say what will help thee." Phocas said: "The power of thy authority, O Trajan, is it given to thee from God, if at least thou hast come to know Him that bestowed the gift on thee?" Trajan said: "My empire is given me by the many gods,[1] to whom it is right to sacrifice. It is right therefore to give due honour to our saviours, and on that account are we bound to sacrifice because of our salvation." Phocas said: "It is just and right, O Emperor, to sacrifice to Almighty God and to obey His commands; but withal we ought to obey the government, not unto impiety, but unto true religion." Trajan said: "Wast thou summoned hither to philosophise, or to sacrifice?" Phocas said: "To whom hast thou to sacrifice, or to what gods?" Trajan said: "To Asklepius." Phocas said: "Where is this god of thine? Show him to me that I may behold him." XII. And when they had come into the temple of the idols, Trajan said: "Lo, here are the gods who preserve all." Phocas said: "I say unto thee, Ho, thou stock and stone, dost thou desire to eat, dost desire drink, dost desire to dress, dost desire to smell, hast thou need of sacrifices? Behold thy gods are vain; they stand erect and sit not down; they have open mouths and speak not; we pray and they hear not; eyes have they, yet see not; hands, yet they take not up the offerings. Wilt

---

[1] In the Greek ἀπὸ θεῶν simply.

The Acts of S. Phocas.

thou that I destroy one of them? yet are they incapable of exacting redress for the deed; they grieve not, nor call upon the autocrat to succour them. And were he summoned, then the god is proved to be powerless. A god who needs mankind to assist him in avenging himself, how can he save mankind? Behold, O Emperor, the emptiness of thy religion."

Trajan said : " Thou hast astonished us by thy words. Wast thou not a sailor, and didst thou not worship Poseidon ?" Phocas said : " I was not only a sailor, but a captain of sailors, and in all things I am piloted by the Lord and offer up such sacrifices as are meet." XIII. Trajan said : "We, too, would know to whom thou art willing to sacrifice." Phocas said : "Thou canst not know, for it is written: "Ho, cast not your pearls before swine." Trajan said : " Then we are swine as thou sayest."[1] Phocas said : " 'Twere fortunate if ye were dumb beasts, for then ye would not fall under judgment as worshipping yonder stones, for which the dumb brutes have no concern at all. But tell me, which is the better, thou that hast all that power of thine, or they who give no answer to what ye say ? " Trajan said : " We command that thou be hung from a tree, and we will see what thy vain philosophy avails thee." Phocas said : " I, if I be hung from a tree, will be above all mountains and winds with the Lord; but thou along with thy gods wilt be

---

[1] The Gk. adds βιωθάνατε, "thou wretch."

in hell in outer darkness, and then wilt thou know that the God in heaven is mighty." XIV. So they excoriated [1] his body all over, yet he did not make the denial, nor was any utterance heard from his lips, but only his lips moved in prayer. And when he had finished his prayer and uttered an Amen, there was a noise from heaven, and a voice, which said : " Be of good cheer, Phocas, for I am with thee. Behold for thee is prepared a place in the garden along with the holy pontiffs and with those who deny not Me and My Father. But Trajan shall go to the place that thou hast portended, there to undergo tortures eternal." Then Trajan was smitten with fear and ordered the saint to be taken off the rack, and commanded four guards to watch him.[2] And they took and put him in prison and he was fixed very securely in the stocks.

But the saint continued to praise and glorify God ; but they shut the doors and kept watch outside the prison. XV. And about midnight the saint fell to praying, thus :[3] " Jesus, Son of God, Christ Lord, whose name is holy, Lord of angels and of every name that is named ; Shepherd of spiritual sheep, keep Thy flock firm, drive away the many-footed wolf, who seduces and ravishes

---

[1] σπαθιζόμενον κατὰ πᾶν μέλος.
[2] The Greek adds : "and one centurion by name Priscus."
[3] Gk. Κύριε Ἰησοῦ Χριστέ, τοῦ μεγάλου θεοῦ υἱέ, τὸ ἅγιον καὶ ἄρρητον ἐν ἀνθρώποις ὄνομα, τὸ κυβερνητικὸν ἐν πελάγεσιν ὄνομα, τὸ ποιμαντικὸν ἐν ποίμεσιν ὄνομα, θεὸς ἀγγέλων, θεὸς ἀρχαγγέλων, θεὸς παντὸς ὀνόματος ὀνομαζομένου, ποιμὴν τῶν λογικῶν σου προβάτων, τήρησόν σου τὸ ποίμνιον ἄσυλον.

The Acts of S. Phocas.

them. Yield not aught to him in Thy labours.[1] Let not the wild boar destroy Thy vine planted by Christ; let it not pollute Thy holiness, as did Nebuchadnezzar. Let not the many-spotted serpent bespot Thy spotless dove. Let not the all-spotted contaminate Thy servants with the parching blast of the south. But preserve Thy vineyard, which Thy all-powerful right hand hath planted.[1] Suffer not thy cross[2] to be destroyed, which with Thy great and precious blood thou didst win. Suffer not Thy ark to be wrecked, of which thou alone wast captain and pilot.[3] I thank and glorify Thy Father and Thee, that Thou wilt make me worthy this day to sup with Thee, for I shall come unspotted to Thy couch.[4] Drive me not without on this day in my coming to Thee. Keep my spirit, as Father, as God, as Lord, as Shepherd, lest there breathe upon[5] me the dragon, and lest his feet dance upon me. For he could not persuade me by gold or silver to lose the precious pearl. But lo, I have abandoned all, that I may possess thee alone, that art all-precious, thee, Lord, the pitiful, the light-giving.[6] Bring me near to Thy Father. Lead me in by the narrow door into the temple of the King, and to Thee be glory and to Thy Father and to Thy Holy Spirit.[7]

---

[1] εἰς τοὺς σοὺς τόπους. What follows as far as "right hand hath planted" is omitted in the Greek.
[2] ἀγέλην = "flock," instead of "cross."
[3] The Gk. omits this clause. [4] παστόν. [5] συρήσῃ. [6] ἐπιφανῆ.
[7] ὅτι διὰ σοῦ ἡ δόξα τῷ μεγάλῳ θεῷ καὶ πατρὶ σὺν ἁγίῳ πνεύματι νῦν καὶ εἰς τοὺς αἰῶνας.

XVI. And when he had said the Amen, the prison was opened and a torch[1] was lighted in the fortress. When the soldiers saw it, they rushed in, and throwing themselves at his feet, they sought of him the washing of the font.[2] And the blessed bishop took the men and went as far as the edge of the sea outside the city, and gave them the seal in Christ,[3] to whom also the Lord manifested Himself. Having come and having fulfilled all the law, we entered again into the prison.[4] And at dawn all the multitude of the city mustered in the public place, looking forward to the martyr-struggle of the blessed Phocas. And Trajan called him into the court and said: "Sacrifice to Poseidon."

Phocas said: "To demons I sacrifice not." Trajan said: "Are the gods demons, and we too?[5] Tell me then what other god is there left?" Phocas said: "He that gave thee thy authority. For ye are dumb irrational animals, and know not the benevolent God." Trajan said: "Then sacrifice at least to thy God." Phocas said: "My God needeth naught, except only prayer and fasting and holy hearts. For all things that have come into existence are His creatures. He giveth breath to all things that are and to whatever shall hereafter come to be." XVII. Trajan said:

---

[1] The Gk. has: "more than ten thousand lamps."
[2] τὸ λουτρόν.   [3] τὴν ἐν Χριστῷ σφραγίδα.
[4] πορευθέντες δὲ καὶ ποιήσαντες τὰ κατὰ τὸν νόμον εἰσῆλθον πάλιν εἰς τὸν Ἅγιον.
[5] Gk. = "we swine."

The Acts of S. Phocas.

"Now hast thou begun to philosophise. Sacrifice to the gods, for crucified god there is none." Phocas said: "Thou hast heard the voice of the Crucified One, and wast terrified. If He should be stirred up against thee, who shall be able to withstand Him? For His threatening consumes the mountains and His wrath dries up the sea." Trajan said: "Thou knowest not to whom thou speakest, or with whom thou hast words." Phocas said: "Because I know with whom, on that account I sacrifice not. But no word more art thou going to hear from me; do whatsoever thou wilt. But this I avow to thee, that I am a Christian."[1] XVIII. Trajan said: "The baths are being heated for thee, and lo, the water is hot. This three days has no one opened them, and into them I bid them throw thee." And Phocas made the Lord's sign upon himself, and entered into the bath, and it was like a brick glowing among gleaming fires. And the blessed one stood there in the midst, and began to praise God and say: "I thank thee, Lord, Lord, that Thou hast made me worthy because of Thy name to be tormented and imprisoned and bound and subjected to many trials. And now, my Lord, send Thy angel and save me from the hand of Trajan, lest haply the enemy say: 'Where is their God?'" And having finished his prayer,

---

[1] The Greek adds a miracle here: "Trajan said: I bid thee be cast into unquenchable fire, and I will see if thy God will take thee out. And when he had been cast in and had made three hours in it, they took him out, and he was just as if they had freshly cast him in."

and said the Amen, he surrendered his spirit at sunset.

Then Trajan bade open the baths, and having entered in, he found the remains of the body of the holy Phocas like a fragrant rose,[1] and like the frozen ice and like fragrant and precious oil. And the baths were cool, just as if they had not been heated at all. XIX. Trajan gazed on the body of the blessed Phocas, and fell to meditating on so long-suffering a faith, and he cried out and said to the soldiers who were with him: "Truly there is no other God, except the one alone who is in heaven." And he became afraid, and trembling quitted the baths. But Phocas appeared to him on the threshold, and said to the despot Trajan: "Go to thy appointed place, unto that impossible abyss. For to me is opened the garden of delight, but to thee is opened the pit of destruction as for thy idols. But there is not for thee a time of pardoning,[2] but only three days. For much righteous blood has been shed in thy lifetime." And Trajan went to his palace in terror, and was in great tribulation, suffering from a violent fever, and betaking himself in pain to his litter, he was devoured of worms and so perished.[3]

XX. Such was the uprightness of life and bravery in martyr-struggle which the blessed

---

[1] νάρδον εὔπνουν, ὡς μύρον πολύτιμον καὶ ὡς κρύσταλλον πεπηγός. Cp. the Apocalypse of Peter, § 3, in which we read of the Blessed that: τὰ γὰρ σώματα αὐτῶν ἦν λευκότερα πάσης Χιόνος καὶ ἐρυθρότερα παντὸς ῥόδου; and see M. R. James' *Apocrypha Anecdota*, p. 150.

[2] ἔνδοσις.   [3] σκωληκόβρωτος γενόμενος ἐξέψυξεν.

The Acts of S. Phocas.

Phocas was the first to display in Pontus,[1] and it is related unto this day. A captain of sea-farers and a shepherd of all good sheep was he, and his martyrdom is true, and is glorified and bruited abroad in the regions of Armenia and Pontus and Paphlagonia. An apostolic man did he show himself to us, and as from some squadron of the saints[2] he took the standard of victory and the earnest of the life to come as promised by the Lord God.[3] To whom glory and power for ever and ever. Amen.

---

[1] πρῶτος τῶν ἐν Πόντῳ λαλεῖται ἕως τῆς σήμερον ἡμέρας γυβερνήτης τῶν ναυτιλῶν, λαλητὸς ἐν παντὶ τῷ κόσμῳ. Οὗ τὸ μαρτύριον τῆς ἀθλήσεως λαλεῖται δοξαζόμενον ἐν τοῖς κλίμασι τῆς 'Αρμενίας.

[2] εἰς τὸν χόρον τῶν ἁγίων μετατεθείς.

[3] The Gk. has: "by Christ, to whom glory and power and adoration, with the Father and the Holy Spirit now and ever, and for all eternity. Amen."

ACTS OF S. POLYEUCTES.

INTRODUCTION.

THE Greek text of these Acts, of which the Armenian is a translation, has been published from Paris MSS. of it in a volume called: *Polyeucte dans l'histoire. Etude, par B. Aubé*, Paris, 1882. I owe the following remarks on these Acts to M. Aubé's introduction.

There are signs that the text of these Acts, as we have it now, can hardly be contemporary. For example, it is alleged therein that the martyr suffered under the Emperors Decius and Valerian. Now these Emperors were not together. And the Acts, if they were really contemporary, would hardly contain such an error. In the appendix moreover of the Greek MS. 513, which is mainly followed by the Armenian version, the persecutions of Decius, Valerian and Gallienus are all confused together under the one appellation of the "first persecution in the East." The author of such a confusion could not be contemporary. The introductory words, "a certain Nearchus," also militate against such a view. It must further strike a reader as somewhat odd that Nearchus survived to tell the tale of his companion's martyrdom. But in spite of all these solecisms, these Acts are certainly based on an early account sent round, according to regular custom, to the churches, to be read aloud on the feast day of the saint. On such feast days a homily commemorative of the deceased saint's virtues was delivered in church, and it is clear that the following piece is such a homily, and that it was so read as early as A.D. 363; for the exordium suits the years A.D. 363-5, when Julian was dead and Christian emblems once more figured on the standards of the army. The earliness of

Date and form of these Acts.

Not contemporary in this form.

the homily is good evidence of the antiquity of the document embodied and embedded in it; as is also the care exercised by the old Latin translator of the fifth or sixth century to eviscerate the document. The metaphrast had the same text as we have in the Greek MSS. collated and published by Aubé, but he curtails the homiletic exordium.

We meet with notices of this martyr in several ancient writers. For example, Gregory of Tours (*H.F.*, vii. 6 *in fine*, *De Glor. Martyr.*, § 103) mentions him; and in the fourth and fifth centuries many churches were dedicated to him, one at Melitene as early as 377; another in Constantinople before the end of the fourth century (Gregory of Tours, *De Glor. Martyr.*, § 103); a third in Ravenna according to Tillemont, *Mém. Eccles.*, t. iii. p. 426. Sacred lamps have also been dug up bearing the inscription τοῦ ἁγίου Πολύοκτος on the site of the ancient Coptos in Upper Egypt, which probably belong to the fifth or sixth century. The ancient Coptos was also called Cana, or Chana. Perhaps Cana neos = New Cana, and was the place alluded to in these Acts as the city of the Cananeots.

The last section of these Acts contains the testimony of Nearchus the friend of Polyeuctes, which I believe to be genuine, although the paragraph which precedes it, and which mentions Philoromus, is clearly an interpolation of the fourth century. The homilist in his exordium plainly refers to the original document or Acts which he is about to read out to his congregation; some of his sentences even quote the letter of the document. This proves that we have here an earlier document embedded in the homily. In the same way the Acts of Theodore the Soldier, along with the testimony of Abgarus his notary, are embedded in a homily, and so preserved to us.

The Armenian Text agrees very closely with the Greek MS. 513 of Paris edited by Aubé. In some places the Greek text explains obscure passages in the Armenian.

The Armenian version. I have translated the latter rather than the Greek direct, because I think that the original document which the Armenian used frequently gave another text than the Greek MSS. preserve;

Acts of S. Polyeuctes.

for I doubt if all the differences of the Armenian are merely due to loose translation.

The story of Polyeuctes is familiar to many, because it has been dramatised by Corneille, whose tragedy however hardly bears comparison with these Acts in real pathos and dramatic representation. Indeed, in his portraiture of the martyr's wife and of his relations to her, the French dramatist went out of his way to be insulse and offensive.

Corneille's drama on Polyeuctes.

The doctrinal drift of these Acts, so far as there can be said to be any, is of a gently heretical type. For Polyeuctes is saved and goes to heaven without having received baptism or any other of the sacraments, and his dialogue with Nearchus tends to make it clear to the reader that none of these things are really essential. If a man only have faith, then he will go to heaven like the thief on the cross. Such doctrine was strong meat for a later age, and accordingly we find it toned down in the old Lation version edited by Aubé. The dialogue between the saints is largely recast to make it more orthodox, and instead of the passage on page 139, we have the following,—

Doctrinal tendency of these Acts barely orthodox.

Ad fontem autem uitæ sic fideliter uenire, salutare probatur, ita etiam non accedere procul dubio creditur. Quibus autem imminet persecutor, nec suppetit facultas adeundi mysterium, sed sub uno et eodem temporis spatio, et conuersionis causa ex divina inspiratione agitur et persecutionis discrimen intendatur, his profecto fidei anchora arctissime tenenda est, ut, cura defuerit fidei famulatrix aqua, sacramentum baptismatis proprii sanguinis aspersione compleatur.

MARTYRDOM OF THE HOLY POLYEUCTES.

By now has the bounteous grace of God and likewise His might been manifested unto all through the holy martyr Polyeuctes. Now are the heathen[1] cast down and full of sorrow, and they that put their hope in their soulless idols and went astray after their graven images are put to shame. In so much as they have been compelled against their wills by the divine might to become imitators of the holy Polyeuctes, in order that unto God the Creator and Maker of all, in accordance with divine writ, every knee may bend, of them that are in heaven and on earth and under the earth. For the tidings of the divine power have been brought to men, and are in recent events ever more and more praised and glorified. For lo! the blessed Polyeuctes, who was esteemed a heathen in life and religion, even he on a sudden set himself to confirm the religion of Christ. He that was soldier of an earthly king, in the twinkling of an eye flouted his human warfare and with all zeal elected in place thereof to bear the armour of Christ, and decked his brow with the never-fading crown, symbol of his struggle bravely borne.

For the Saviour summoned him to His own

---

[1] Gk. the Hellenes.

Acts of S. Polyeuctes.

kingdom by a certain revelation, and bade him doff the earthly cloak of war which he wore, and array himself instead in the martyr's garb of mystery and ineffable honour. Yea, He bade him put off his sordid earthly cloak of unbelief, that he might don that of the holy martyr, which is more honourable and holy and pleasing to God. Then with self-born zeal the blessed one hastened forth at the summons of the Saviour, and by his very readiness forestalled the call, spurning at once and unhesitatingly all that is earthly and human. Him neither wife nor children, nor store of riches nor military discipline, nor honour and high command, nor any human glory and greatness could draw away from the true service of God. (For he esteemed more highly the life and citizenship of heaven, and gave up without delay of one moment the life of foolishness and idolatry for the true and spotless worship of God.) But what is even more wonderful in the economy of his salvation is this, that the saint Polyeuctes was living with the very daughter of the Persecutor. And this Persecutor was inducing all others by his violence to worship idols, but he could not bend the good resolution of the saint. Wherefore he then took his daughter and her children, and brought them to him; wishing by means of them to humble and ensnare him. But he remained firm and immovable in the faith of Christ, and spurned the ties of his human kinship and affections; striving only to follow and serve the heavenly King, who had chosen him out to be his own soldier. Nor was it without divine providence that he was even in this life pressed into the service of the camp, in spite of the many hardships which the life entailed. For God wished from the first to test the martyr's resolution and prove him, as pure and choice gold is proved in the furnace; and therefore He threw him from the first into a life of warfare, such as many deemed likely to displease him. But instead he was proved by means of this very life on earth to be a faithful and firm servant of God. And, lo and behold, it was just by reason of his good conduct and devotion to arms, that he became a martyr, and passed from the humble army of this earth to yonder greater one.

O pious martyr, all holy, witness of God revered in all places, of whose memory we all weary not. O Godlike martyr and true, who bestowedst so much more honour and glory on the human race, than thou didst derive therefrom. For thou didst trample on the head of the serpent, even as did also the holy martyr Thekla, and Perpetua[1] who ascended along that brazen ladder, which led to heaven, until she reached her Saviour. Unerring are the prophecies in all that they foreshadow. For the prophets knew that the trials of this earthly life are many and wearisome, and that they encompass the race of Christians. And after a long and honourable[2] life on earth a man will

---

[1] The Armenian omits the reference to Perpetua, but retains that to the ladder. There must therefore be a lacuna in the text.
[2] The Arm. = dishonoured.

Acts of S. Polyeuctes.

yet scarcely be able to reach heavenly honour. Well, along this ladder the blessed Polyeuctes ascended. He likewise smote the head of that same dragon, and spurned idols, mounting upwards by the mysterious and ineffable ladder; and thus in miraculous wise he confirmed the utterance of the apostle, who says, that by faith they shall quench the power of fire and shall shut up the mouths of lions.

O armour of the heavenly faith, which the sword of Satan could not touch! O pupil of Christ, tried by fire, true and genuine soldier! Thus it is that for his virtue and true faith he is eternally honoured in deathless memory, as one who is still near to us. Wherefore this day will we celebrate the true festival of his birth, and so reap the fruit of his deeds, in order that he may bestow upon each of us his helpful and goodly prayers.

What gift then shall we offer to the saint comparable to that which he bestowed on us? How shall we display our gratitude for the love of God manifested unto us, and prove our goodwill? Let us dance our customary dances, if it be our pleasure so to do; and let us recall to memory the deeds of the saint and all that regards his history. Thus we shall fix in our minds the very words he spoke and participate in his holiest memory agreeably to the document, and shall be able to establish our souls in the true faith.

Now the origin of his martyrdom was as follows. A certain Nearchus, for that was his name, and Polyeuctes the blessed martyr, were

K

called brethren; not as being so by blood relationship, but as being so by choice and love of each other. And because of their true friendship for one another they were called comrades and familiar friends, while according to the mysterious will of God they were proved to be sharers of His mysteries. Now Nearchus was a Christian, but the blessed Polyeuctes in matters of religion reckoned himself a Greek, though he was such in name only, for he was not far from the true faith, and was destined to transcend many dubious Christians in his fervour in its behalf. How wonderful is the divine economy! For before the Saviour came to dwell among us, sent down by God from heaven to earth for our salvation, all men sat in the gloom of idolatry and in the depths of impiety. But at the advent of the Saviour, all on a sudden rose up as it were out of a steep well from their idolatry. My brethren, think of that advent! Think of the faith of Polyeuctes, of the king coming down from heaven to dwell among us, of His soldier who freely ran to serve Him. What then was the trial which the martyr underwent? What was the occasion of the call which summoned him from Paganism to bear witness all on a sudden immediately after the advent of the Saviour?

Decius [1] and Valerian were abusing the authority

---

[1] I omit here some flowers of rhetoric given in the Armenian and absent from the Greek MS. 513. The passage omitted incidentally states that Polyeuctes suffered on the fourth day after the Lord's appearance to him.

committed to them by God in an impious manner; and with the cruel violence of despots had enacted a new law, to the effect that those who consented to sacrifice to idols should be advanced in the service, while those who should refuse to sacrifice were to be put to death by beheading.

Now on the publishing of this iniquitous edict against the Christians, Nearchus the friend of the martyr was in confusion and bitter straits; and he sighed and wept continually, and shrank from his usual converse with Polyeuctes. The latter was surprised and was moved to sympathise with him; and several times he went to him and asked him the reason of his sorrow. But the other found it not easy to answer the questions of the holy martyr; who, after a spell of silence during which Nearchus remained plunged in profound grief, repeated the question as follows: "What is this mood of thine, so unlike the warmth of frank and open friendship? Hast thou renounced thy old friendship, that thou dost not deign to answer me? Have I given thee any cause to sorrow or shrink from me in this wise?"

It was only then and with difficulty after repeated questionings on the part of the martyr, that Nearchus unbent and began to speak and say: "Because I foresaw the separation between us which this impious and iniquitous edict will at once bring about, therefore, O Polyeuctes, I kept silent, because henceforth we cannot maintain our old friendship for one another."

Then the holy Polyeuctes answered him and

said: "O·Nearchus, thy words to me are contrary to all that I hoped or expected. For even though we are about to be parted by death, still no one can dissolve the bond of friendship and love which unites us." Nearchus said to him: "Aye, this is just what I was brooding over, that the separation I had in mind is something above and beyond that entailed by human death." But when the holy Polyeuctes heard this, he fell on the neck of Nearchus and prayed and besought him to tell him the reason of the impending separation. But Nearchus, when he received the supplications of the holy martyr, wished to tell him all, but was prevented by the difficulty he felt and by his tears, and full of confusion, he gazed at Polyeuctes, and such was his affliction that he threw himself on the ground. And the holy Polyeuctes could not bear to see this, yet was at a loss how to console him, and he thought that perhaps he had taken offence in some way at his friend; and accordingly he fell to reflecting thus: "Surely I have not incurred reproach in the blameless life of Nearchus." So after reflection, he said: "Surely no one has traduced Nearchus, and it is not for that or because of any calumny or loss of property that Nearchus is plunged in dejection and tears. I am ready, said the holy martyr, to help him in such case, and to bear accusations and death for my true love of Nearchus. Nay, had I even a child, I would not spare him, if I could indulge my love of Nearchus. Faith, I would reckon it lower than my love of him, and would sacrifice all to keep my affection for him whole and unimpaired."

And when Nearchus heard such language from the holy martyr, he rose up, and with difficulty opened his lips, for he was much weighed down with care and sorrow. And he began to speak thus: "O Polyeuctes, on the morrow are we to be parted from one another?" But Polyeuctes could not believe the words of his friend, but was much perplexed and disturbed at his strange agitation and at his shedding so many tears, and he besought him to say what had happened to him, and what reason he had for speaking in such a manner. And after he had besought him many times, Nearchus began to tell him with many tears about the iniquitous edict against Christians. And when the other heard of these iniquitous edicts, he rallied his spirit, and resolved to become ✗ a spectator of God and of heaven. Moreover he recalled the revelation which he had received, and found that it had been concurrent in time with the edict. And forthwith he was filled with grace, and began to tell Nearchus about it. "This day," he said, "I beheld, O Nearchus, our Lord Jesus Christ, whom thou worshippest in holy wise and with fear and trembling. He approached me, and stripped off me the filthy human cloak which I wore, and clad me with one far more precious, and bright as light, and flashing with gold; and at the same time that He thus arrayed me He bestowed upon me also a winged horse." When Nearchus heard this he rejoiced exceedingly, and said to his friend: "I trow that thou also hast a knowledge of Christ, the God in heaven, who is for ever and ever, and is rich with heavenly riches, and who apportions His grace without stint or grudge to all who call upon Him." And in reply Polyeuctes said: "Yet when did I forget my Lord and Saviour, Jesus Christ? And whenever thou hast told me about Him, did I not listen with wonder and admiration? And whenever thou hast read to me the Divine Scriptures, have I not on hearing them forthwith shed tears and trembled? Although I was not in name called a Christian, yet by disposition and in reality I was eager to range myself among the servants of the Saviour; for everywhere and always was I anxious to put to shame the vain folly of idols, with their false and crafty deceit."

And when Nearchus heard this, his soul was filled with rejoicing, and he said to the blessed Polyeuctes: "With regard to the foul and false idols, we are compelled now to sacrifice to them by the iniquitous emperors; and for those who may refuse to sacrifice, and resolve to serve Christ, it is ordained that they should die by the sword. What then dost thou now say, O Polyeuctes? Restrain me not from weeping, and from lamenting on account of thee, for I am in doubt whether I shall not lose thee on account of my love. For a presentiment came over me that thou wilt submit to the edict of the Emperor; for thou art not yet a perfected

The Acts of S. Polyeuctes. 135

Christian, and thou wilt be compelled to sacrifice to idols."

But when the blessed Polyeuctes heard this there was kindled in his soul an impulse towards God, and with his fleshly eyes he looked to Nearchus, as if he were vexed, and he caught him by the hand, and said : " These then were Thy apprehensions, O Nearchus ? Were these from the first the opinions Thou entertainedst of me ? How couldst Thou harbour such a presentiment about me, Thou who on every occasion wast wont to read to me the divine and ineffable mystery, and I, when I heard it, repudiated the foul and abominable images? How then, O my comrade Nearchus, have we been content until now with the knowledge of that which is fleshly, while we have ignored all along the spiritual and ineffable through which we converse with God ? Why then do we not carry out our feelings, O Nearchus, or why do we not proclaim publicly and before all the world the faith which is in our Lord Jesus Christ ? "

But Nearchus was aroused as it were from sleep by the words of the blessed Polyeuctes, and rallied his soul, and said to the saint : " To me, O Polyeuctes, neither wealth, nor military honour, nor the life of this world appears more precious than the life of Christ. Nay, I would fain give the preference to immortality, and salvation, and eternity, over life that is human and transitory." But Polyeuctes, on hearing this, resolved to test the faith of his friend, and explore his resolution. So he said to him: "And art thou not sparing, O Nearchus, of this honour?"[1] But the other thinking that he asked this question seriously, and not merely to try him, replied: "If thou only knewest the honour which I have had bestowed on me[2] by Christ, and the progress He has vouchsafed to me!" (For He spoke openly and spiritually with him, and even in accordance with the divine will guided him in his resolutions.[3]) The holy Polyeuctes said to him: "Thou imaginest that I am ignorant of the progress which thou hast made in Christ, and the honour which awaits thee from Him. But before thee, O Nearchus, have I made progress with the Saviour; for this very day have I received from the Saviour, through a revelation, a heavenly and royal cloak. But I would fain put to thee one capital question of a spiritual kind; for I have a fear and suspicion in my mind, lest if I should come to the Saviour unbaptized,[4] He should not receive me with the rest into His spiritual host. Is it then possible for those who are not baptized, neither have partaken of the holy mystery, to be found acceptable to God?"

But Nearchus, seeing what was in the mind of the blessed Polyeuctes, forasmuch as he was

---

[1] The Gk. runs, καὶ οὐ φείδῃ σοι, ὦ Νέαρχε, τῆς τοιαύτης ἀξίας.

[2] The Arm. adds "at home."

[3] The Gk. MS., followed by Aubé, omits the words bracketed.

[4] The Arm. = "imperfect." The Greek has ἄνευ τελετῶν καὶ μυστηρίων, "without the rites and mysteries."

The Acts of S. Polyeuctes. 137

not yet actually a full Christian, and had had no experience of the divine mystery, resolved to spur him on to yet greater faith, and he reminded the saint of the divine writings, and exhorted him with still greater urgency to believe. And he began to address him thus : " Spare thyself," he said, " Polyeuctes, all apprehension on this point. For God is able, as the divine writings say, to raise up children to Abraham from these very stones ; that is because of a choice and decision, which was neither hoped for nor expected, he can make the very Gentiles soldiers of Christ. ✕ For behold, dearest friend, unto all the Gentiles[1] the doors of heaven are opened, and the approaches to deathless salvation are not shut to any one. Although a man may have believed but for a little time, yet for that little he shall receive a great reward, if his faith be genuine. This is why the Saviour also in the gospel commands that the same reward should be given to the labourers who had entered the vineyard in the first, and ninth, and eleventh hours ; signifying that even though you come in unto the Lord at a late hour you shall receive the same reward as the rest." And when he heard this Polyeuctes recollected a passage which accorded with what Nearchus had said, and he said : " In truth I once heard you read from the Divine Book that some of the labourers worked for a single hour

---

[1] The Gk. has πᾶσιν ἔθνεσιν ἀνέῳκται, and just before τοὺς ἐξ ἐθνῶν ἀνθρώπους. In the homiletic exordium the words Ἑλληνισμός and Ἕλληνες were used to denote paganism and pagans.

only and that to them the Saviour commanded the very same reward to be given as to those who had borne the heat and burthen of the day." And Nearchus said to him: "Yes, and thou mayest remember yet another history, of a kind to stir and urge thee still more strongly to believe, and this is from the history of the Lord. Bethink thee of the thief[1] who was crucified on the right hand side; what did He say to the thief who was crucified on the left, and who reviled the Lord? 'We suffer justly for what we have done, but our Saviour was guiltless and sinless of the cross,' and as he said this he turned and said, 'Remember me, Lord, in Thy

---

[1] The story of the penitent thief is told in Luke's gospel only, which was therefore in the hands of Nearchus. In Luke, however, the term κακουργοί is used, not λησταί, whence we may perhaps infer that Nearchus had Mark or Matthew as well. John's gospel simply says ἄλλους δύο. Luke does not add that it was the thief *on the right hand* of Jesus who repented and that it was the one *on the left* who scoffed. This is either an addition of the Acta, or drawn from some form of the gospel which we have not got. The Greek text runs, according to MS. 1449: 'Ἰδοὺ γὰρ τῷ λῃστῇ, τῷ ἐκ δεξιῶν αὐτοῦ προσηλωθέντι καὶ λέγοντι· 'Ἡμεῖς μὲν ἀξίως τῶν ἑαυτῶν ἁμαρτιῶν ἐκτιννύομεν δίκας, ὁ δὲ Σωτὴρ ἡμῶν ἀναίτιος ὢν καὶ ἀναμάρτητος, διὰ τί ἐσταυροῦτο; καὶ πρὸς τούτοις εἰπών· Μνήσθητί μου, Κύριε, ἐν τῇ βασιλείᾳ σου, εὐθέως ὁ Σωτὴρ ἀπεκρίνατο πρὸς αὐτόν· Σήμερον μετ' ἐμοῦ ἔσῃ ἐν τῷ παραδείσῳ. MS. 513 has a variant ἄξια ὧν ἐπράξαμεν ἀπολαμβάνομεν, ὁ δὲ, so agreeing with the text of Luke, and also εἰπόντος for εἰπών, and ὅταν ἔλθῃς ἐν τῇ βασιλείᾳ σου. The Armenian text follows MS. 513 in the first of these variants, but for the rest follows MS. 1449. Though it is fuller than either text, and corresponds to the following Greek: προσεῖπε γὰρ τῷ λῃστῇ τῷ ἐκ δεξιῶν προσηλωθέντι καὶ λέγοντι τῷ λῃστῇ τῷ ἐξ ἀριστερῶν προσηλωθέντι καὶ βλασφημοῦντι· Ἡμεῖς μὲν κ.τ.λ. Also after καὶ πρὸς τούτοις the Armenian adds words similar to those found in the Codex Bezæ, στραφεὶς πρὸς τὸν Κύριον, The Textus Receptus of the N.T. has ὅταν ἔλθῃς ἐν τῇ βασιλείᾳ, but Codex Bezæ and other sources omit ὅταν ἔλθῃς. The coincidences of the text of the Martyrdom with the Acta Pilati are very striking, *e.g.* the Act. Pil. have ὅταν ἔλθῃς, and have μετ' ἐμοῦ ἐν τ. παρ. ει.

kingdom.' And then what answer did the Lord make unto him? For his simple and unpretending faith what great things did He not promise him? for He said, 'This day art thou with Me in Paradise.' Dost thou see, O Polyeuctes, what great good tidings He bestows in return for how short a spell of faith? Lo, according to the gospel, if a man possess faith, even though it be small, he is yet able to move mountains."[1]

And thereat the blessed Polyeuctes cried out, and said: "And is it possible, O Nearchus, for men to attain unto such things without baptism?" Nearchus replied: "Everything is holy to the holy, as again the Divine Scriptures say.[2] But to those who are defiled in their will nothing is holy, because their mind and consciences are destroyed. Behold, we see the Lord, when they brought to Him the blind that they might be healed, had nothing to say to them about the holy mystery, nor did He ask them if they had been baptized; but this only, whether they came to him with true faith. Wherefore He asked them, 'Do ye believe,' He said, 'that I am able to do this thing?' With genuine love of man did He manifest His power, and addressing to them a single word he commanded their fleshly eyes to see, and immediately their eyes were opened."

---

[1] The Greek has Ἰδοὺ γὰρ πίστις ἀληθινή, κἂν μικρὰ τυγχάνῃ, ὁλόκληρα ὄρη,' κατὰ τὸ Εὐαγγέλιον, μεθίστησιν. This recalls 1 Cor. xiii. 2, rather than the equivalent passage in the gospel, Matt. xvii. 20.

[2] 2 Tit. i. 15.

Then on hearing these things the blessed Polyeuctes rallied and encouraged his soul; and he forgot all earthly concerns, and said, crying out on a sudden:[1] "I have been one with Christ from the beginning, and He will care for me and guard me. For I have renounced all mortal things, and henceforth 'tis meet that I should bear witness (*i.e.* be martyred) for Christ's sake. But the law of the Saviour was made manifest beforehand, which taught us, saying, 'Whilst thou wast still being formed in thy mother's belly I knew thee; and before thou camest forth from the womb I loved thee.' Therefore it is manifest that He has called me into heaven. For behold, the heathen who hate God[2] saw the Lord Jesus appear and standing near me, saw my face shining with the resplendent light of His countenance. Now, therefore, it is time for us to depart; go and read the unholy edict of the Emperor."

And when the blessed Polyeuctes read it, he began to make mock of such human legislation as that, and seizing the writing he tore off a portion[3] of it. And after that, looking in another direction, he saw the idols, referred to therein,

---

[1] The Greek has, "Let us then agree with Christ to be martyred (μαρτυρῆσαι), O Nearchus, by whom indeed we are also foreknown (ᾧ δὴ καὶ προεγνώσμεθα). For His code of law teaches, saying, Before I formed thee, etc." πρὸ τοῦ με πλάσαι σε ἐν κοιλίᾳ, ἐπίσταμαί σε, καὶ πρὸ τοῦ ἐξελθεῖν ἐκ μήτρας, ἡγίακά σε.

[2] The Greek texts are here different and confused, but both MSS. omit this reference to the heathen. MS. 513 has τὰ θειότερα φαντάζομενον ἑαυτὸν βλέπω κ.τ.λ. "I behold myself having a vision of diviner things, and I have a vision of the Lord Jesus Christ standing near me."

[3] Greek = tore it into bits.

being borne on high into the temple, where they usually were, and they were decorated with boughs and leaves in order that men might be deceived by such a show, and come to behold the so-called gods. Such were the idols at which the holy Polyeuctes looked, and beholding, he was filled with divine scorn and began to mock at them. And every one voluntarily approached the idols; but he seized every one of the figures in turn and hurled them to the ground, and in an instant crushed and ground them all to powder.

And when this happened his father-in-law, Felix, came up, who had been appointed persecutor by the iniquitous emperors, and he was dumb-foundered at what had been done by the holy Polyeuctes, and said to him: "I have lost both my children, and now I, Felix, am bereft of children. For I who formerly was proud, and boasted of my children and son-in-law, am now, alas! childless; for no one henceforth will take pity on Polyeuctes, not the gods, nor the autocrat emperors, seeing what sort of deeds he has dared to commit, breaking and destroying all our gods." But Polyeuctes said: "Long ago I have spurned them, and now have demonstrated their impotence by actual deed. But, O Felix, see if you have any other gods, and, if so, make haste to bring them forth, in order that I, the servant of God, may insult and annihilate them."

Then Felix turned to the saint, and said to him: "Concern thyself, O Polyeuctes, to live yet a little while, and seclude thyself quietly, in order that thou mayest behold thy wife before thou diest." But the holy Polyeuctes reasoned according to the divine wisdom, and replied: "What wife or child have I to look upon[1] save only those spiritual and heavenly ones whom Christ has made ready for me? But if thy daughter would follow me, let her also follow me in my resolve, and display a zeal that is blessed and glorious. But if she has any other intentions, then shall she be overtaken by the same fate as thy so-called gods." But Felix wept when he heard these words, and he saw that Polyeuctes had cast off all human ties as alien. He said to him: "But thee, O Polyeuctes, the trickeries of Christ have deceived." And the holy Polyeuctes said to him: "I admit that by His power He has drawn after Him my mind and will. For Christ has such irresistible might that He has brought me under His ineffable sway and detached me from the folly of idols, nor has He disdained to make me His chosen soldier." And as he spoke these words he was himself filled with the divine and heavenly power.

Then he was given over to the persecutors and their servants, who smote him piteously on the lips with green switches. But the saint cared not at all for this torture, for he beheld Him who was crucified for him standing near him. Then the saint with deep indignation began to say to Felix as follows: "O thou foul, and unholy, and

---

[1] ποίαν ἐγὼ γυναῖκα ἢ τέκνα φαντάζομαι.

The Acts of S. Polyeuctes. 143

abominable mystery-monger,[1] who art the minister of kings miserable and of brief span, why dost thou try to cajole me with thy crafty tears, who in thy secret heart art full of guile; because of my wife and children dost thou try to drive me from the hope of Christ. From this day forth weep not for me, Polyeuctes; but if thou believest me, 'tis thyself that thou must weep for, who art destined by thy foul and disgusting services to the children of this world to be condemned to darkness and the eternal fire."

And when the blessed Polyeuctes had said this much, he dismissed the things of earth and betook himself to the contemplation of heavenly things alone. And at that time a certain woman, whose name was Paulina, ran up in haste, with tears and full of sympathy, and said to the holy martyr: "Why art thou mad, O Polyeuctes, or who hath befooled thee into such hardihood, and into doing such deeds as to destroy the ten and two gods?" But the blessed Polyeuctes ridiculed the words of his wife, and said to her: "What if I have destroyed your dozen of gods; have you not then met with other gods on the face of the earth? However, if thou wilt obey me, O Paulina, follow me in my resolution, and believe, and have regard for thyself, in order that instead of this transitory life thou mayest receive the life which is eternal and deathless." And after using these words, as well as many others

---

[1] μυσταγωγέ.

spiritual and full of mystery, he ceased.. And many unbelievers, when they beheld his unblenched and inflexible faith, were confirmed in the faith. And then all the body of the persecutors met together and decided that the blessed saint should be put to death by beheadal.

The holy martyr knew of this unholy command, and contemned the tortures of the human body; nay, he welcomed them as the road to perfection;[1] and he stood full of joy awaiting the sentence of death, for he was rejoicing with the Saviour in heaven. But because he was full of sympathy, as long as he was in the flesh he continued to converse with us, and actually addressed the brethren who stood by him, as follows: "I see," he said, "a certain youth leading me on, and eager to converse with me, and he teaches me to forget and pass away from human things.[2] Therefore it is clear that I am about to die in the Lord, and it seems to me that by means of His precious blood in a mysterious manner the seal both of the divine baptism and of Christ is herein set upon me."

But Nearchus never forgot his friendship and love. For they were in their bodies twain one spirit and one life. Then the martyr gazed on Nearchus, and said: "Farewell to thee, and

---

[1] προκοπάς.
[2] The Greek = "The martyr then of Christ, being about to be consummated and to receive through His holy blood in mystical and ineffable wise the divine baptism and the seal of Christ, did not forget his friendship for Nearchus." Note the representation of Jesus as a youth.

forget not, my brother, the ineffable joy that is mine and thine."[1] And these last words he left behind him, as it were a seal set upon Nearchus; and himself was slain with the sword. Then the brethren buried his precious and holy body with honour in Melitene, a city of the Armenians, and bestowed it on them as it were an eternal heritage of their own. The saint was buried on the fourth day after the Sabbath;[2] forasmuch as it was also meet that he should end his life on such a day. For in all respects he showed a faith that was four-square in its strength and unshakeableness. And thus they laid to rest his holy body; but his precious blood Nearchus caught in clean napkins, and took it to the city of the Cananeots (as some precious heirloom, and they treasured it up as a weapon of salvation for all from far and near).[3]

All this was wrought, in the days of Decius and Valerian, in the East, during the first persecution.[4] And be it known, the first saint who suffered was Stephanus, in Jerusalem; and the second was the holy Philoromus, in Alexandria; and the third saint was Polyeuctes, in Melitene,

---

[1] μνημόνευε τῶν ἀπορρήτων ἡμῶν συνθηκῶν.
[2] ἐν ἡμέρᾳ τετράδι, ἐννάτῃ τοῦ Ἰανουαρίου μηνός.
[3] Greek omits words bracketed.
[4] The MS. 1449 has ἐν τῷ πρώτῳ διωγμῷ τῆς ἀνατολῆς, after which it adds, "in the reign of our Lord Jesus Christ, to whom glory and might with Father and Holy Spirit now and ever for eternity. Amen." This MS. does not contain the words which follow: "And be it known, etc." These are only found in MS. 513, and in the Armenian. Aubé points out that they must be an interpolation of the fourth century, since Philoromus suffered 305 A.D.

before the fourth of the indiction of the month Aratz,[1] in the reign of our Lord Jesus Christ, to whom power and glory for ever and ever. Amen.

[2] And after the holy Polyeuctes had suffered, I, the humble Nearchus, gave the records of the same to Timotheus, the Cananeot, and to Saturninus, and adjured them by the judgment of Christ and by the triumph in Christ of the holy Polyeuctes, that they would year by year keep his day, and read the record with care. But Timotheus received that record, and deposited it in the church, wherein it is read twice a year, on the fourth day before the ides of January,[3] the day on which the holy Polyeuctes suffered, and on the eighth day before the calends of January,[4] when his holy blood was deposited in the city of the Cananeots. But may the beneficent God who presides over the contests of His martyrs, establish us also and make us the foundation stones of His churches in Christ Jesus, imperishable God, with the Holy Spirit, to whom glory and power for ever and ever. Amen.

---

[1] The Greek MS. 513 has πρὸ τεσσάρων Ἰδῶν Ἰανουαρίων. The practice of reckoning dates by Indictions (or terms of fifteen years) only came into vogue in the reign of Constantine. To import it into the reign of Decius is an anachronism. The Armenian perhaps explains the curious expression of MS. 1449 : ἐν ἡμέρᾳ τετράδι, ἐννάτῃ τοῦ Ἰανουαρίου μηνός. The word ἐννάτῃ is a corruption of Ἰνδικτίωνι.

[2] This paragraph also is only in the Armenian, and in MS. 513 ; not in MS. 1449. In the Armenian, owing to a break in the text, it ends at the words "in the Church." This paragraph probably belongs to the third century.   [3] *i.e.* January 10.   [4] *i.e.* December 25.

THE ACTS OF SAINT EUGENIA.

INTRODUCTION.

THE history of Eugenia has never, like that of Saint Polyeuctes, been dramatised, though it abounds in characters and positions well adapted to a French stage. In translating it I have followed the Armenian version, which gives a more ancient form of the text than either the Greek Acts of the metaphrast or than the old Latin version made probably by Rufinus the presbyter of Aquileia, about A.D. 400. A comparison of these three forms of the text shows that we have in them three distinct stages of its development, of which the Armenian is the earliest, the old Latin intermediate, the metaphrast's the latest. In my notes I have been content to indicate the divergencies of the old Latin version only from the Armenian, for it was not worth while to enumerate the many omissions, amplifications, substitutions and additions by which the metaphrast, after his manner, adapts the older narrative to the taste of his tenth century readers. Similar examples of his method are presented by the Acts of Theodore, of Callistratus, and Demetrius. *Various Texts of these Acts.*

One palmary proof of the superior antiquity of the Armenian form of these Acts of Eugenia lies in their frequent references to the history of Thekla. Eugenia sets herself from the first to copy Thekla, whose history, falling by chance into her hands, leads her to break away from the polytheism of her parents, to espouse virginity and don male attire. She refers to the history of Thekla as being an inspired book, and the writer of these Acts more than once imitates that history. In a subsequent age, when the old Latin Version was made, Thekla had become a somewhat *The Armenian, the oldest Text, As proved by its references to Thekla.*

heretical saint, and accordingly all references to her and to her Acts were obliterated, and references to S. Paul and his Epistles substituted. The metaphrast's recension has yet more markedly been freed from references to the heretical saint.

The poems of Venantius Fortunatus, however, a poet of the second half of the sixth century, juxtapose the names of Eugenia and Thekla in a way that suggests that he had before him the Acts in the same early form as the Armenian, *e.g.*, we read, *Carmina,* Ed. Frid. Leo, Berol., 1881, *Monum. German. historica,* tom. iv., pars prior, p. 192 :

> Unde magis, dulcis, hortamur ut ista requiras
> Quæ dedit Eugeniæ Christus et Alma Theklæ.

Fifty years earlier, Avitus, Bishop of Vienne, in his poem, *De laude Castitatis* (Migne, *Patrol. Lat.*, vol. lix., col. 378 B), gives an outline of the story of Eugenia agreeing in all respects with our text.[1]

In regard to a history written with so much evident literary art as these Acts, the first question that suggests itself is : Can any of it be true? Has it any basis in fact?

Credibility of these Acts Is it not a pure and rather skilful romance?

It must be allowed that there is a basis of fact underlying the story; for, (1) of one or another of the actors in it, viz.: Philip, Eugenia, Protus, Hyacinthus, and Basilla, there is to be found mention in the very earliest catalogues of saints, *e.g.* in the old Syriac menologion translated by Wright, in the kindred list of Jerome and in the fourth century Depositio Martyrum.

Proved by modern discoveries in the Roman Catacombs.

(2) The actual tombs of Protus and Hyacinthus were found by Father Marchi, in 1845, in the Catacombs of Basilla. It cannot be mere chance which unites all three names both in the cemetery and in the legend.

---

[1] I owe these references to an art. by Dr. Franz Görres on " Das Christenthum u. der Rom. Staat," in the *Jahrbücher für Protest. Theol.* —Leipzig, 1844.

How then does the history of Eugenia cohere: 1. with itself; 2. with independent records?

(1) The internal chronology of these Acts is clearly impossible. Philip is sent as Eparch to Egypt in the seventh consulate of Commodus, *i.e.* 196 A.D.; and Eugenia is then aged sixteen. After two years and three months Eugenia is made superior of the monastery. We may allow two or three years to elapse before the charges of Melania bring her before Philip. After that Philip is bishop for one year and three months. When Philip became bishop, the Christian church—there was only one—in Alexandria had been closed for eight years. These are all the indications of date given by the Armenian up to the end of § 19, when Eugenia, with her mother and brothers, returned to Rome after the murder of her father Philip. Such as they are, they agree with the old Latin version, which says that Philip, at the date of his death, had been Eparch between nine and ten years, and that Severus and Antoninus Cæsar ordered him to be slain; for in 205–206 these were the reigning emperors. Note that the Armenian speaks of the emperors in the plural, but without naming them. The eight years during which the churches had been shut carry us back just to the date of Philip's mission from Rome. The Armenian text explains that he was sent out to set affairs to rights according to Roman customs; and this may mean that Christianity was to be repressed. The old Latin and the metaphrast explicitly say so; but they add that the Jews were more rigorously treated by Philip than the Christians, an amplification of this part of the text due perhaps to a vague recollection of the Edict of Severus, issued A.D. 203, by which Jews were forbidden to make proselytes and Christians to make converts.

Chronology of these Acts impossible,

So far, the narrative, as given either in the Armenian or in the old Latin form, is consistent with itself. It ceases however to be so when the heroine arrived in Rome, in § 20. Let us enumerate some of the points of difficulty which now obscure the narrative.

Especially that of the last chapters.

1. Avitus and Sergius, sons of Philip, whom the Emperor had just had murdered, are welcomed by the Senate. This is unlikely, seeing that their father had just before been murdered by order of the Emperor.

2. One of them is made Consul, or Proconsul, in Carthage, the other Vicarius Africæ. Now we first meet with the latter title in the Notitia dignitatum, and 409, Codex Theodosii 7, 15, 1. Of course the title may have existed earlier, and Mommsen (*Das Römische Militarwesen seit Diocletian*, Hermes, xxiv., p. 200), hints that it was earlier than Diocletian. It cannot however be as early as 210 A.D. On the other hand we actually find in the consular lists that Pompeianus and Avitus were both consuls A.D. 209. If Avitus was sent by the Senate to govern the consular province of Africa rather later than 209, which is likely enough, we have here a confirmation of the Acts. For if Avitus was about the age of his sister Eugenia, he may have been of sufficient age in 209. The Acts, however, rather hint that he was younger, or anyhow not very senior to her. The mention of a Pompeianus, as Consul, A.D. 209, also agrees with the Acta, for he may easily be the Pompeius to whom Basilla, a kinswoman of the Emperor, was betrothed.

3. The rest of the chronology is less possible. Basilla, whom the story requires to be a young virgin, is, according to the Armenian, a kinswoman of Gallus, and, at the same time, a contemporary of Eugenia. But C. Vibius Trebonianus Gallus succeeded Decius towards the end of A.D. 251, when Eugenia would have reached the age of seventy-one years. Yet the story represents her as martyred in the bloom of youth, and her mother survives her, and her brothers are still young men! The absurdity is still greater if with the old Latin and the metaphrast we read the Emperors' names under whom they all suffered, as Gallienus and Valerian, who reigned together 254–260. In A.D. 260 Eugenia would have been eighty years old. 4. The Armenian, moreover, hints that one Nestor was bishop of Rome at the time of the martyrdom of Eugenia, of Basilla, and of the eunuchs, and that this bishop hid himself on hearing of the condemnation of Cyprian by

The Acts of S. Eugenia.   151

the Consul Maximus. Now this condemnation was in 258, on Sept. 14. The Latin substitutes for Nestor, Cornelius the Pope of Rome, who suffered Sept. 14, A.D. 252.

According to the old Latin version the eunuchs Protus and Hyacinthus are tried before Nicetius, Urbi Præfectus. According to the Armenian, Eugenia is brought before Anictus, Prefect of the City. There is nothing to prevent there having been a Prefect of the City of the name Anicetus or Nicetus, though I can find no trace of him.

There is but one explanation of the chronological discords of the latter half of the piece. It is this : The events narrated must belong to the first half of the third century; but about A.D. 280, a recension of the document was made in which it was attempted to connect the martyrdom narrated in it with the great persecution of Decius; for the latter was then fresh in men's memories, and eclipsed the recollection of earlier persecutions. *Anachronisms of the story due to a late recension of it about A.D. 280.*

In the same way the memory of the persecution of Decius was, in some parts of the Roman empire, eclipsed at a later time by the persecutions under Numerian. Thus we find the martyrdom of Babylas which Eusebius puts in the reign of Decius, set down in the exordium of the Acts themselves to the time of Numerian. And after every fresh outburst of fury against the Church there was a tendency at work to connect the memory of the older and already popular saints with the most recent of the crises through which the Church had passed. Such an explanation as the above is favoured by the disagreement which we find within the interpolated part itself. Thus the Armenian names Gallus as the kinsman of Basilla, so implying that her death took place in his reign; the old Latin, on the other hand, mentions Gallienus and Valerian in the most explicit way. Again the Armenian makes Nestor bishop of Rome; the Latin has Cornelius, the well-known correspondent of Cyprian. Of Nestor we have no mention in any other source. Perhaps he was an anti-Pope early in the second century.

Returning now to the first part of the narrative, let us see if we can trace any of the persons named therein in independent history. We have no mention by name of a Prefect of Egypt appointed at the end of the reign of Commodus and named Philip. From the introduction to Part XXIX. (the Inscriptiones Ægypti) of Boekh's *Corpus* (tom. iii., p. 313), we learn that about 184 A.D. M. Aurelius Papirius Dionysius became Prefect of Egypt, and was, through the enmity of Cleander, the Prefect of the Prætorium, deposed, apparently by Commodus. In 194 A.D. M. Ulpius Primianus was appointed. He was succeeded A.D. 202 by Metius Lætus, and he A.D. 204 by Atianus Aquila, he in turn by Flavius Tatianus A.D. 215. It has been supposed by Labus that Primianus was preceded by an unknown prefect who held his office but for a short time. In the above list there is no room for Philippus, unless the very name Philippus be a corruption of Ulpius. It is possible that Philip was only the name adopted by the prefect, whoever he was, when he became a Christian; for it was customary to take a new name on being converted, and it is by this new name that a person would be handed down in Christian legend. Another way of surmounting the difficulty would be to suppose that Philip was not prefect of Egypt, but only one of the judges whom the emperors sent out to superintend all judicial processes in Alexandria. The Armenian, however, styles Philip Eparch, and the Latin Prefect. We know from Eusebius, *Hist. Eccles.*, Bk. vi., Chap. 1, that there was a persecution of the Christians at Alexandria during the reign of Severus, in the first years of the third century, in the course of which Leonides, the father of Origen, perished, along with many others. The focus of this persecution was Alexandria, though it extended to the Thebaid. This may have been the persecution in consequence of which the church in Alexandria had been shut up for eight years; but no prefect of that date held office for ten years.

We read that Eugenia was betrothed to Aquilius, son of the Consul Aquilius. This agrees fairly well with the consular lists in which we find an Aquilius to have been Consul in A.D. 168. His son might have been betrothed to Eugenia

No trace in general history of Philip,

The Acts of S. Eugenia. 153

in the year 195. Of the Bishop Helenus, called in the Latin form, Bishop of Heliopolis, we know nothing. But our knowledge of the bishops even of the great sees, like Rome, and Alexandria, and Ephesus is very fragmentary and incomplete for the first three centuries. This fact would also explain the absence of Philip from the list of the bishops of Alexandria. There seems to have been a question whether he was a proper bishop, to judge from the somewhat apologetic language in which the Latin version mentions his appointment. Perhaps the assurance from heaven given in a dream to his wife Clodia, that God had given her husband a place among the sacred pontiffs in heaven, points in the same direction. We probably should read between the lines of such an assurance. It may have been a reason for dropping him out of the list of bishops or overseers of the church of Alexandria, that his wife and family were so prominent in the legend; whereas the usage of the Church at a very early time required that the Patriarch of Alexandria should be celibate. It has been objected to the entire story of Eugenia, that there were no monasteries in the neighbourhood of Alexandria as early as the end of the second century. Here again the paucity of our records is such, that we must not pronounce dogmatically against the possibility of there having existed in Egypt some such establishments. Philo of Alexandria describes such a colony of pious men and women, living together as monks and nuns, over the Lake Marea near Alexandria, as early as the first half of the first century; and these settlers so closely resembled the Christians that Eusebius imagined they were converts of St. Mark. There is no mistake so great as those commit who imagine that they have an exhaustive knowledge of all the religious movements that went on in Alexandria in the first century, and who therefore pretend that Philo's description is a forgery of the third century and really meant as an apology for the Christian monastic institutions of the late third century.

But some of the other Actors admit of being identified in historical records.

Early Monastic Institutions near Alexandria probable.

There is nothing to be said in favour of such a view, and it rests on nothing except the assumption, that we know every detail of the religious life of Egypt in that age so thoroughly as to be able to impugn the genuineness of any one of Philo's most characteristic writings, which may chance to tell us something which we have not learned from other sources. We may with great plausibility suppose that the community which Philo describes had lasted on and become Christianised, for the transition from the one to the other was easy. To some extent therefore the legend of Eugenia and the description left by Philo confirm one another. There can be no doubt that the growth of such monastic communities was natural in the climate of Egypt, and we know of the existence of similar institutions among the Egyptians as early as the third century before Christ.

Signs of antiquity in these Acts,

There are some other points in the Armenian narrative which smack more of the second century than of the third or fourth. There is first the position accorded to the Acts of Thekla, which are actually called a sacred book. Now the Church was beginning to suspect these Acts as early as the time of Tertullian. Secondly, there is the extreme simplicity of the dogmatic teaching, and the stress laid on the moral teaching of Christ.

e.g. Position accorded to Acts of Thekla,

And Absence of dogmatic teaching.

Eugenia does not instruct her monks to believe in the birth of Christ from the Virgin Mary, or in the Trinity. Humility and abstention from use of oaths are the staple of her teaching. Rufinus, or whoever was the author of the old Latin version, omits the precept against oaths, and evidently felt so much the absence of orthodox dogmatic teaching in the narrative, that he undertakes to supply it; and in my note on ch. 27 I give a specimen of the way in which at the end of the fourth century older documents were brought up to date. Thirdly we have in the Armenian text a quotation from the Gospel, where Eugenia opened it at random and read it aloud, so remarkable in its form as to deserve a passing notice. I print it as it must have stood in the original Greek.

Early form of N. T. citation.

The Acts of S. Eugenia.

Ἰησοῦς εἶπεν τοῖς μαθηταῖς, οἴδατε ὅτι οἱ ἄρχοντες τῶν ἐθνῶν κατακυρίουσιν, καὶ οἱ μεγάλοι κατεξουσιάζουσιν αὐτῶν. οὐχ οὕτως δὲ ἔσται καὶ ἐν ὑμῖν. ἀλλ' ὃς ἐὰν ἐν ὑμῖν θέλῃ πρῶτος γενέσθαι, ἔστω ἔσχατος ὑμῶν καὶ διάκονος πάντων.
This agrees in part with Mark x. 42–44. But notice how vv. 43 and 44 are fused together and juxtaposed with Mark x. 31, where alone we find the saying, that the first shall be last. In Matthew we in the same way find scattered and apart these texts which Eugenia in her gospel found set together in one whole. It looks as if we had here the reminiscence of some older gospel, for the context forbids us to believe that it is merely a bit of inaccurate citation. The old Latin version and the metaphrast conform the citations to the canonical texts.

In the *Philosophumena* of Hippolytus, ix. 12, we read of an eunuch priest of the name of Hyacinthus, who was a trusted agent of Marcia, Christian concubine of the Emperor Claudius. By her he was sent to Sardinia to release the Christian convicts in the mines of that island. **Possible testimony of Hippolytus.**

In the Depositio Martyrum of the 4th century we have the entry: x. Kal. Oct. Basillæ Salaria Vetera Diocletiano ix. et Maximiano viii. Coss. P. Allard (*La Persécution de Dioclétian*) says that this date marks the burial and probably the martyrdom of Basilla. **Evidence of the Depositio Martyrum.**
This is inconsistent with the legend, which expressly represents the eunuch to have taught the faith to Basilla. Probably the date in the Depositio Martyrum is not that of the martyrdom of Basilla, but of the transference of her remains to the same cemetery in which Protus and Hyacinthus were interred. In ch. xix. of these Acts the name Perennis is given as that of the prefect who succeeded Philip and contrived his assassination. Perennis was Prefect of the Prætorium under Commodus, and was together with his son assassinated in Rome long before Commodus ever **Mention in the Acts of Perennis.**
entered on the sixth consulate, during which he sent out Philip to Egypt. The difficulty is not removed even if we

follow with Baronius the reading of the metaphrast, and suppose that Philip's mission was in the sixth year of the reign of Commodus. The simplest way of explaining this anachronism is to suppose that Perennis was introduced into the narrative at the time of its recension, about A.D. 280, by one who was familiar with the name of Perennis as that of the prefect under Commodus who sentenced to death the martyr Apollonius.

It will be seen from the notes to what an extent the Latin version supplies details not in the Armenian. It adds not only names like those of the emperors in chs. 17 and 18, or of Helenus the uncle of Basilla, in ch. 25, but it supplies topographical details in ch. 29 as regards the cemetery of Eugenia. It exaggerates, as when in ch. 4 the multitude escorting Helenus is stated to be over 10,000. It also, like the metaphrast, introduces many citations from the canonical scriptures which are not in the Armenian form. If a conjecture may be allowed, I would suppose the Latin form to be a version made at Rome about A.D. 400. The text from which it was made was in substance identical with that which the metaphrast used, and already substituted the Epistles of Paul for the Acts of Thekla. The Armenian form is earlier than the text used by the Latin translator and the metaphrast, but is not the earliest text. I should conjecture also that the earliest text went only so far as ch. 19 inclusive, for so far only is the narrative fresh and lifelike, and free from chronological inconsistencies. This earliest narrative may have been composed in Alexandria early in the third century. The nucleus of chs. 20–30 may have been also written about A.D. 225, but about fifty years later a recension was made of the last part of the tale, fitting it in awkwardly with the great persecution of Decius. The Armenian is a first draft of this recension of about A.D. 275 or 280, the Latin form and the metaphrast represent a second draft of the same.

Characteristics of old Latin version.

The Armenian the earliest text we have, yet only of a late recension.

ACTS OF S. EUGENIA.

THE martyrdom of the virgin Eugenia, and of her father Philip, and of her mother, and of the brothers whom she had.

I. In the course of his reign over the great city of Rome, the Autocrat Commodus, in his seventh consulate, despatched the influential and famous Philip to the city of Alexandria to bring back to obedience and submission to government the land of Egypt, in order that all might bow to the power of his edicts, and his alone. This Philip, along with his wife Clodia, and their two sons Avitos and Sergius, and Eugenia their daughter, came from Rome to Alexandria, and he forthwith set in order the province of Egypt in accordance with Roman customs.[1] II. Now his daughter, Eugenia, was sixteen[2] years of age, and shone so much on account of her singular intelligence, being instructed in both Greek and Roman letters, that she excited the wonder of philosophers.

---

[1] The Latin adds that Philip: " Cunctis quidem magicam curiositatem sectantibus finem imposuit, Iudæos uero nec nuncupationem nominis habere permisit, Christianos autem procul ab Alexandria tantum debere esse constituit. Ipse uero plus licet philosophorum amicus quam fautor idolorum, Romanis tamen superstitionibus, ac si religiosus cultor, instabat, non rationi, sed traditioni concordans." The phrase, "over the great city of Rome," used above, shows that these Acts, at least in their earliest form, were not composed in Rome. The Arm. spells Avitus *Apitos*.

[2] The Greek and Latin Acts say fifteen years.

Now one day her father asked her if she would marry Aquilinus,[1] a consul. Eugenia answered and said to her father : " The honour of chastity is more choiceworthy than wedlock."[2] But they strove to beguile her holy soul by all sorts of promises and tricks.

Now it chanced that there fell into her hands the history of the holy Apostle Paul and of the blessed Virgin Thekla,[3] and as she read it in secret, day after day, she wept, the more because she was subject to heathen parents. But when she went on reading day by day the history of the holy Thekla, it occurred to her to imitate her conduct ; and having made her choice in the depths of her soul, she set herself to study the teaching of the Christians. III. And she besought her parents to allow her as a favour to leave the city and visit a certain country place ;[4] and it chanced that as she was on the way in her litter, revolving in her innermost mind the life of the blessed Thekla,[5]

---

[1] The Latin has Aquilius, son of the Consul Aquilius.

[2] Eugenia's answer in the Arm. is obscure. I have given what I believe to be the sense. The Latin gives it thus : Maritus moribus, non natalibus eligendus est. A husband is to be selected for his character and not on account of his birth and family.

[3] The Latin and Greek Acts ignore Thekla. The former runs : pervenit ad manus eius beatissimi Pauli Apostoli doctrina.

[4] The Latin has : Et quoniam iussi fuerant Christiani ab Alexandria urbe discedere, rogat parentes ut spectandi gratia permitteretur prædia sua in suburbano Alexandriæ posita circuire.

The Arm. says nothing of this prohibition to Christians to live in Alexandria.

[5] The Greek and Latin again omit this reference to Thekla, and instead of it introduce the incident narrated in the next §, as if that suggested Eugenia's address to her eunuchs. The Latin and Greek thus transpose § § 3 and 4.

The Acts of S. Eugenia. 159

she said to her eunuchs, Protus and Hyacinthus : " You must surely know all that the poets invent about the so-called false gods,[1] and all that the philosophers say about the true God ? Do we find even in these such truth as is set forth in this divine book about God? " 'Tis a very grovelling and counterfeiting mind which believes in carved stones or seeks aid from wooden images made with hands."[2] But whilst they were in this mind, they began to reflect and speculate about the true God and about divers religions, and they decided in their souls that there is nothing preferable to this power.

And as they were engaged in such arguments and reflections as these, they heard some Christians who were worshipping say, " All the gods of the heathen are devils, but the Lord made the heavens." And when she heard these words, Eugenia bade them halt her litter, and for a long while her mind was full of awe, and she said : " How apt is this testimony to the holy book,[3]

---

[1] Literally "no-gods."

[2] This speech of Eugenia's is very different in the Greek and Latin texts: Scio vos mecum litteris eruditos et digna simul et indigna hominum legimus gesta, philosophorum quoque syllogismos vano labore constructos studio scrupulosissimo transegimus : Aristotelica argumenta et Platonis ideas, et Epicuri sectas, et Socratis monita et Stoicorum, and so forth.

The Armenian text has much more the tone of a third century document than this.

[3] Note how for a second time the Acts of Thekla are here referred to as a "holy book." The Latin makes one speech out of this and the preceding speech ; and instead of this reference to the Acts of Thekla, has as follows : Igitur iubet conferre sermonem : et apostolus legitur, et propheta laudatur ; fit concordia fidei, et qua arte ad penetralia sapientiæ divinæ absque sui separatione perveniant, consilio ardenti definitur.

which we have met with in pursuing our road, and have learned of the vain perniciousness of the harmful and misleading cults. But come, let us carry out what has occurred to me, let us see if we cannot in this way compass so lofty a design. Or how long are we to wander round in the cycle of unsubstantial words, arguing vainly about the true God and about unanimity of faith. Here is a plan by which we will be able to achieve the blessed flight we look for, and repel the savagery of the devil, and embrace the faith of Christ."

Then Eugenia said to her eunuchs Protus and Hyacinthus as follows: " The honour which springs from man made me your mistress, but wisdom hath made me your sister. Now, therefore my brethren, with one soul and with all unanimity let us cast away the empty glory of

---

Dominam me, inquit, vobis usurpata potestas attribuit, sed sororem sapientia fecit. Simus ergo fratres, sicut divina sapientia ordinavit, non sicut se iactat humana temeritas. Pergamus pariter ad Christianos, et sicut ordinavero properemus. Helenum audio dici episcopum, cuius est habitatio illa in qua die noctuque audiuntur Deo suo cantare, quos etiam nos, quoties transimus, psallentes audimus. Sed hic episcopus variis dicitur ecclesiæ suæ occupationibus detineri. His autem qui in divinis laudibus vacant, Theodorum quemdam presbyterum constituit, cuius tanta miracula narrantur, ut etiam cæcos suis orationibus illuminet, et dæmones effuget, et infirmantibus afferat sanitatem : sane ad diversorium huius congregationis, in quo Deus canitur, nullam patitur venire feminarum. Hoc ergo considerans, tondere me arbitror, etc. This narrative presupposes an intimate knowledge of the Christians on the part of Eugenia. The Arm. does not ; nor does it mention Theodorus. It moreover represents as her motive for cutting her hair and dressing as a man, the desire to emulate Thekla. The Latin and Greek texts, since they eschew mention of Thekla, have to invent another motive. They accordingly introduce the touch "nullam patitur venire feminarum."

The Acts of S. Eugenia.

human honour, and hasten to the service of the true God, that we may not be undone by the opposition of the adversary. But do you divest me of the tresses of my hair and make yourselves ready at dawn. Perhaps this very night will be our departure, in order that our journey to the men of God may prosper. And you must walk, the one to the right and the other to the left; and so put me down from the litter unperceived, and then let the litter go empty. But we three will then hasten to the men of God." And they approved of the plan, and at dawn everything was done according to the plan.

IV. Now Christ gave His grace to reward their faith. For it chanced just as she descended from her litter, the holy bishop Helenus[1] was making a progress along the road, along with a multitude that were singing a psalm and saying altogether with one voice: "The paths of the just are straight, the paths of the holy are made ready."[2] Then Eugenia said to Protus and Hyacinthus, "Behold ye the might of the psalmists? Con-

---

[1] The Latin has : Et quia mos est apud Egyptum, quando circumeunt monasteria Episcopi, psallentium eos sequatur exercitus ; supervenit idem Helenus Heliopolis episcopus, et cum eo amplius quam decem millia virorum. Contrast this with the Armenian, in which the narrator himself simply says "a multitude," and puts the natural exaggeration, "thousands," into the mouth of Eugenia. In the Latin it is the narrator who is quite definite, "amplius quam decem millia." Görres, accepting the Latin as the original form of text, finds in this statement an argument against the antiquity of these acts: "Widersinnig ist ferner die Mittheilung, damals wären die Bischöfe bei ihren Besuchen in den Klostern von tausenden von Christen begleitet gewesen." This argument is abolished by the Armenian text.

[2] Isa. xxii. 7.

sider if that which ye heard from the Christians, who were singing a psalm to their God, be not intended as a sign unto us; for just as we were pondering over the true God in our minds, we heard from the men of God, as they worshipped, the words: 'All the gods of the heathen are devils, but the Lord made the heavens.' And lo! at the very moment when we separate ourselves from the worship of idols, thousands have met us saying with one accord, 'Straight is the path of the just, and ready is the path of the holy ones.' Come then and let us mingle with the multitude of them that give praise, and we shall be reckoned to belong to their ranks, and we will enter as participators with them into their truth, though it be late evening."

V. And so they united with the worshippers and began to ask, who was the aged man who alone in the midst of the multitude sat under an umbrella.[1] Then they heard from one of them that he is Helenus, the bishop, who in his childhood frequented the monastery of the Christians, and who destroyed the wild beasts of the neighbourhood.[2] "But," he continued, "why do I

---

[1] The Latin has: qui solus vehiculo aselli uteretur in medio populi sequentis et precedentis.

[2] The Latin has: Helenus episcopus, ab infantia Christianus: qui dum infantulus in monasterio cresceret, tantæ sanctitatis virtutibus augebatur, ut si quando missus fuisset ignem e vicino petere, ardentes prunas vestimento deferret illæso. The very same story is told by Rufinus in the very same words of the monk Helenus in the second book of the Lives of the Saints. This fact only proves (as Rosweyd notes) that Rufinus was the author of the Latin text of the Acts of Eugenia, and does not warrant the argument based on it by Görres and Baronius against their antiquity. That

speak of or relate his virtues of long ago, when only a little time back a certain wizard called Iras[1] came and tried to turn away the people from the holy books, and ventured to oppose with counterfeit arguments the holy bishop Helenus. And the holy bishop discerned his deficiency of understanding, but being unable to undo him in argument, said before all the multitude : 'Of what use is it for us to wrestle in argument with this son of perdition and unbeliever?[2] He who believes not in that which is set before us in the midst, not only does not raise the fallen,[3] but by his vain teaching he ruins and does violence to those who have been so raised. But I will first try to save him (and shew him) that there is a God who governs all things rightly and who by the hand of me, His humble servant, reveals the unspeakable message of His might." And he said : 'Therefore let there be kindled in the middle of the city[4] a flaming fire, and before your eyes let us both enter it without shrinking, and let him who is not consumed be believed to be His true worshipper.'

---

the Armenian omits the miraculous incident and gives a different one empties such an argument of all weight.

[1] The Latin and Greek call the wizard by the name Zareas, and add that he tried to pass himself off as a bishop sent by Christ to teach; statements barely consistent with the fact which they also relate, that he de Scripturis divinis populum seducebat.

[2] Instead of what follows the Latin has: Et ait ad populum : Pauli apostoli in hac parte monita omnino tenenda sunt; dicit enim Timotheo discipulo suo, and then cites 2 Tim. ii. Noli verbis contendere; ad nihil enim utile est, nisi ad subversionem audientium.

[3] Eccl. iv. 10.

[4] The Latin has: in media Heliopolis civitate.

And the entire people approved of this resolution, for a large part of them believed in the magician and took his side. Now immediately the fire was lit and flamed up, the holy bishop Helenus bade that both enter it without fear. But Iras the impostor said: 'Not so, but let us each go into the midst of it separately; and do you go first and foremost, for it is you that proposed it.' Forthwith the holy Helenus raised his hands to heaven, and weeping, said:[1] 'Thou knowest, O Lord Jesus Christ, Son of the living God, who didst appear fourth in the furnace to the three children, that I was not covetous of human glory, but only of the salvation of Thy people, unto whom Thou hast made me worthy of praise, and whom the betrayer seeks by means of his minister to lead astray from the just path over a precipice. For the sake of their salvation I willingly enter this fire, trusting firmly that I shall find Thee there shedding Thy dew upon me, so that the fire may not touch me who remember Thee.' And when he had said this he crossed himself, and went into the fire, and stood in the midst of the flame a long while, and was in no wise hurt by the fire. When the multitude beheld the superb miracle, they took Iras, and although he resisted, they threw him into the fire, and he began to burn. And the blessed Helenus, although his tortures were well deserved, none the less made haste and rescued him still alive; and he was insulted by all and left on the

---

[1] The Latin omits the prayer which ensues.

spot. And he whom ye see yonder continually glorifies God."

VI. Then Eugenia, with her eunuchs Protus and Hyacinthus, fell on her knees, beseeching the holy Helenus[1] to confirm them also in the faith; and they besought him that through him they might become acquainted with the Lord. But he said to them : " Devote yourselves of a habit to praising Him at dawn, in order that there be granted a joyous vision to thee by His grace." But Eugenia besought him to pray for them. " For," said she, " we three are Romans by birth, and have abandoned the worship of idols, and in pursuit of thee have come hither." VII. And while they were relating their story the old man was silent, because he had seen in a dream all that they were about to tell him. But while he was meditating, they came to the spot and

---

[1] According to the Latin, Eugenia fell on her knees at the feet not of Helenus, but of him that had related to her the story of Helenus. She prays him to bring her before Helenus. He answers that he will do so after the bishop has entered the monastery and rested awhile. Eugenia with her eunuchs then enters the monastery with the rest of the throng. It continues thus, cap. VII.: Perfectis igitur matutinis laudibus, paullulum requievit episcopus, et iussit sibi ad sextam præparari, ut divina mysteria celebraret, ut dum sextam cœpisset, nona ad refectionem ieiunantium opportune perveniret. Requiescens autem episcopus, somnium vidit, in quo ad simulacrum feminæ ducebatur, ut illi sacrificaret. Tunc dixi, inquit, in somnio his qui me tenebant. Permittite me ut loquar cum dea vestra. Et cum me permisissent loqui, dixi ei : Cognosce te creaturam Dei esse, et descende, et noli te permittere adorari. At illa his auditis, descendit, et secuta est me, dicens : non te deseram, quousque me creatori meo restituas et conditori. The narrative continues that Eutropius, with whom Eugenia had already spoken, now approached Helenus and told him of the tres pueri fratres who had left their idols and come thither. " Christo servientium numero in isto monasterio se sociari desiderantes.' The Latin then continues in fair accord with the Armenian.

found a reverent man, who had been with him, whose name was Eutropius. He said to him: " There are come and stand in our presence three youthful brethren who have denied the worship of idols. They desire to serve Christ the Saviour and pray to be enrolled in the congregation of believers ; who are fain to be made worthy by means of thy holiness of repenting and of being made participators in the pure faith."

Then the holy Helenus said : " We thank Thee, Lord Jesus Christ, for having made me worthy to attain unto this and to witness this which Thou lately revealedst to me through grace and by Thy holy will." But they came in to him and offered prayers ; and he, when he had finished his prayer, took Eugenia by the hand along with the others, and said : " On what pretence chiefly did ye wish to visit the humble servants of God ? However, inform me of why ye are come on a visit to me, for I would fain hear, that I may reap the fruit of your proposal." The wise Eugenia made him answer, and said : " We were convinced that the nature of God cannot dwell in wood and stones, and we were discussing among ourselves apart, which is the true religion, in which the worshipful and heavenly God acquiesces, when we heard a sound at this spot ; for you were with one accord singing a hymn and saying : ' All the false gods of the heathen are devils, but the Lord made the heavens.' Invited by these wise words we abandoned the service of idols, and came in haste hither along with a multitude. We follow your

The Acts of S. Eugenia. 167

reverence, believing in God and desiring to be associated with them in your pious faith and true counsels. But there is one brotherhood between the three of us, and one of us is named Protus and another Hyacinthus, but I am called ✗Eugenius." Said the blessed Helenus: "Well wast thou called Eugenia, for 'tis a noble act of ✗ thine to pass through combats achieved to the Lord. But know thou this, that God has already revealed to me concerning thee, Eugenia, whence thou art and whose daughter thou art and who are come with thee;[1] all this the Lord showed to me, and how these men were encouraged by thee to come to God." And the holy Helenus bade them spend three[2] months in the church and in the convent, and then he made them because of their true faith worthy of holy baptism. And after that he sent them to the convent and confided them to the principal thereof, but he told no one the real facts.

VIII. But now let us return to the time when Protus and Hyacinthus took Eugenia and sent back the litter home empty to her mother. Well, her household thought that Eugenia was come, and they all rushed out full of joy to meet her. But when they did not find her in the litter they

---

[1] According to the Latin Helenus turned to the eunuchs and said : In corpore servitutis positi, ingenuam dignitatem animi tenuistis fortiter et tenetis. Unde vobis, me tacente, Christus dominus loquitur, dicens : Amen, amen, dico vobis, iam non dicam vos servos, sed amicos (Joan xv.). It is noticeable that this quotation from the canonical N.T. is absent in the Armenian.
[2] The Latin does not specify the time which elapsed before baptism.

with one accord began to weep and lament. And there was a tumult and disturbance all over the city, and there was huge lamentation and violent sorrow, and everyone was plunged in profound grief. The parent mourned for a daughter, and the brothers for a sister, the slaves for a mistress,[1] and everyone of the citizens mourned because of the parents' bereavement and of the affliction which had befallen the family. Never before had such a catastrophe befallen them, and they sent about to every government looking for Eugenia, and they questioned the seers, and sought out the ventriloquists and offered victims to the idols, and they all began to declare that Eugenia had been translated by the immortal gods. And the father credited this,[2] and ceased to mourn, opining that she was now really numbered among the gods, and he set up a statue to her of pure gold. But her mother Clodia and her brothers Avitos and Sergius could not cease at all from their grief, but continued to mourn most bitterly.

IX. But Eugenia disguised as a man remained in the aforesaid monastery, locked in spiritual union with Protus and Hyacinthus. And they progressed so much in the divine love in Christ, that in two years' time they took into their minds the whole book.[3] X. But in the third

---

[1] This is imitated from the Acts of Paul and Thekla, ch. 10.
[2] This is the germ of the Bishop Helenus' dream as given in the Latin text.
[3] Latin: omnes Scripturas dominicas memoria retineret. The Latin

The Acts of S. Eugenia. 169

year while they were still pursuing such a life, the elder[1] of the monastery died and passed from this world to his Lord. And after his death it seemed good to all the brethren to appoint the blessed Eugenia to the principalship. But Eugenia declined, for she was restrained by scruples of conscience and felt that a woman ought not to be head of a congregation of men of God. And yet she feared to become a source of aversion and strife and turpitude to those who invited her to take the post.[2] Then they all with one will and accord assailed her, and she returned them the following answer again and again: "In the congregations of Christians ye said that Christ will of His own accord define that which is to be according to His pleasure. Wherefore, if ye so command, let the gospel be brought forward, and let us open and read it, and whatsoever command first meets the eye, let us give ear thereunto." So they brought the holy gospel, and the blessed Eugenia took it and adored, and they all held their peace and prayed. Then she opened and read the place in which it is written: "Jesus said to His disciples, Ye know that the rulers of the heathen are lords, and the great ones oppress them. But let it not be so in your midst also; but he that shall among you

---

continues with a long and stilted eulogy of Eugenia, not given in the Armenian.

[1] Latin : abbas qui præerat fratibus in monasterio.
[2] The Latin simply has : timens ne omnes unanimiter deprecantes sperneret.

desire to become first, let him be least of you and servant of all."[1] But after she had read this, Eugenia said : "Make up your minds upon this model that I shall be so."[2]

And all the brethren sharing her persuasion, she assumes the title of principal in order not to grieve them. For they all besought her to remove the anxiety of the convent and she acquiesced.

But she made herself a pattern of humility; and herself discharged in excess all the services which the juniors were required to perform for her, such as bringing water from the well, cutting wood, keeping the floor clean and ministering to all the wants of the brethren. But she also made herself a little room at the door of the monastery, that she might not appear to be better off in any way than the other associates. And when they came to evening service[3] they would find her already come, and there was not one of all the brethren who was found to transcend her in humility. At all seasons she devoted herself, and was accessible to the brethren, and would exhort

---

[1] Latin : Et revolvens codicem venit ad locum, et coepit legere, dicens : Dixit Iesus discipulis suis ; Scitis quia principes gentium maiores sunt his quibus dominantur, et principatum eorum gerunt (Matth. xx. 25) Apud vos autem non est sic, sed si quis in vobis vult primus esse, sit vester ultimus : et si quis inter vos voluerit esse dominus, sit vester servus (Lucæ xxv. 25).

[2] Ecce inquit et vestris iussis obtemperans, decrevi primatum suscipere, et Domini iussionibus obedire, ultimum me vestræ charitati constituo.

[3] The Latin translator here sees his chance : et tertiæ, sextæ, nonæ, vespertinis vel nocturnis atque matutinis horis tam cautissime insistebat, ut videretur iam perisse Deo, si horarum vel quidpiam spatii absque divinis laudibus aliqua præteriisset. On the other hand the Latin omits what follows about Eugenia's teaching the brethren not to use oaths.

The Acts of S. Eugenia. 171

and advise them continually not to say anything to anyone under oath, but to use sober speech ; and she would say to them : " Let us learn from His commands how much reverence we the servants of God ought to shew. Let us therefore be careful to have in our hearts all due zeal and enthusiasm, for in no wise ought God to be neglected by us ; for it is in this wise that a man denies his Lord, who teaches others to do what He has forbidden." So when they learned from her all this, they were confirmed in the faith, and from morning to night they remitted not the study of the divine writings. But she was so precious to God that she could cast out devils, and to the sick healing was through her vouchsafed by God.

XI. There was a certain wife of one of the senators whose name was Melani,[1] that had suffered a long time from a quartan ague. She came to Eugenia, who made the sign of the Christ on her breast[2] and dispelled all the languor of her sickness and raised her up whole. And after that the blessed Eugenia hastened to the convent. XII. Melani returned and continually called Eugenia, and she in a spirit of pity would go to her. And Melani, not knowing that she was a woman, longed to behold Eugenia from a corrupt

---

[1] Melanthia in the Greek and Latin. "Matrona quædam Alexandrina, cæteris matronis præstantior, nomine Melanthia.

[2] Lat. " quam cum beata Eugenia oleo perunxisset." In the sequel the Latin represents Melanthia as sending silver cups full of money to Eugenia, which she returns.

motive ; and not because she had been healed by her intercession, but because she believed her to be a man, she would send to her such unholy messages as this: " Why dost thou smite and waste thyself with vain labour, destroying all the bloom of thy youth ? Surely God does not love melancholy. Does He really bid all men to pass all the time of their life without joy or relaxation ? Not so ; but do thou come and let us enjoy the gifts of God, lest as those who have turned ungrateful, we account ourselves unworthy of the gifts of God. Wherefore for thy own benefit comply with my demands, so that thou mayest be with me and put an end to all this thy hard toil, and that we may enjoy a brilliant and fair time. And thou shalt be lord of all my possessions, yea, and shalt be lord also of my person. For I am of high and splendid rank and of distinguished family, and my wealth is enormous ;[1] and I do not think that I shall offend before God, if thou wilt become my husband, and casting away melancholy enjoy a good time."

This and the like was the pleading of Melani, but the holy Eugenia arose to avoid such deadly and destructive words, wishing to save the other's soul from the suffocation of death, and signifying to her how vile a thing is worldly desire. For

---

[1] The Lat. adds : dignitas generositatis est mihi : hoc anno absque filiis viduata sum, succede pro eis in facultatibus meis, et non solum rerum mearum, sed meus esto iam dominus. The Arm. does not represent Melanthia as a widow, but in this detail the Latin may be more correct, for it would not have lost the opportunity of adding adultery to her offences.

The Acts of S. Eugenia. 173

while a person thinks to gain something by means of temporal desire, he robs his soul of perpetual love and of the delights which pass not away. And it is in no wise right to embrace fleshly desires, for by means thereof the traducer flatters us in order to shatter and destroy the spirit of man. But to these words addressed to her by the blessed Eugenia, Melani turned a deaf ear and would not listen to them, for she was possessed by a spirit of bitter shamelessness, as it is written : " Into the malicious soul wisdom entereth not."

But Eugenia endeavoured in every way to save her from death and destruction, and shunned her company. But Melani pretended that she was sick in body, and besought the blessed Eugenia to visit her as one sick. And then when the saint had come in and sat down in her chamber with her, Melani ventured to approach her with secret embraces of a shameless kind and began to allure her to impiety with unholy words. Then the blessed Eugenia understood the deceitfulness of the evil demon and the wickedness of the traducer that was in her, and stretching out her right hand she made the sign of the cross on her forehead, and with a loud cry and violent tears and groaning she began to say : " Right fitly wast thou named Melani, for the blackness of sweaty vice and the filth of wickedness exudes and drips from thee ; for thou art a daughter of darkling sins and a leader of destruction and a darling of Satan, a flame of lust and a sister of unrighteousness, doomed to unending death, a daughter of eternal

Gehenna, a fountain darkened and clouded with shameless desire, an enemy of God, a welcomer of the devil. Away with thy madness from the servants of Christ."[1]

XIII. But when Melani heard this she flamed up with wrath and she could not contain her shame, and she was afraid lest the rumour thereof should reach many ears and she herself become an object of scorn in the eyes of the multitude. So she went to Alexandria, and in the public court laid her complaint before the Eparch[2] Philip to this effect: "I fell in with a certain unbelieving youth, who called himself a Christian. Him I summoned for my health, for it was rumoured that he can assist the sick. But when he was bid come near me, he began to use obscene and shameless language to me and tried to seduce and outrage me. But why should I use many words? For he was the aggressor and dared to lay hands on me as if I were a slave, so that if there had not happened to be in my chamber a certain One of my slaves, who saved me from being overmastered by his violence, he would probably have carried out his vile desire on my person."

But when the Eparch heard this he was very angry and sent a large force of soldiers, and ordered that Eugenia and all who were with her should be bound in iron fetters,[3] and after a few

---

[1] The above narrative is much abbreviated in the Latin.

[2] In the Lat., præfectus.

[3] The Latin exaggerates here as usually: Deponuntur itaque omnes in vinculis: et quia unius carceris eos non ferebat locus, per diversas custodias dividuntur.

days, the number of which he fixed, be brought into court before the people in the theatre, so that he might hear what they had to say, and then order them to be thrown as food to the wild beasts. So when the time came, the blessed Eugenia and all her associates were brought in iron fetters into the court in the presence of all. (And the multitude, not knowing the righteousness of their cause, cried out against them, especially those who were on the side of Melani. For the multitude had various minds, and some cried out to burn them with fire, and some to throw them to the wild beasts, and others cried out for them to be subjected to all kinds of tortures.)

XIV. Then the Eparch silenced the crowd, and had Eugenia set before all and interrogated her thus : "What temerity led thee to act so insolently? Thou wast visiting from afar Melani that hath the rank of our national senators and was nigh unto death, and thou didst enter in unto her in the guise of a Christian, as being skilled in the art of healing, and then didst thou invite this freeborn woman to acts of wanton iniquity. Surely your Christ does not enjoin on you any such deeds? or is this the service of your confession, to work the works of perdition?"[1]

Then Eugenia made answer to the Eparch, and said : " I have prayed earnestly for this false in-

---

[1] The Latin does not give these words from " Surely your Christ," to "perdition." In the rest of ch. XIV. the Latin differs a good deal from the Armenian and is more diffuse, but there are no differences of consequence.

dictment which has befallen us. I was resolved to overcome my scruples, and reserve for the future Judge this infamous fiction; for true holiness need not fear aught that malice can bring against it; nor again can chastity conjoined with holiness lie hid, for it will reap not only the praise of men because of its light and splendour, but also the honour of reward from its God. For the chastity of the wise is kept safe and in innocence, by those who have made it theirs by strenuous effort, and it nobly guides the soul of the Christian as it were to the love of God. XV. For I will reveal before all that which I have concealed in my bosom. For I am a woman by sex, and because I could not attain my desire and serve God as I deemed necessary and in fair security on account of being a woman, therefore I disguised myself as a man, and in a just and fitting way concealed my charms; in emulation and after the example of my teacher Thekla,[1] fleeing from what is destructible and fleeting I was resolved to attain to the good things of heaven. It was to win such glory and to satisfy my craving after the Divine virtues that I disguised the frailty of my sex under male attire. For this cause and because I was pricked with a longing

---

[1] "As before so here the Latin eliminates Thekla: "Tanta enim est virtus nominis Christi, ut etiam feminæ in timore eius positæ virilem obtineant dignitatem; et neque ei sexus diversitas fide potest inveniri superior, cum beatus Paulus apostolus, magister omnium Christianorum, dicat quod apud Dominum non sit discretio masculi et feminæ, omnes enim in Christo unum sumus (Galat. iii.). Huius ergo normam animo fervente suscepi, et ex confidentia quam in Christo habui nolui esse femina."

after Divine worship I took the form of a man, in order that in masculine wise I might bravely keep my virginity intact."

When she had said this she rent the garment with which she had attired herself from her head downwards, and exposed her hidden countenance[1] and her beautiful virginal breasts. But for one moment only, and then she hastily veiled them again with her rent garment. And, continuing, she addressed the Eparch and said : " Thou art my father after the flesh, and Avitos and Sergius are my two brothers. But I am thy daughter Eugenia, who for the love of Christ spurned the things of earth along with my two servants, who, behold, are here, Protus and Hyacinthus, my eunuchs, who along with me have joined the ranks of Christ's army. And I pray that Christ may draw thee to Himself with such power, that under my teaching thou mayest before all men become in Christ a conqueror of all desires ; even as I myself trust to be kept safe and scatheless even to the end."

XVI. And thereupon the father recognised his daughter, and the brothers their sister ; and they ran before all and embraced her, and with tears they clasped each other in their arms. And forthwith one ran and told her mother Clodia ; and she on hearing it rushed pell-mell in her hurry and came post-haste into the theatre, and quick as lightning they snatched up a gold-embroidered

---

[1] The Arm. is here obscure, and literally=et incognitos uultus faciei, manifestabant pulchra pectora uirginis.

shawl and attired Eugenia in it against her will, just to shew to all who she was. And then they raised her aloft and carried her away, and all the multitude shouted out, saying: "There is one Christ, one Lord, one true God of the Christians." But the bishops and elders along with a great congregation of Christians were standing by the theatre and kept a fast until such time as they should be slain, when they hoped to gather up the relics of the saints, that they might wrap them up and bury them. But even they came into the theatre glorifying God, and with one voice cried aloud, saying: "Thy right hand, O Lord, is glorified in its might; Thy right hand, O Lord, hath scattered[1] Thine enemies." But they lifted her up on high for all to see, that none might ignore her wondrous purity. And while all gazed a sudden fire came down from heaven and consumed Melani and all her household. And when they furthermore saw this, great joy mingled with fear filled the multitude, and they opened the church which had been closed for eight years, and the Christians won the confidence of all. Moreover Philip the Eparch was baptized, as well as his sons Avitos and Sergius. Her mother also, Clodia, was baptized along with her handmaids, and (an innumerable number of heathen turned Christian.[2]) And all Alexandria was like a single church.

---

[1] Lit. pulverised.

[2] The Latin adds that Philip restored their privileges to the Christians, et mittit relationem ad Severum imperatorem de Christianis, et memorat

The Acts of S. Eugenia. 179

XVII. Now at that time all the elders were leading and governing the church, because he that was previously chief guardian of the divine laws had departed to the Lord. So they made him (*i.e.* Philip) bishop and he greatly honoured the church, even as it had become worthy of honour. But he also continued to administer the government; for he had the power and authority of Eparch, and his successor was not yet arrived. But at once the Egyptians took the cue from him and forsook the folly of idols and turned to Christ, and in all the cities churches were opened and day by day Christianity flourished and increased.

XVIII. But when all this took place under the guidance of the grace of God, the devil, who is jealous of the good and is teacher of evil and co-worker therein, inspired certain of the heathen who were chief men in the city, and caused them to go and prostrate themselves before the emperors[1] who were then ruling, and to pour out before them a tale of envy and hatred against the holy church and the god-fearing bishop Philip.

XIX To supersede Philip was sent an Eparch, whose name was Perinos, who had orders from the emperors, in case things were as reported, to

---

satis reipublicæ Christianos prodesse, ideo debere eos absque persecutione aliqua in urbibus habitare. Consentit relationibus Imperator. Of all this the Armenian knows nothing.

[1] The Latin gives their names : Severo et Antonino Augustis. The Alexandrians complain that Philip has restored their privileges to the Christians, and that cum nono anno in fascibus irreprehensibiliter administraverit, nunc decimo anno perdidit omnia.

slay Philip. Now Perinos came, but was not able to effect this, because Philip was beloved by all the multitude of citizens. So he sent certain men to him disguised as Christians, who entered the church, and, finding Philip therein engaged in the service of God, they went up to him as if to receive his blessing, and slew him just as Zacharias was slain between the altar and the shrine. But he filled the office of bishop one year and three months, and as a martyr and confessor passed away to the Lord.[1]

But Eugenia took the body of her martyred father and laid it in the hospice,[2] which had been built by her mother Clodia, near to a certain spot called Tiranas,[3] which was a house of prayer of her brothers for the glorification of the Lord Christ, and they had built it in regal style on the aforesaid spot. And when this had been done, all who were near to the blessed Eugenia as well as her mother and brothers with one accord joined together and loosed unto Rome, led by the grace of God.

XX. Wherefore Avitos and Sergius were welcomed with joy by the senators, so much so that

---

[1] The Latin omits the reference to Zacharias, and relates that Philip lived three days after being stabbed. The metaphrast gives the name of his successor and assassin as Terentius, probably a false spelling of the name Perennius. We have the same false spelling of the name in the Armenian Acts of Apollonius.

[2] The Latin also relates that Eugenia established on the spot a monastery for Christ's virgins.

[3] The Latin does not mention the place Tiranas, nor the shrine erected by the brothers.

the one of them became Consul in Carthage, and the other was appointed Vicarius[1] of Africa. But Clodia and Eugenia went on living according to divine counsels, and day by day they would exhort others to the life of virtue, and brought many persons to God, and they were marvelled at by senators and virgins and were foremost in zeal for Christianity. And one Basilia, a virgin, who was a kinswoman of the Emperor Gallus,[2] of great intelligence and famous for her wisdom, came privily to Eugenia, and, having heard from her the word of truth, believed so firmly that no one could detach her from the faith. But because she could not continually see the blessed Eugenia, she took and accepted as if it were a free gift from Eugenia her two eunuchs Protus and Hyacinthus; and in their company early and late she studied the divine hymns and questions and prayers and passed her days therein. Then a certain bishop,[3] a man fully perfected in holy and divine precepts, came to Basilia and illumined her with holy baptism as well as all who were with her; and unintermittingly he instructed her in the divine writings, confirming her in the faith of Christ. XXI. And thus it was that all

---

[1] The Latin and Greek have Vicarius Africæ; also Proconsul, not Consul. The metaphrast makes Avitus Proconsul of Carthage and Sergius to be Vicarius Africæ. The Arm. has the spelling Bitaritos.

[2] The Latin simply says: quædam ex regis genere virgo, Basilla nomine, and does not mention Gallus.

[3] The Latin names him, "Cornelius cum esset in urbe Roma sacræ legis antistes," and just below "Cornelius papa urbis Romæ."

unanimously made such progress in the life of virtue, that all were ready for martyrdom.[1]

XXII. But so long as the bishop sat at the head of the church and led it, the Christians were at peace, and there was no hostile agitation against them. But Cyprian[2] when bishop suffered many afflictions for the faith, and one Maximus by name, a Consul, received an imperial command by letter and slew him. But when the bishop Nestor heard of the same he kept in hiding and apart, for he was aware of many highly placed Romans who were Christians in secret.

But one day Basilia came to Eugenia and she welcomed her with much joy and said to her: "This day hath the Lord revealed to me, that blood will flow over the rose-coloured image of thy youth,[3] which means that thou wilt suffer for the confession of Christ and receive the crown and symbol of victory." And the blessed Basilia on hearing this raised her hands to heaven and rejoiced in God with exceeding joy. And when they had prayed and ended the Amen and were sat down, Basilia said to Eugenia: "For each of us, as we see, our Saviour has revealed the crown of glory, for as to thee concerning myself, so also

---

[1] The Latin here inserts many lines of commonplace eulogy of Eugenia, Clodia and the eunuchs.

[2] The Latin has: Valeriano itaque et Gallieno imperantibus orta seditio de Christianis est, eo quod Cyprianus Carthaginem everteret, et Cornelius Romam. Data est ergo auctoritas ad Paternum proconsulem, ut Cyprianum occideret. Cornelius autem quia a multis Romanis etiam illustribus fovebatur erat in abditis.

[3] The Latin omits this sentence.

concerning thy departure from earth hath Christ revealed to me. For I beheld that thou didst receive a twofold symbol of victory from heaven ; partly because of the struggle for virginity that thou didst win in Alexandria, and partly because of the shedding of blood which shall overtake thee."
XXIII. Now the blessed Eugenia was delighted to hear thereof and called to her all the virgins, who through her had in holy wise espoused the life of spotless chastity, and invited them to share her victory. And after finishing her prayer, she lifted up her voice and spoke to them as follows : " Behold the time of vintage, when the ripe fruit is gathered in,[1] for ye are my bowels[2] of pity and grape-clusters sprung from me. Convoy me first away and then make yourselves ready with watching. For this is the chief proof of virginity, to liken yourselves to the angels and to draw nigh unto God. For this excellence is love of the life to be, and mother of modesty, teacher of holiness, mistress of repose from care and guide to joy ; the goal of virtue and crown of faith, succour of hope and guardian of honour, glory of the soul and rest eternal, inviting us to the goods and leading us on to the kingdom of heaven. There is not therefore any difference in the labour which it will be for us to abide in our virginity and holi-

---

[1] In Latin: Ecce vindemiæ tempus est, quo succiduntur botri, et pedibus conculcantur, sed post hæc regalibus conviviis apponuntur.

[2] The Latin has: Et vos palmites mei, et meorum viscerum botri, estote parati in Domino.

ness.[1] For these are the seductions of the world and fleeting joys. By reason of which those here below are encompassed with woes and tears. For they rejoice a man's heart to begin with, but at the last they overtake and thrust him into torture. In the present they lull him into repose, that they may doom him to eternal torments. Wherefore my honourable virgins, who have so bravely run with me in the race of virginity, remain ye firm in the love of God in which ye now stand and enhance it yet more. For that was a time of lamentation, when ye were caught in folly. But ye have been filled with the unfading joy by Almighty God.[2] But I will commit you to the care of the Holy Spirit, and I trust that in His kingdom He will prove you perfect and spotless. But keep me ever as a pattern before your eyes, having in mind the teaching of me that am lowly and following the same all your days.

Such was the tenour of the exhortations which she addressed to them ; and after kissing them all with tears she further said : " Farewell, my sisters, for Basilia and Eugenia depart from you in the flesh." XXIV. And at the same time one of the maids of Basilia came to Pompeius, to whom she was betrothed, and said to him : " Dost thou know, that my mistress Basilia, who was engaged

---

[1] In Latin : Nihil ita nobis laborandum, nihil ita est enitendum, nisi cum virginitate vivamus, aut quod est gloriosius, pro virginitate etiam moriamur.

[2] Tempus flendi temporaliter, sine fastidio et horrore sufferte, ut tempora gaudii eterni cum omni possitis dilectione suscipere.

to thee, has been cajoled by Eugenia, and has utterly refused to wed thee?"[1] XXV. When Pompeius heard that, he was inflamed with wrath, and he came and wished to enter the chamber in which was Basilia with Protus and Hyacinthus engaged in prayer and praise. XXVI. Then they took Protus and Hyacinthus, and put pressure on them to sacrifice, threatening, if they refused, to give them to the sword. But they sturdily refused to comply, so they inflicted all sorts of tortures upon them. And after enduring many torments they suffered the death-penalty by the sword. And so they died in the holiness of martyrdom.[2]

---

[1] The Latin has: Quia te dominam nostram Basillam novimus ab imperatore meruisse, sextus et eo amplius est annus quam tu in tenero ætatis anno ut postea acciperet distulisti; sed patruelem eius Helenum scias esse Christianum, et hanc ita factam Christianam, ut tibi omnino non nubat. It goes on to relate that Basilla was wont to kiss the feet of the eunuchs, and that Pompeius on learning of all this statim concurrit ad Helenum patruelem eius, quia et nutritor eius erat et tutor. Helenus replies that Basilla is grown up and must decide herself. After learning of her refusal, Pompeius omni pene senatorum favore usus presents himself before the Emperor and urges that Eugenia has brought novos deos from Egypt, and that the Christians iura ipsius naturæ pervertunt, separant coniugium, gratiam sponsarum sibi associant; et dicunt iniquum esse, si sponsum suum sponsa accipiat (a common and well-founded form of complaint against Christian teachers of that time).

In ch. XXVI. the Latin goes on to relate that decrevit Gallienus Augustus ut aut sponsum suum Basilla acciperet, aut gladio interiret. She replies that her bride is Christ, and is at once put to the sword. Of Basilla's death the Arm. says nothing, though in the Latin it occurs before that of the eunuchs. It should be noticed that the metaphrast has Protas instead of Protus as the eunuch's name, while the Armenian has Proteus. I have adhered, however, to the Latin spelling Protus.

[2] The Latin has iubet eos decollari Nicetius urbis præfectus, but they were first brought to sacrifice to a statue of Jove, which immediately fell down and was broken. This miracle is not in the Armenian. The metaphrast also gives the Eparch's name as Nicetius.

XXVII. Next they seized Eugenia as well,[1] and tortured her before Aniktus, prefect (Eparch) of the city. XXVIII. And he commanded her to come and sacrifice to Artemis. But the blessed one came to the spot and entered into the temple, and having come opposite the image and having spread out her hands to heaven, she remained in prayer a long while. And when she had finished her prayers, forthwith the image of Artemis fell down and was broken into such fine fragments that even the dust thereof was not apparent.[2] But they did not comprehend the power of God, but thought that such things took place through the arts of wizards, so they commanded that a big stone be hung round her neck and that then she should be thrown into the Tiber. But the moment they threw her in, the bonds were broken and the stone fell from her and sank. And the holy Eugenia remained on the surface of the water. And all the Christians when they saw the miracle were filled with great joy, and

---

[1] In this ch. the Latin puts a long defence of herself into Eugenia's mouth: Polliceor tibi quod ars nostra vehementior magis est: nam magister noster habet Patrem sine ulla matre, et matrem absque patre. Denique sic eum genuit Pater, ut omnino feminam nunquam sciret; sic eum genuit mater, ut masculum omnino non nosset: hic ipse uxorem habet virginem, quæ illi quotidie filios creat . . . quotidie suam carnem eius carnibus coniungit. Oscula eius circa eam sine intermissione sociantur et cet. We then read that: "Audiens hæc Nicetius, obstupuit"—not unnaturally! The metaphrast concocts a different speech about demons and magic, and attributes it to Eugenia.

[2] The Latin is not content with so everyday a miracle, but relates that there was an earthquake and that the temple, foundations, idol and all, sank and vanished, only the altar being left, which was at the door, and before which Eugenia stood.

uttered hymns of praise, saying : " This is God who is with Eugenia and saves her from destruction ; the same God who was with Peter in the sea and saved him from being engulphed." But the water bore Eugenia up, and she reached the bank, and she came out and stood on the dry land. XXIX. Then they seized her a second time and put her in prison and ordered the royal baths to be warmed, which were called Tiberian (or "whose name was Tiberianus")[1] And they heated them so that they glowed like hot iron ; and then they ordered her to be thrown in and consumed by the flame. But the moment she entered, the fire went out, so that they were not able after that to heat the royal baths by command because of the icicles which formed in them. And when the grace of God triumphed over these means and wrought so mightily in behalf of Eugenia, they ordered her once more to be imprisoned. So they threw her into a dark house without bread or water, and all the house was illumined. And the blessed one was in the prison twenty days, and a light shone there every day. Then an angel of God appeared to her and strengthened her, and said : " Be of good cheer, Eugenia, servant of Christ ; for the Lord Jesus Christ, whom thou servedst with all thy heart, has sent me to thee, saying : ' Be of good cheer and be strong, for on this day I receive

---

[1] The Latin has: in thermarum Severianarum fornacibus. The metaphrast does not give this piece of information.

thee into heaven, when thou hast fulfilled the course of victory.'"[1] And on the very day of the birth of Christ, they sent an executioner, who came and slew her in prison. And when the Christians heard thereof, they gathered together and took the body of Eugenia, and wrapping it up carefully laid it in a special place, not far from the city opposite the road which was called Latina.[2] XXX. But her mother Clodia went and sat over the tomb and wept; but the blessed Eugenia appeared to her[3] and said: "Rejoice and be glad, mother mine, for the Lord Jesus has led me into joy and into the resting-place of His saints. And He has set my father in the ranks of His holy pontiffs; but thyself He will welcome in peace on the forthcoming Lord's day. And do thou instruct thy sons, my brothers, to keep safe the seal of Christ, whereby they may be worthy to receive the heritage of His saints." And it came to pass when Clodia had returned to her house, she taught her sons all the commands

---

[1] The Latin makes Christ Himself appear, bringing for her in His hand panem nivei candoris et immensæ suavitatis et gratiæ.

[2] The Latin has: non longe ab urbe via Latina in prædio eius proprio, ubi multorum sanctorum ipsa sepelierat membra. The metaphrast simply has: In a place not far from Rome, and the road is called the Roman road. In Kraus' Roma Sotteranea, p. 547, we read that the Cemetery of Eugenia, called also of Apronianus, is situated on the Via Latina. No trace remains of the church which contained her relics, until Stephen VI. (V.) transferred them to the Church of the Apostles inside the city. Boldetti thought that he had found the entrance to her catacomb a quarter of a mile outside the Porta Latina, where the road bifurcates, and where on the right hand under the Casa and Vigna Moiraga there was to be seen an old but ruined catacomb.

[3] The Latin adds, of course: cum multo populo virginum.

which the blessed Eugenia had given. And on the Lord's day at the hour of the completion of the sacrament, while she was in church and was offering prayer, she gave up her spirit into the hands of Christ, the Lord of all spirits.[1] And when she had thus died, her sons Avitos and Sergius took her and laid her beside their sister. But they themselves progressed in zeal for the Lord with all virtue, so as to detach many of the heathen from their unholy sacrifices and turn them to the faith of Christ; and hallowing them with holy baptism, they were themselves made worthy to imitate the lives of their parents and blessed sister, and mingled in the ranks of the saints. And may we also become worthy to enjoy the kingdom of heaven and praise God, Father of our Lord Jesus Christ. For to Him must all life give glory, and every knee bend of those in heaven and on earth and under the earth, that every tongue may confess Him who is above all, and to Him belongeth glory for ever and ever. Amen.

---

[1] The Latin does not relate the death of the mother Clodia, though it gives the daughter's prediction that it will be Die dominico.

ACTS OF S. CODRATIUS.

INTRODUCTION.

THE Saint Codratius, according to the Menologium of Basil Porphyrogenitus, suffered in Nicomedia under Decius and Valerian. His festival is celebrated on the ninth day of May, under which in the Bollandist Collection (May 2, p. 362) is to be found all that is known of him apart from the Armenian Acts, which I now translate for the first time. A Greek Synaxarium, translated by the Bollandist editor, gives a meagre outline of what the Armenian contains. The Bollandist editor remarks as follows: Hæc autem elogiorum diversitas reperta in Synaxariis, mutuos defectus quadam tenus supplentibus, omnino persuadet exstitisse olim, quae forte etiam nunc alicubi lateant, prolixiora martyrii Acta, unde Singuli Auctores Synaxariorum diversa illa Elogio decerpserint. In the Armenian we have probably preserved to us the missing document here referred to. The Latin notices name the Saint Codratus or Quadratus.

The Armenian Acts supply new matter.

The miraculous element in these Acts is very small and may easily be referred to the subjectivity of the Christians who witnessed the martyr's trial and recorded its details. On the whole the narrative seems very genuine, and Prof. W. M. Ramsay, in his *Historical Geography of Asia Minor* (p. 180), refers to the meagre Latin form of the Acts, as given in the Bollandist Collection, in support of his contention that the port of Prousa was called Cæsareia.

They are entirely credible.

These Acts contain little that is of doctrinal interest, except the single statement of the martyr that after ten days he will be in Paradise. I cannot find in any other source indications of this belief, that the journey occupied exactly ten days; though it was a common belief that a certain period must elapse. Codratius, like S. Phocas and in similar words, is invited to sacrifice to Poseidon.

The name of the Consul in these Acts before whom Codratius is tried is named in the Armenian, Prineos. In the Latin forms the name is spelt Perinius, which must be the same as Perennis, for the Greek spelling was Περέννιος. This is suspicious, seeing that Perennis was Prefect of the Prætorium under Commodus, and was murdered A.D. 185. However it may have been a fairly common name. O. Hirschfeld (*Römischen Verwaltungs-geschichte*, I., p. 228) notes that the name of a son of Perennis, Legate of Pannonia, has been erased in an inscription of the year 185, but he had perhaps other descendants. The Acts of Eugenia, probably by an anachronism, refer to a Perennius as having been Prefect of Egypt early in the third century. The Acts of Codratius also mention a judge Maximus, whose position in the proconsular court must have been that of adsessor. A Quæstor is also named; but it is impossible to identify any of these personages, so scanty is our knowledge of the Fasti of the Roman provinces. The date prefixed to the Acts, "under Decius and Valerian," must refer to the whole period of persecution which continued from Decius to Valerian. The same heading attaches to the Acts of Polyeuctes of Melitene.

MARTYRDOM OF SAINT CODRATIUS.

IN the time of Decius the Emperor, and of Valerian, the Christians were carried off from many cities and taken to Nicomedia, the metropolis of Bithynia, and were cast into prison. And there they were kept under custody and were dragged before the court. If they consented to eat of the unclean meats offered to idols, they were then released without torture and sent to their respective homes. In consequence whereof great terror fell upon the Christians of the above-mentioned city, and some hid themselves in the mountains and some in the fields. But there were goodly champions and worthy servants of God, who, with good courage, walked about the city with great joy, saying, "O that we may be worthy to glorify God by an avowal of His love for man!"

And there was one of them whose name was Codratius, who was of goodly stature and fair to see, and eloquent, and was held in great distinction by all men, and was the leader of all in his reverence to God, and was ardent in his faith. He approached the turnkey and the soldiers, and gave them much money, that they would allow him to minister to the prisoners, his brethren who were in prison, and to dispense to each of them his due of care. So he went boldly and ceased not from going in unto them; and thus he encouraged those who were of good heart and willing, to suffer martyrdom for their Lord. And he besought them to remember him without fail; but the weak in heart, and them that were cast down, he encouraged, and comforted, that they might not have fear, but rather rejoice the more. And he told them that most men do not leave this life at their own good pleasure, but with great trouble and in pain, and yet here in this transitory life they have not met with rest, and they have not forestalled nor made themselves worthy of the life to come. But he who mortifies himself for the sake of God, wins many and great goods both in the temporal life and in the life to come. All this he did as champion of the faith.

Now the Consul of that province came forward and sat down in public on his throne of judgment, and ordered the servants of God to be brought before him. And when they came and stood before him, the Consul said to them: " Let each of you tell his name and his race, his rank and his country." But the blessed Codratius could not restrain his enthusiasm and his religious fervour; but on a sudden, at that very moment, came forward to hasten to the Lord. And pushing himself forward in front of all the brethren, because he was last of all, and without anyone constraining him so to do, he leaped forward, fearing lest some one of those who had already engaged in the struggle should faint in heart before the torture, and deny his faith. For he saw some of the

Acts of S. Codratius. 195

brethren pale and stupefied by the diverse tortures they had undergone, and he feared that they might yield in their resolution. So he came forward to assist them, like a noble champion and knight of Christ that he was. And before they could any of them make answer, he said : " We are called Christians, this is our name ; but there is one honour for all of us and one freedom ; we are servants of Jesus Christ, our heavenly King, and of the unseen God ; and our city is the heavenly Jerusalem, in which Christ giveth mansions to His true soldiers. Behold, thou hast heard everything." But the Consul wondered at the man's boldness, and said to the turnkey : " Bring forward this presumptuous man, let us see what his impudent arrogance will benefit him." But he of his own freewill pushed the brethren this side and that, and boldly stepped forward, and crossed himself, and said to the Consul : " Of my own free will I stand before thee, O Consul, having made myself the antagonist of thy father, Satan. I am ready to meet all means to which thou mayest resort against me. Therefore do what thou wilt, for thou shalt learn from the very trial of them that the soldiers of Christ are invincible ; for we have taken upon us His seal, and are willing and ready to combat thy machinations."

But the Consul said : " Tell me, thou miscreant, first thy name and thy rank and fortune." Codratius answered, " Hear first that we are Christians ; but fortune we know not, for we are servants of our Lord Jesus Christ." The Consul said: "It is not meet that thou shouldst call thyself a Christian, because, if so, the edict of the Emperor slays thee. But since I behold that thou art a clever man, and of fair seeming, wherefore I think that thou must be of great family. Therefore obey me, and I will write about thee to the Emperor, and will win for thee a judicial post, if only thou wilt sacrifice to the gods." But Codratius answered: "Hold thy barbarous tongue, O Consul; there are not many gods, but one God our Father, from whom are all things, and one Lord Jesus Christ, through whom is all, and we through Him." The Consul said: "Nay, but there are many gods, and there are twelve chief gods, in whom thou must trust, and to them do homage." But the Holy Codratius made answer by citing the words of Homer (*Il.*, ii. 204): "'Tis not a good thing, a many of rulers, let there be one ruler." And the Consul said: "Aye, but there is another passage which thou hast not seen, so turn thy regard to this further verse." Codratius said: "What verses?" The Consul replied, "Those which Homer utters about Poseidon, how that he mustered the clouds, and stirred up the sea with all the winds and canopied it with mists; and the Father of gods on high thundered frightfully, and Poseidon came and shook the earth and the city of the Trojans and the ships of the Achæans. Much also did he say concerniug Zeus, what deeds of valour he wrought. Dost thou behold his greatness?" Codratius replied: " Is it all true or

Acts of S. Codratius.

false, that which Homer said about them?" The Consul replied, "It is true." Codratius answered: "And all that he said concerning their foul desires and adultery, and their filthy and lewd debaucheries? Must we believe that all this was said truly, when it is conduct which becomes not the gods, but only becomes madmen and disgusting beings? And I blush for thee, that thou permittest thyself to worship the semblance of foul devils, abandoning God. And if thou wilt, I will convince thee from the lips of thy own poet, that they are filthy demons." The Consul answered: "Thou hast begun to scold and abuse, and I fear lest the king may be angry with me, because I have permitted thee in my forbearance thus to speak. But however I will at once make away with this presumptuousness of thine." Codratius said: "What thou callest my presumptuousness, neither thou nor thy king nor anyone else shall be able to take from me."

Then the Consul bade them strip him and pinion him upon a board, and beat him with bludgeons, and ask him saying: "Tell us thy name." But he gave them no answer. And the Consul said to the turnkey: "What is he called?" But they say: "Codratius is his name, and moreover he is of a great family." The Consul said: "Spare him then, and raise him up from the block." And he said to him: "O good fellow, what is this that thou hast done, allowing thy rank to be insulted?" And he called him near unto himself, and said to him: "Consent to obey us, and do not abase thy rank and family by the superstition of the Christians, by which thou art ensnared." Codratius answered: " I have chosen to be an outcast from the house of God rather than dwell in the tents of the sinful," Then said the Consul: "Obey me, and sacrifice to the gods, since thou art equal in rank to the great Senate of the Romans, that thou mayest not die like one of the evil doers. Thou knowest the edict of the emperors, and of the great Senate, how many thousands they are of good men, that have resolved that not a single one of the Christians shall live." Codratius replied: " Blessed is the man who hath not walked in the councils of the impious and in the paths of the sinners; that hath not stood, nor sat, in the seats of the wanton." The Consul said: " Do not deceive thyself with metaphors, O Codratius, for this edict touches all Christians alike, whether a man be poor or rich, whether humble or of high rank; the tribunal spares no one." And Codratius replied: "It is as thou sayest, for the book that is given by God also says: 'neither bondsman nor free, neither rich nor poor, neither Barbarian nor Syrian, neither Greek nor Jew, for we are all one in the Lord.' But I pray thee to carry out upon me the edict of thy emperors and of the Senate; for I am a Christian, and my family and my rank depends upon my Lord, who keepeth whole my bright renown, and not upon them who are to-day, but to-morrow are not." The Consul said: " Obey me, and sacrifice, and rejoice in the good things

Acts of S. Codratius. 199

of life, and in the brightness of this daylight." And having thus spoken, the Consul wept, and drew deep sighs, and wiped his face with a napkin. But the brave Codratius said : " Shed not thy tears, for they are the odious malice of the serpent and of Beliar who slayeth men. O thou ravening wolf, thou canst not devour the servants of God." Maximus the judge said : " Out on thee, wicked man ; my august master pities thee, and thou revilest him." " Codratius answered : " Let him weep for himself and for the day of his birth, for I am no fitting object for his tears ; but who art thou that speakest in his presence ? The Consul is enough for us ; but if thou wishest to judge me, the Lord will prevent thee." Asterius, the Quæstor, said : " I swear by thy good Fortune, my lord Consul, if thou thus permittest him, he has no reverence for the Autocrat and Emperor, but will revile him and insult the gods, and bring upon us great peril." Codratius answered : " Well saith the scripture that is sprung from God : ' wherefore were the heathens puffed up and the peoples filled with vain thoughts? The kings of the earth were arrayed against me, and its rulers were gathered against the Lord and His anointed.' For behold even now Christ is judged by impious and vain rulers." The Consul said : " Strip yonder boaster and again smite him, that he may obey our lords the emperors."

But the blessed one in his torment thanked the Lord, and said : " Glory to Thee, my Lord God Jesus Christ, that Thou hast made me worthy, who am unworthy and sinful, to bear these tortures for Thy holy name, in order that I too may become a partner with Thy servants. I thank Thee, Lord, and falling before Thee I pray Thee, my God, fulfil my career in Thy holy name, and set upon my confession the seal of the grace of Thy Holy Spirit. Bestow upon me an understanding mind, and unswerving faith; make me wise with Thy immeasurable wisdom; watch me with Thine eyes, Thou that art on high. Now is the time of my deliverance and of my being holpen; now is the time of Thy promises. Receive my prayers, that I also may be glorified by Thy holy name. Fulfil my calling, guide aright my desires, bring me near unto Thy father; avow me as Thine before Him, O my Lord Jesus Christ."

But the torturers helped one another to scourge him, and five times they took one another's places, till the flesh of the back of the holy martyr was raised up a palm's breadth, and the blood flowed down like a river with shreds of His flesh. The Consul said to him: "Dost thou yet believe then in the gods?" But the blessed Codratius answered: "The idols of the heathen are gold and silver, the works of men's hands; mouths have they and speak not, ears have they, and may not hear; nostrils have they, but shall not smell; hands have they, and may not feel; feet have they, yet walk not; and their throats shall utter no speech. Like unto them shall be they who make them and all who put their trust

Acts of S. Codratius. 201

in them." Then Prenios, the Consul, said: "Methinks thou wouldest deceive us, since thou utterest such dark words; but obey me, and sacrifice to the gods." The holy Codratius said: "Since thy light appeareth to be darkness, and thy truth to be folly, hear a bright and clear saying; be it known unto thee, that I reverence not thy gods, and do not obey the edict of Cæsar and of the Senate. Do then quickly whatsoever thou wilt do, and send me on my way direct to the heavenly King." The Consul said: "Thy horoscope hath dealt out unto thee a great share of shamelessness. I swear by the gods I will not spare thee; but with new-fangled tortures and with a cruel death I will destroy thee."

And then he waited for a day and bade all the Christian prisoners to be cast into prison. And they brought with them the blessed Codratius, and they took potsherds ground small, and sprinkled them on the ground, and stretched out the saint, and placed a single great stone upon his loins, and made fast his feet and hands in the four holes of the stocks, and fastened chains to his neck. And he lay there many days. But the blessed Codratius, like the noble martyr that he was, endured these bitter and pitiless tortures with piety and fortitude, and swerved not from the faith of Christ. And the Consul set out on a journey to the city of the Niceans, and ordered that the holy martyr be brought in his train. And as he entered the city, he had the saint led in front of him. But the saints walked in great joy, among whom was also the blessed Codratius, like a goodly warrior boasting in his strength. So he entered the battle array in the sheen of his armour, and looked sternly on the hideous fray; and by the mere look of his terrible countenance struck panic into the phalanx of his enemies. Thus also Codratius bore his manacles as if they were a fair badge of honour, and he made merry and was of good cheer and to the fore. So that the Greek philosophers wondered at the fortitude of the Christians and at their endurance, and said: "Truly this faith of the Christians and this ever-present hope of theirs, is a great thing; on account of which they thus endure torture and pain." And many of them believed in the Lord.

And when they had set the saints before the magistrate, he ordered them to bring forward the holy Codratius; and when he was set before his tribunal, the Consul said to him: "Sacrifice to the gods, O Codratius." But the holy Codratius said: "I am a servant of Christ, who declares by the prophets that the gods who made not heaven and earth, shall be destroyed." The Consul said: "It is incumbent upon thee to obey the edicts of the emperors, and not of Christ whom thou callest God." Codratius answered: "I believe in my Emperor Christ, and not in men, who know not God; it is written that we should pray for them, but in no wise at all sacrifice to them. For what good do ye do to the Cæsar, if ye sacrifice to foul idols; nay, rather ye even do much harm, especially to yourselves." The Consul said: "If thou

Acts of S. Codratius.

prayest for the Emperor, it is right that thou shouldest also listen to his commands and be obedient to them, for it is written for thee, to give unto Cæsar the things that are Cæsar's, and unto God the things that are God's." Codratius answered: "All fitting debts upon earth, and whatsoever is right, that will I fulfil unto the Cæsar; but unto my God I strive to fulfil every service of reverence which is due to Him. The Emperor has commanded us Christians either to sacrifice or to die; and we are ready for the sake of the confession which is in Christ to die, not once only, but a thousand times." Then the Consul said: "Dost thou see how many multitudes of Christians have sacrificed to the gods?" Codratius answered: "Yea, more than all of them am I good and wise, if I sacrifice not. But, however, where are they who have sacrificed, for I would fain behold them." Then the Consul ordered that they should be led before him; and when they were come, those who had denied their faith, the blessed Codratius fixed upon them a glance full of passion and indignation, and said to them: "Ye miserable wretches, wherefore have ye thus fallen suddenly into trangression, and given yourselves over to Satan, abandoning your rank and station, and denying the Lord Jesus Christ, who for our salvation became our ransom and bought us with His blood? Have ye not learned the resurrection of the dead, and how that Christ cometh a second time with glory and with hosts of angels, to judge the just and the sinners ; and to lead the just into life eternal, but to cast the transgressors into fire everlasting and into outer darkness, where the worm endeth not, and where there is weeping and gnashing of teeth ? What answer will ye give in the peril of that day, when the hosts of the angels will stand before Him in fear and trembling, and will quail at the sight of us and of the dread tribunal ? Open the eyes of your heart and know from what ye have fallen. Ye have abandoned the Eternal King, and have sold yourselves to be worthless slaves, who, finding your Lord without, smite and slay his fellow servant; whom the Lord when He cometh shall cut asunder and give their portion to the infidels. Learn ye, what ye have done from fear of temporal tortures, how that ye have given yourselves over to everlasting tortures. Look ye to yourselves for that which shall happen to you at the hands of the just Judge. Have ye not heard the voice which said : ' Fear not them who slay the body, but cannot slay the soul ; fear rather Him who is able to destroy soul and body in Gehenna ' " ?

When the blessed Codratius said this, they all with one accord began to cry out with loud voice with tears and to say : " We were afraid, master, of torture, and we were ensnared like the senseless animals, and like sheep that are hemmed in among wolves. Our sins have found us out and surrounded us ; we wished to live the temporal life, and we have died to the eternal life. But what we shall do now in our wretchedness, this we know not." But the blessed Codratius was filled with great joy over their return, and seeing their tears said to them: "Be of good cheer, brethren, for our Lord Jesus Christ is full of noble pity and is compassionate; He is free from vindictiveness and merciful. With many tears, cast yourselves before Him; and stand up even now firm in the confession of Christ, and by His blood shall each of you be saved from his sins. Even though once ye rejected Him with the flesh, yet now be valiant in spirit and conquer."

But they raised a great lament and bewailed themselves for a long time, and cast themselves on their faces on the ground, and poured dust over their heads, and beat their breasts with stones; and so terrible was the spectacle, that not the Christians only joined in their lamentations, but the very heathens and the pitiless soldiers; so that one would have thought that the very stones cried out and sorrowed with them. For the whole city was aghast at their lamentations, and there was gathered together to the place a multitude of men and women and of children, of Jews and of heathens, and of Christians, who were in hiding, so that the streets and the alleys and the roofs were filled with the multitude of them. But the Consul was wroth thereat, and ordered that the blessed Codratius be hung up and flayed, and the torches be applied to his side. But the brave Codratius recked nothing of the torture, but with great boldness exhorted them to be brave, and said: "Thus is it right, brethren; pray unto the Lord without ceasing, for He is merciful and hears you." But they said: "We are not worthy to name the holy name of Christ, because we have offended Him." But he strengthened them, he the holy martyr, and kept saying: "Cry aloud, brethren, cry aloud; our Lord and God is kind; He draws nigh to those who cry out unto Him for help. Despair not, brethren, but come near unto me, and ye shall be emboldened and trust in the Lord." And they ran and fell down before him in violent trouble, and the whole multitude of those who were come to see wept.

But the holy Codratius lifted his eyes to heaven and cried aloud with tears and said: "O Lord, thou God, who art great and terrible, kind and full of noble pity, who didst send forth Thy only born Son, our Lord Jesus Christ, to shine upon us as the Sun of Righteousness, and didst illuminate us who were before in darkness, and didst through Him reconcile us unto Thee, and didst call us who were before in darkness to a holy calling; O merciful One, and compassionate, long-suffering and full of pity, and true, who passest over our sins and wipest out our proud iniquities; for Thy exceeding love of man, O Lord, cast out him that is first in evil and slayeth man, that hateth the good and is full of envy, Satan, the father of idols, and prince of darkness; and receive Thy soldiers back, who for a little were seduced by the snares of Satan, but have now

Acts of S. Codratius. 207

taken refuge in Thy all-powerful goodness. Be not wroth with them, as with rebels. Albeit they were wilful, they stand now unchanged. And if Thou receivest them in Thy loving kindness, receive me also as an offering for the sinful, and make them worthy to mingle with Thy heavenly and true host, and shew to them a sign in Thy goodness, that Thou hast not abhorred, but hast pitied and received the repentant. O Lord Jesus Christ, hear me Thy servant, and instead of them take my soul, that Thy holy name may be glorified for ever." And all the brethren with one voice cried out aloud a great Amen. And on a sudden the brands were extinguished, and the hands of the torturers flagged, and a cloud of light appeared over the heads of the saints, along with great darkness and grievous smoke which spread itself over the heads of the Consul and of the heathen; so that the Consul on his seat of justice, and all who were with him, were aghast with fear, because they thought that the city was going to be destroyed. And after a long silence, a voice of angels was heard, who praised and glorified God, so that all the Chrisians believed that there was great rejoicing in heaven over those who had returned to repentance. And after two hours had passed, little by little the darkness cleared away, and the heathen began to see the light which was around the saints. But those who were in iniquity began with loud voice and lamentation to cry out to God and say: "We have sinned, O Lord, expiate our sins; we have transgressed, be propitious unto us." And the Consul came to his senses, and ordered them all to be cast into prison, and to be carefully guarded. But he ordered the blessed Codratius to be taken down from the tree and confined along with them; for all this time the goodly champion was hanging there. And he commanded him to be watched carefully as before. But the crowd of citizens followed after the saint.

But on the next day the Consul took his seat in the tribunal, and ordered that they should be brought before him; and he questioned them, and examined them straitly, and having found out their obstinacy and their immutable resolution, he commanded that they should all be bound and taken to their several villages and burnt alive. And the saints went on their way with great joy, glorifying God and thanking Him for their unlooked-for deliverance. But the blessed Codratius, along with certain of his companions, he bade them take in front of him to the Hellespont. But the multitude of the saints, according to the command of the ruler, went to their respective villages and died in Christ.

But the Consul came to the city of Apamea, and, as he sacrificed to the foul idols, he ordered the holy martyr to be brought before him. And they brought first of all and before all the rest, the blessed Codratius. Then said the Consul to him: "Sacrifice therefore now to the gods, and thou art delivered from the tortures, that await thee if thou remain obstinate. Codratius answered: "I am a Christian and I sacrifice not to devils." And when the Consul saw all his flesh lacerated, he wondered and said: "But what more shall I bestow upon this self-murderer?" But the soldiers hesitated to answer, for they saw that tortures had no longer any power to influence his body. Then he ordered that haircloth should be brought and that Codratius should be wrapped in it, and that a hole should be made, and that he should be cast into it, and there scourged with cords. And after one hour he ordered him to be brought out of the cloth, for he thought that he was dead. But he rose up and stood before him; and the Consul said to him: "Do you no longer feel the tortures?" But the holy champion thanked God and said: "Glory to Thee, O Lord Jesus Christ, for the arrows of children but wound themselves, and their power is weakened in them. It is Thou that hast given me strength, my God, unto the glory of Thy power." And the Consul was wroth and said to him: "I will tear all thy limbs asunder piece-meal, thou wretch, if thou still trustest in thy wizardry." Codratius answered: "Blessed is the Lord my God." The Consul ordered that he should be again brought before him to Cæsareia on the Hellespont.

And when he came thither he sacrificed there also to the foul devils as he had done at Apamea. He commanded also that the blessed Codratius should be brought before him, and began to question him what he would have; but finding that the holy martyr was firm, he said: "Thou hast had enough now of the tortures which thou hast suffered, so come and sacrifice to the gods." But the blessed Codratius said: "Inasmuch as thou didst mock me with these tortures, dost thou really suppose that I shall obey thee?" Then the Consul ordered that he should be stretched upon stones, and that they should put upon his hands and feet enormous stones, and beat him for a long time with cudgels. But the blessed one in his torment sang psalms and said: "Many a time they fought with me in my childhood, but mastered me not. On my back the sinful smote me." And when he had finished the psalm, the Consul said: "Let him be beaten longer, since he has not felt anything." Codratius replied: "Smite, smite my flesh, which thou thinkest to torture; for thou makest glad my spirit in a way thou knowest not." Then the Consul said: "Thou hast mastered, O wretched one, an evil demon." Codratius replied: "I swear by my Saviour Christ, that Jesus Christ my Lord hath mastery over one still worse, and not over one only, but over all his host. To Him be glory everlasting." And the multitude of the brethren sent forth the Amen.

The Consul was very wroth and leaving alone the blessed Codratius, he ordered a certain two of them to be taken and hung up and flayed, namely, Saturninus and Rufinus, and he commanded that they be hung from one tree.

Acts of S. Codratius.

Then they tore them with nails, until the inner parts of them began to pour out. But they in their torments uttered no word, but only besought the holy Codratius and all the brethren who stood near to pray for them. And last of all, the blessed ones themselves fell to praying and said: " Lord Jesus Christ, Son of God on high, send unto us also help from Thyself and protect us Thy lowly servants, our God, and give us endurance and victory unto the end." And after a long time when they gave no answer, for from the stress of torture they were not even able to speak, then at last the Consul ordered that they be taken to the high road which leads to the Hellespont, and there slain with the sword. And thus did the blessed ones end their life. And God-loving men met together and gave gold to the executioners, and took their relics and bore them to their respective cities, and with great honour placed them in caskets. But the blessed Codratius he ordered to come after him, along with others also, to a temple of Apollo; and when he had come into the shrine of Apollo he began to constrain the saints to sacrifice to the foul idols. And he said to the blessed Codratius: " Now therefore obey me, fellow, and forsake this madness of thine. Wherefore dost thou insult thy rank and family; recognise the gods and live, and I will bid the physicians take care of thee. Offer sacrifice to Asclepius, and he will heal thee; fear the great Apollo, and the god Hercules, and the king of all, Zeus, and the ineffable Ares, and the ruler of the sea, Poseidon. Didst thou never embark in a ship and know the fear of him?[1] Do homage to the sun; surely he is not dead according to thy blasphemy, even though he be not in the heavens." The blessed Codratius answered: "I do homage to the true and unseen God, and to His only born Son, Jesus Christ, our Lord and Saviour. And I dread His menaces, and I quail before His all-powerful Godhead, and I will not deny the name of His ineffable power. In dead idols I believe not, and of devils I have no fear. I despise the works of men's hands, and thee also, who hast but a temporal power. For I, after ten days, go to my Father, but thou wilt end thy life in the bitterness of evil. For thou hast not known the true God, thou son of Satan and brother of Beliar, who sharest with foul devils, more senseless than a hog, mad hound, blood-drinking dragon, fiercer than the wild beasts that devour men. Art thou not ashamed before such a multitude as this, who taste not of anything? The cooks are to be more respected than thyself, who, in name, are the servants of men; for they place the flesh of the slain animal in decent manner drest for the benefit of men, and not of devils. You sacrifice to stones, and you tear and bite yourselves. But let one of them come forward and take your offering, let him appear and seek it of himself, and let him take and eat it.

---

[1] Compare the address of Trajan to Phocas, p. 115.

Let your gods that are made of stone say what he wishes that anyone should sacrifice to him, whether a goat, or a bull, or a fowl. Blush, ye sons of shame, for ye are mad and think that we are mad."

And when he had said this, the Consul ordered the executioners to sprinkle vinegar and salt water upon his wounds, and to rub him with a rough cloth, and to bring red-hot irons and plunge them into his sides. But the blessed Codratius bore the pain bravely and fell to praying gently, and his lips alone moved; and no sound whatever was heard to issue from him. But when the torturers were weary, he ordered them to unfasten him. And on the morrow he first of all bade them carry him to the Hellespont in a vessel (*or* basket).[1] And after that the Consul made a journey, and came to the river Rhyndacus, where there met him a governor with a crowd of common people, ostensibly to praise him, but really for the sake of the servant of God; for he longed to see the blessed hero, the fame of whose martyrdom had reached Asia and all the land. And the Consul ordered them to carry him to the village close at hand, which was called the village of the Temple. And there he dressed, and at daybreak he took his seat on the tribunal, and ordered them to bring before him the holy Codratius; and all the crowd was

---

[1] Or translate thus: "he commanded a vessel to be brought to the Hellespont."

gathered round and looked upon the heroic contest of the holy martyr. But the blessed one shewed to the multitude a face full of joy, though running with blood, according to that which is written. "The countenance of him that rejoices in heart is joyful." Again he was carried by the torturers; for from the excess of the tortures which he had suffered, he could no longer walk; but they bore him along the road in a cart. And when the saint was brought before him, the Consul said: "Hast thou gained wisdom, O Codratius, or art thou not yet healed of this madness of thine?" But the blessed one with a loud voice replied: "From my childhood am I sane, and from my mother's womb am I the servant of Christ."

Then the Consul made them bring an iron brazier and set it upon the fire till it was like fire, and commanded them to set the saint upon it. But the blessed Codratius said: "Away from me, ye ministers of Satan; of my own accord I go." And making upon himself the sign of Christ, he rose up. But they sprinkled in the brazier pitch and oil. But the holy Codratius began to sing a psalm, and said: "O God, look upon me to help me, and O Lord, hasten to assist me; let them be ashamed and confounded who sought my life: let them be turned back and ashamed who will to do me evil." And having finished his psalm, he said to the Consul: "This fire of thine is more liquid, and the iron of this brazier is softer than thy heart." And when long time had passed by, and the fire came not nigh at all unto the holy one of God, the Consul ordered them to take him off the brazier and to bear him a little way outside the village to a certain rising ground, and there to behead him. And as they carried the blessed Codratius, he continued to sing psalms and to say: "Blessed is the Lord, who hath not given us to be the prey of their teeth." And the brethren who stood by sang psalms and went with him as far as the place where he was to die. And having come thither, and having thanked God, and having prayed for a long time, then he finished his blessed course in Christ. But the brethren took his holy body and laid it carefully in a fitting place.

Let us continually glorify the Father and the Son and the Holy Spirit, now and always, and for ever and ever, Amen.

ACTS OF THEODORE.

IN the Bollandist Acta SS, the pieces relative to the martyrdom of S. Theodore are to be found under February 7th (February, vol. 2, p. 23 seq. and p. 890 seq.), where the Bollandist editor calculates the true date of the saint's death to have been A.D. 319, in which year the 7th of February was a Saturday. But we must not try to be too precise in fixing the date, for the earlier Armenian form of the Acts give the 27th of August, and the old Latin form assigns November 4th.

In the Acta SS. two forms of the narrative are given; first, a Latin translation of the metaphrast's recension of the Acts, and then in the appendix of the volume an older Latin version taken from the Codex 79, " Serenissimæ reginæ Sueciæ," which the editor without very good reason considered to be earlier and more trustworthy than the metaphrast's form.

Both of these forms however agree together in three points. (1) The first six sections, as far as § 7 of the Armenian give particulars of the persecution of Licinius. There were slain, we read, in that time four hundred martyrs and seventy centurions and three hundred in Macedonia. (2) They also relate at great length how Theodore in his youth slew a dragon, which was the terror of his native town Eukhaita. (3) In § 17 the saint is represented as delivering a long sermon to Abgar and the rest of the brethren, in the course of which he gave the instruction that his body be taken to Eukhaita. In the Armenian text, points (1) and (2) are entirely omitted and their place supplied by particulars of the saint's training and promotion in the Roman service, and as to (3) it is simply related that they took the saint's remains to Eukhaita in accordance with instructions long before given by the saint to Abgar.

In the Armenian form we have probably a fourth century homily delivered on some feast day set apart to the commemoration of the saint. We gather from the exordium (§ 2) that the church is still in danger of persecution; so that this homily was probably composed prior to A.D. 363, when all fears of persecution ceased. The first six §§ of the Armenian contain nothing about the dragon, and are altogether more sober than are the corresponding §§ of the later forms of the narrative. In general outline the last part of the narrative (§§ 7–18 inclusive) is the same in all three forms. A comparison of these §§ in all the three forms shows that the Armenian must be nearest to the original form, from which are derived the metaphrast's and the early Latin form.

I think that the last part of these sections found in all three forms, from § 13 as far as the words "with a sword" in § 17, may be reckoned an interpolation inserted at an early time by a hagiologist, who after the manner of his class was eager to assure his readers that the persecutors after the saint's death paid the penalty of their cruelty. According to the original narrative the saint died on the cross. The words given to the angel in § 13 : "Why then didst thou say that thou wast abandoned by me?" resemble a later hagiologist's corrective to § 12, which has a very genuine ring about it.

The original Acts, no doubt composed by Abgar, the saint's notary, must have begun about where § 5 of the following begins, and have ended soon after the beginning of § 18, omitting however the interpolation which I detect in §§ 13–17. The document, however, which the metaphrast, the old Latin translator, and the Armenian translator alike had in their hands, already included this interpolation.

Prof. W. M. Ramsay has identified Eukhaita with the modern Tchorum on the old road from Amasia to Nicomedeia and in easy communication with Gangra and east of the Halys. The Abbé Duchesne has cited the Latin form of these Acts, in proof of his contention that Eukhaita was west of the Halys. Prof. Ramsay (*Geography of Asia Minor*, p. 318) answers that "the Acta Theodori contain little or no local colour. His history is divided between Eukhaita, Nikomedeia and Herakleia (Pontica), which is said to be a city near the others." And again (p. 321) the Acta Theodori "is really one of the most contemptible documents in the entire Acta SS. It is quite clear that nothing whatsoever was known about Theodore except his name and a tale that he had slain a dragon." To this criticism it is sufficient answer that the Armenian Acta, (1) mention no dragon, but give instead thereof very probable and sober details of the saint's life; (2) say nothing of the proximity of the three cities to one another, but on the contrary imply that Herakleia was a very long way from Nicomedeia. The saint could not spare the time from the affairs of his province in order to visit his Emperor at Nicomedeia. Nor would the latter have made the conduct of the war a pretext for visiting the saint in Herakleia unless it had been a long distance. Lastly, the Armenian proves Herakleia in Cappadocia to be the city in question.

Thus the Armenian text rather supports Prof. Ramsay's geographical views than not, and constitutes one more proof of the danger of condemning a document until you have got back to something like its original form.

I have supposed that the Armenian text is a fourth-century homily in which are embodied the original Acts, just as the Acts of Polyeuctes are embodied in a similar homily. Now in the last § 19 the words: "Writing down the history of his martyrdom and handing it on to future generations," seem to imply that the Acts were being then for the first time written down when the homily was composed. However these words do not really preclude the view that the homilist made use of an already existing record of the saint. He is simply insisting on the general necessity of keeping alive the memory of the martyrs by copying and distributing the records of them. This last § 19 is absent from the metaphrast's recension and from the earlier Latin form. It is anyhow inconceivable that § 12 should be anything but what it pretends to be, namely the personal narrative of the slave and notary Abgar. It is a passage instinct with genuine feeling, such as no hagiologist ever composed in cold blood long after the events narrated.

THE MARTYRDOM OF THE HOLY THEODORE THE SOLDIER.

1. UNSEARCHABLE and wonderful are the heavenly gifts which the Creator has freely bestowed in miraculous wise on the ranks of His holy martyrs. Unspeakable is the patience with which they entered and won the struggle, and too varied are their virtues for it to be possible to relate them, even for those who loved them and fought beside them. Nor is it easy to tell even in metaphor of the fair seeming and brightness of the richly burgeoning wreaths and of the unfading and varied chaplets which they wove. It is hard to relate how, by their strength in martyrdom, they locked together and surrounded themselves with the shields of the Spirit, and were tried like gold which is tried in the fire. Thus they crossed over the dark sea and turbulent of this wicked life, and displayed their victory over the antagonism of the devil. None of those who are in the flesh can worthily commemorate their excellence; for the Divine Spirit alone is able to describe it.
2. Yet although it is beyond the compass of man to relate it, we must not be altogether silent. Nay, let it be told as according to the apportioning of the divine grace of the Spirit one has ability to publish it to pious souls. In order that by means

Acts of Theodore. 221

of the recollection of the valiant and spiritual soldiers of Christ, the children of the church may be awakened, and may aspire to enter into the pavilion of rest to which they are called, armed with the armour of God; in order that in the time of persecution, and when trials arise, they may be able to participate with those who were found to share the cross of Christ. 3. Let us then begin the commemoration of this noble martyr of Christ, the holy Theodorus, albeit we are not able to do full justice to his bravery and excellence. Yet we may tell a little out of much. We can say who he was, whence he came, and how his martyrdom began and ended, and we will relate the story of the time of his persecution. For he was not the Theodorus the Tiro,[1] whose commemoration is held on the first sabbath of the forty days' fast; but our saint was his nephew, and was held in high honour by the emperors from whom he received a command in the army. For he (*i.e.* the Tiro) was martyred under the King Maximianus, in the city of Amasia in Cappadocia; so that they were not far from one another, either in point of time or of family.

4. But in the times of the lawless and impious Emperor Licinius, a blazing storm of cruel persecution swept over the church of God, and everywhere the altars all over the Roman empire were heaped up with the molten images of devils, and

---

[1] The Armenian spells Tyrion. Theodore the Tiro, or recruit, was a saint much celebrated in Cappadocia. His Acts are not, so far as I know, preserved in Armenian.

in all places the edict of apostasy was circulated, and commands of the following kind posted up in every village and city with all sternness, to the effect that they should do homage to stones, and to trees fashioned by the hands of men, and that they should offer up holocausts and sacrifices to the so-called gods, and should content themselves with foul food. And those who obeyed this edict received honour and promotion from the Emperor, but those who refused to do so were compelled, and were subject to stripes and to torture, and punishment by sword and fire. For an inextricable mist of darkness and disturbance encompassed us all, for they took many of those who believed and gave them over to the judges, that they might confine them in dark places, and subject them to cruel and pitiless tortures, and after long tribulation die by the sword.

5. At that time there blazed forth a star of dazzling brilliancy, a lamp that scattered its radiance far and wide, and illuminated the mist and darkness of idolatry, appearing victorious over all, I mean the brave champion and soldier of the King Christ, the holy Theodorus. For when this edict of the impious and lawless Emperor Licinius went forth, that all who believed in Christ should be taken and thrown into prison, and bound and subjected to intolerable privations and tortures; then the blessed and famous witness of Christ, Theodorus, had been born of Christian and religious parents, in the village of Eukhaita. He was brought up and trained in all good discipline

in Christ, and grew in stature and wisdom, and was schooled in the teachings of religion. While he was still in the flower of youth and prime of life, fair to look upon and filled with all wisdom, he became on that account the friend and intimate of the kings and princes of that day. For in the wars of the barbarians, the saint was ever victorious and won all praise; for which reason he received the very highest honour in the army, and was promoted to the very highest grade of command. 6. Now some malignant satellites of the devil obtained the ear of the Emperor, and laid information that the saint was a Christian, and not only he, but his whole country and city; "for under his influence," they said, "they have been perverted by him along with your army, and have turned away from the worship of idols, and have disobeyed your commands; they no longer keep the mysterious festivals of the gods, nor do they taste of their holy sacrifices." 7. When the Emperor heard this, he was dumbfounded; and, though he was full of wrath, he wavered in his counsels, and did not know how he would be able to take in his deadly net so conspicuous a man. He did not think it suitable to write and summon him to come before him, for he feared that he would see through his crafty designs, and be afraid, and disregard his commands. So he formed this plan, that he would make the conduct of the war a pretext for his coming to those regions, and so take him in the city itself. And having formed this design, the lawless prince determined to send some of his nobles together with a force to Heraclea, a city of Cappadocia, where the saint dwelt. And he wrote to him a letter in complimentary terms as follows: "If it should be pleasing and acceptable to you, come and see us, and do homage to our gods in the city of Nicomedia, and come with a great suite and with much pomp. But if there is any reason to prevent you, it is meet that we should come and see your district, and the city in which you dwell, for we are very desirous to see you and enjoy your good will." And when the captains came to him, and brought the letter of command, Theodorus took and read it, and was delighted and thanked God; for he had thought already in his heart of declaring himself for the true religion, and of becoming a witness of Christ; and now on a sudden the good will and pleasure of God was about to be really accomplished. So on that occasion he received the king's men with great honour, and made them presents; but he excused himself from going to meet the king on the score of the requirements of the province, and begged them, and promised them riches, if they would go and persuade the Emperor to come to the city of Heraclea, bringing with him the full number of his gods. "You will behold," he wrote, "all the population of the town and country, and they will be glad and rejoice, and will hold a great festival with sacrifice and adoration." So the men went back to the Emperor, and gave him the answer which had been despatched to him. And this the ruler took and read, and was deceived and taken

Acts of Theodore. 225

in by it, like an unreflecting child; for he determined to set out for those regions, thinking in his wickedness that all his designs were already accomplished. So forthwith he took a number of cavalry, and arrived at the city of Heraclea. And when the holy Theodore heard of the arrival of the Emperor, he went out to meet him with great pomp and rich suite. 8. But on that night, as he slept in his house, the saint beheld in a vision that the ceiling of his house was lifted up, and a shower of corruscating sparks of fire descended upon him; and a voice was heard saying to him: " Be strong, and of good cheer, Theodorus, for I am with thee." And when the saint woke up, he told his dream to those who were nearest to him, and said : " God is pleased that in this place my blood should be shed for the name of Christ." And then he arose and knelt down, and prayed ; and when he had finished his prayer and wept, he thanked the Lord.

9. And then he arose, and washed the fair glory of his countenance, and put on precious raiment of byssus, and he ordered them to equip his horses in gold trappings. And then he rode out with his horses and met the Emperor. And when he beheld his ruler, he did homage to him, and after the manner of kings, he wished him well, saying, " Hail to thee, most powerful and autocratic Emperor, sent by God." But the Emperor, when he heard this, and saw the magnanimity of the saint, instantly embraced him with much tenderness, and welcomed him fondly, and kissed him, and said :

"Hail to thee, O prince, fair as the sun to look upon, for it is meet that thou also shouldst reign along with me." And they entered together into the city along with the multitude of their men, who had gone out to meet the king; and he prepared a resting-house in the royal quarters, decorated after the manner of the palace, with canopies and imperial throne. And when the Emperor saw this he was overjoyed, and praised the city and the citizens, and he bade Theodorus sit down, and said to him: "Behold, according to the prayer that thou hast written to me, O Theodorus, I have come as the guest and recipient of thy hospitality to visit thee and thy city; and I have brought with me the most precious and the most illustrious of our gods, in order that thou mayest worship them, and offer sacrifice to them." The holy Theodorus made answer, and said: "O victorious and great Emperor, thou hast done well in fulfilling the request of thy servant, by making us glad with thine advent; and yet more hast thou honoured us by bringing with thee thy gods, in order that all may behold them, and may be confirmed in the ordinances of religion. But I pray thy highness to rest a little from the labour of the journey, and to give me thy most illustrious gods, all of them, in order that I may take them to my house, and anoint them with fragrant oil, and offer frankincense to them, and cense them, and in order that I may prostrate myself and offer sacrifice in my own private house, and then after that may bring them out into public before all, and sacrifice; in order that all men, marking and beholding this, may be encouraged to emulate me in my piety." And when the Emperor heard this, he was very satisfied and pleased with the words of the saint, and believed that which he had said. And he ordered them to bring and give to him all his idols fashioned of gold and silver. And the saint took them, and carried them to his palace to put them to rest. But he arose that night, and he broke and ground to powder all those gods, and then he took the bits and distributed them to the poor and needy.

10. But after three days had passed, the prince commanded that they should summon before him the great Theodorus, and he said to him: "O most honourable and illustrious of the princes who were before myself, and thou who hast been still more promoted and honoured by my own majesty, now therefore give proof of thy enthusiasm and love which thou hast towards my gods and towards us. Bring a sacrifice and offer it to them before the whole people, in order that they may all behold thee, and may fulfil our edict with all readiness." But whilst the saint was on the point of making answer to the Emperor, a certain man stood forward who was a person of authority, and whose name was Maxentenes,[1] and said: "O noble prince, thou hast not known and understood the treason of this impious general, nor how he hath falsely deceived thy majesty in respect of

---

[1] Maxentius in the Latin form.

thy all-victorious gods; for yesterday night, going forth from my quarters, I beheld a certain poor man, who was going along full of joy, holding in his hand the golden head of our great queen Artemis."

When the Emperor heard this, he was much enraged, and stood agape and could not believe what he heard; but he said to the saint: "Is this that they said true?" The saint made answer and said: "Yes, it is true and just, I deny it not; for I have done justly what I have done. For surely if thy gods have not been able to help themselves, how will they be able to help thee?" Then the countenance of the Emperor changed colour with rage, and filled with wrath he said: "Woe to me, for I have been deceived like a little child, and have been turned to ridicule before the eyes of all. And now I know not what I shall do or how I shall act; for I who am emperor and ruler of all these forces and of the world, have come along with all my forces to be deceived at the feet of this miscreant; I have become the shame of the province and of the city, losing all my victorious gods." And when the holy Theodorus saw the Emperor filled with such folly, he laughed in his soul, and said: "O thou senseless demon, filled full with all lawlessness, didst thou not take note beforehand, that I was a Christian and a servant of Christ; how could I be deceived by thy deceitful and pernicious edicts? But in order that thou mayest know that thou art truly tricked like a simple child, therefore have I shown unto thee the weakness of thy gods, in order to put to shame thy impiety. Thou art puffed up with thy empty and transitory greatness, and thou hast not any hope or expectation of the greatness which passes not and of the light which is eternal, and thou knowest not Him who gave thee thy temporary greatness; but thou art infatuated by the crafty illusion of the devil, and darkened so that thou mayest not see the light of the glory of the only-born Son of God, and in the presumption with which the evil one inspires thee, thou dost not know what thou sayest. But I hold vain all this glory of created things, which estrange a man from God, in order that I may inherit immortal life, which eye hath not seen, nor ear heard, and which God has prepared for those who love Him. But for thee and for thy material gods is reserved the fire eternal, which is made ready and kept for Satan and his hosts."

The Emperor said: "O insolent miscreant, Theodorus, I could tolerate thy insults to me, for as regards obedience to myself, thou shalt be reformed; but why hast thou insulted the gods?" The saint made answer and said: "Herein is the very demonstration of thy want of wit, for thou beholdest the nothingness of thy molten images of demons, and yet after this thou hast the rashness to give them the name of gods, who are like horses and mules, for there is no understanding in them, hewn out by the hands of mechanics."

11. And the Emperor was filled with wrath, and said: "Henceforth I will not tolerate thee, but I

give thee over to miserable torture." And he ordered the executioners to strip the saint, and to stretch out his hands on fourfold pinions, and to scourge him with green switches, without spare, upon shoulders and chest and stomach; and they scourged the blessed one, so that the godless torturers were wearied and faint. And they carded the flesh of the saint with their cruel blows, and the blood poured forth from him. And then the Emperor ordered him to be smitten without spare on the neck with leaden hammers. And as they smote him, he ordered that all that was remaining of the body of the holy martyr should be scraped with iron needles, and then that fire should be brought and that they should burn all the wounds in his body. So they burned and roasted his whole body according to the command of the Emperor. But the holy martyr shewed yet more patience than before amid the throes of his cruel anguish, and thanked God that his desires were fulfilled; and as if he reckoned for nothing all this intolerable torture, he said to the Emperor: "O thou minister and servant of Satan, and enemy of all righteousness, dost thou not see that thy torturers flag, and that thy foolhardy pride is humbled, and thy violence overcome, and thy father the devil Satan is put to shame; and however much my outer man is destroyed by thy torture, so much the more is my inner man renewed unto eternal life?"

But the Emperor was very wroth, and ordered his soldiers to take the saint to prison, in order that he might deliberate about him, by what death he should slay him. And when they had cast him into prison, after a few days he ordered him to be brought before him; and he tempted him with many words and questioned him, but yet could not persuade the blessed one. So then he ordered them to crucify him, and he made the entire number of his army shoot at him with arrows. But the martyr of Christ with great gladness went after the soldiers, and when he came to the cross they bound his hands and feet, and took and fastened him upon the tree. And a number of soldiers shot at him with arrows, and hit the face and eyes of the saint. But the champion of Christ endured it patiently, and gave thanks to God, and reckoned for nothing all the anguish and pain. And after that they came and mutilated his manhood, and all the multitude that stood round wept, all of them. 12. And I Abgar, the slave and secretary of the saint, who had received his command to write down all, point by point, when I beheld such cruelty, I threw away my paper from my hands, and I went and fell at his feet, weeping bitterly; and the saint, when he saw my tears, said to me in a gentle but weak voice: "O Abgar, grieve not, nor be remiss in thy task, but accomplish that which thou hast begun, and obey me yet a little longer that thou mayest see the end of my consummation, and write it down." And when he had said this, he raised his eyes to heaven, and said: "Father of our Lord Jesus Christ, my God, who in Thy unspeakable goodness dost control and arrange all things; who also by the hand of Thy only-born Son, and true and Holy Spirit, hast bestowed upon me strength to bear; for Thou, Lord, didst erewhile make promise to me, saying: "I have not abandoned thee, but for all time I will be with thee, and will save thee; and now, O my God, wherefore hast Thou forsaken me, and hast withdrawn from me Thy pity? For the wild animals have torn my flesh because I loved Thy name; the pupils of mine eyes have been put out, and my flesh has been consumed with fire, and my fingers have been crushed, and my face has been altered so that it is no longer like that of a human being, and my soul reels and trembles with the fear of the tortures of the cross. And now, O my Lord and my God, for Thee have I borne all this, being given up to fire and sword, and to all anguish. Wherefore I beseech Thee receive my spirit forthwith, and refresh me according to Thy good pleasure, for Thou art all powerful."

And when he had said this he was silent, for all the members of the flesh of the martyr were weak, and the hollow of his stomach was lacerated and crushed because of the harrowing and of the tortures inflicted. But the lawless and impious Licinius, thinking that the saint was dead, ordered his guards to remain there, in order that for a whole day and a night his body might be exposed upon the cross. 13. But in the first watch of the night, an angel was sent from God, and took him down from the cross and made whole all his body, and said: "Rejoice and be strong, for the Lord was with thee and is with thee, and shall be for ever. Why therefore didst thou say that thou wast abandoned by Me? Forasmuch as the course of thy martyrdom is accomplished, and thou comest to the Saviour Jesus, and shalt receive the indestructible crown in the kingdom of the just." And when he had said this, the angel rose up to heaven; but the holy Theodorus, beholding his body entirely healed of its wounds, lifted his hands to heaven, and magnified the Lord and said: "I magnify Thee, my God and my King, and I bless Thy name for ever and ever." And after praying for a long while, he uttered the Amen.

14. And at dawn early the Emperor called a certain twain of his nobles, and said: "Go ye along with a force of men, and take down from the cross the wretched body of yonder ill-starred impostor, and drag it before me, in order that I may command it to be placed in a coffin of lead and cast into the depths of the sea, lest the Christians should snatch it away, and take it and honour it according to their custom." And when the captains had gone, and while they were yet afar off, they beheld the cross empty and void of the body of the holy martyr, and they began to gape with astonishment. Antiochus said to Patricius: "Verily it is true, that which the Christians say, that Christ after three days arose from the dead, for now we behold this word of theirs literally fulfilled." But Patricius ran to the cross and beheld the holy martyr Theodorus sitting

near to the cross with his body entirely healed, and he began to tell the multitude of the great miracles of God which had happened unto him, so that both cried out with a loud voice, and said: "Great is the God of the Christians, and there is none other God but He." And they came and threw themselves at the feet of the saint along with the soldiers who were with them, in number eighty and two, and they said: "We too are Christians, and servants of Christ; we beseech thee, receive us who have gone astray through ignorance from the path of truth, and pray in our behalf to God the Creator, in order that He may make us too worthy of the compassion of His grace." 15. When the Emperor heard this, he was exceeding wroth, and ordered the Consul [1] whose name was Cestus, to take three hundred of his soldiery, and to go and behead them. But when they had gone, they too, by the favour of God, beheld the miracle of God, and believed like the others in Christ. And there was there a crowd and great multitude who all cried with loud voice and said: "Great is the God of the Christians; He that hath done such wonders, He alone is God. Come then, let us stone the lawless Licinius; for God is our Emperor, the God whom Theodorus preached." And when this disturbance arose, they began to raise a tumult one with another, and there was much shedding of blood in the conflict of the rabble. But a certain evil-

---

[1] The old Latin has Anthypatos, Pro-consul. I find no Consul of the name in Clinton's lists.

doer whose name was Leander drew his sword and rushed upon the holy Theodorus; but the Consul saw this and drew back his hand, and delivered the saint from him, and slew the lawless Leander. But another, whose name was Merpas, came forward amidst the crowd, and threw himself upon the Consul, and drawing his sword slew him. 16. But the blessed saint, when he saw the disturbance and riot of the crowd, went into the midst of them, and by his entreaties he appeased the crowd; and the multitude took the saint with them and returned to the city with great joy. And as they passed and came near to the doors of the prison, in which were confined all who were in bonds, these all cried out from prison and said: "Pity us, servant of God on high." But the crowd, when they heard it, said: "Command us that we at once pull down the doors of the prison, and set free them that are confined therein." But the saint restrained them from carrying out their counsel; and he himself approached the door and prayed to God, and made upon it the sign of the cross. And of its own accord it opened wide, and their bonds were loosened, and those who were confined came forth and threw themselves at his feet, and gave thanks to God and to His saint. But he said to them: "Go ye in peace each to his own place"; and many other miracles did God accomplish by means of him, for the sick and the suffering and they who were possessed by devils were healed by his prayers.

17. And when the impious Licinius saw that

all the people of the Greeks repudiated and cast from themselves the worship of the gods, and believed in Christ, he was very wroth, and sent a force of soldiers, that they might go without the knowledge of the multitude and cut off the head of the saint; and they went and at once executed his command, cutting off the head of the blessed one with a sword. And thus ended the victorious and mighty champion of Christ, the holy Theodorus, in the month of August, on the twenty-seventh day thereof, to the glory of God.

But after the martyrdom of the saint, Abgar, his slave, according to his command as he had been aforetime commanded to do, took the body of the saint and wrapped it in clean linen with fragrant spices, and they laid it in a coffin and took it and laid it to rest in his paternal inheritance in the village of Eukhaita. 18. And the multitude of the people of Heraclea followed the relics of the saint with lighted tapers and fragrant incense and spiritual songs, according to the custom of the Christians, and laid it in its resting-place. And many miracles were accomplished by God by means of the tomb in which reposes until to-day the relics of the saint, for those who approach it with faith. For on the day of the commemoration of the martyr, there comes a multitude of people of all races, who keep his memory with great honour and with offerings, for God glorifies those who glorify Him. 19. For this saint outshone the sun in splendour and with inextinguishable brilliancy lit up a life of virtue by his unblemished and correct faith, and repulsed the lawless ruler with all his servants. He kept his confession unshaken in the sure hope, and in his own life glorified the living God. He as martyr shared in the cross and in the death of our Lord, who of his own free will submitted to torture and death, and, following Him, offered up his life as a fragrant offering and pleasing to Him. For his true death was an expiation for angels and men, a lifting of the curse and an act of reconciliation to God. By the shedding of his blood he extinguished the folly of the idolaters and became a pillar of the faith, a seal of the Church, a door to those who would enter into heaven. He it is whom we honour by bearing him in memory and by conducting his festival with splendour; writing down the history of his martyrdom and handing it on to the generations to come, that we may be ourselves witnesses to him who bore witness, until we all come to Christ who appoints the lists of martyrdom (ἀγωνοθέτης). He in our behalf for ever intercedes with the merciful God, that unto us also may be opened the door of pity, so that we may enjoy with him the goods which have no end. Those then who in faith and fear and with all goodwill keep the commemoration of the martyr of Christ, whatsoever they ask of the Lord, it shall be unto them; and they shall be partakers of the reward of their works along with all the saints in Christ Jesus our Lord, to whom be glory and power, for ever and ever. Amen.

ACTS OF S. THALELÆUS.

INTRODUCTION.

THE Acts of Thalelæus are given in vol. 5 of the month of May, in the Bollandist collection, p. 178; where there will be found printed a shorter and a longer Greek form of these Acts. The longer form is quite worthless; but the shorter form, which is printed from a MS. at Florence (Cod. xiv., Pl. ix. of the Laurentian Library), agrees closely so far as it goes with the Armenian; and the Bollandist editor rightly concludes, in view of the simplicity of the Greek and general brevity which characterises it, that this form of the Acts was composed with the help of the Proconsular Acts themselves. The subscription of Tanebus given in the Armenian is not contained in the Greek. *These Acts contain genuine elements.*

The Bollandist editor supposes the martyrdom to have taken place during the reign of Carinus and Numerianus, between November 283 and March, 285; but we shall see that there is good reason to set the date as early as the reign of Hadrian.

In view of the graphic character of the exordium of these Acts, as well as of the attestation at the end of the Armenian form of them, of the slave Tanebos, it seems hasty to deny to them any historical value. The first question, which follows on the admission of an actual historical basis for them, is whether the martyrdom took place under Hadrian or under Numerianus, more than a century later. The Greek Acts begin thus: "In the consulate of Numerianus the king." On the other hand, in the body of the piece the martyr is invited to acknowledge the Emperor Hadrian; it is in the temple of Hadrian that the magistrate *They belong to the reign of Hadrian, not of Numerianus.*

holds his court, and it is hard by the temple of the same emperor that Tanebos buries the remains of the saints. It is therefore certain that the events related took place under Hadrian, if at all; and that some editor at the end of the third century or early in the fourth prefixed the mention of Numerianus. In the same way we have the date of the martyr Babylas, who suffered under Decius, shifted in the exordium of his Acts to the reign of Numerianus. Such a falsification is most likely to' have taken place at the end of the third century, before the persecution of Diocletian had effaced in Antioch the memory of Numerianus. I have before noticed[1] the tendency there was to defer the death of a popular saint, so that he might appear to have suffered in the persecution of which the recollection was uppermost in men's minds. Not only is the later date incompatible with the mention of Hadrian in the Acts, but the detailed account which Thalelæus gives of himself agrees best with the earlier date. Ægæ or Aigai was a seaport and arsenal of the Romans in the second century. It lay opposite the modern port of Iskanderun, and is to-day called Ayash (see Prof. Ramsay's *Hist. Geog. of Asia Minor*, p. 385, who notes that there was there a temple of Asklepius, which was destroyed by Constantine). In the reign of Hadrian there would of course have been in so important a station of the Roman fleet a temple of the reigning emperor, in which the governor would naturally hear a case of *majestas*. But it is the hint which the piece gives of the relations between Edessa and Aigai, which is decisive against the reign of Numerian as the date of these Acts. The city of Edessa was brought under the sway of the Romans in the year 115 by Trajan, who struck commemorative medals with the words on them: "Armenia et Mesopotamia in Potestatem P. R. Redactæ." Hadrian, we read in Spartianus: "Toparchas et reges ad amicitiam invitavit, . . . a Mesopotamia non exegit tributum quod Trajanus imposuit" (Spart., *Adrian*, 13, 17, 21).

Older numismatists believed that Hadrian actually struck

---

[1] See page 151.

Acts of S. Thalelæus. 241

money in Edessa. But although M. Ernest Babelon has shewn that this was not so, yet there is no doubt that during his reign the Roman influence was paramount in Edessa, and that a Roman resident of some sort was kept there. The native prince Manou was the faithful friend and ally of the Romans. These native princes were not called by the Romans kings, but dynasts, phylarchs, or toparchs. (Suidas, s. voce *Phylarch.*; Procop., *Bell. Persic.* 2, 12.) It is more than probable that in the reign of Hadrian a common policy was pursued in regard to the Christians all over the empire, in the dependent client states as well as in the regularly organized provinces.

Under Numerianus there was no Roman authority in Edessa.

It is thus quite conceivable that a fugitive from justice at Edessa might be arrested at Anazarb and brought before the Roman magistrate at Aigai. Whether the judge Tiberius or Tiberianus of Edessa was a Roman officer or a servant of the client prince of Edessa we do not know. Edessa is little over fifty German miles due east of Aigai, and there was a highroad thence to Aigai by way of Zeugma, Castabala, and Anazarb, which lay a little north of Aigai, among the mountains of Cilicia. The concerted action hinted at between the authorities of Edessa and Aigai was possible under Hadrian, but under Numerian it was impossible; for Edessa had finally passed under the sway of the Parthians more than thirty years before, when at the end of 259 Valerian was taken prisoner on his way to relieve it. Such close administrative connexion between Edessa and Aigai as these Acts reveal would be still more intelligible at the beginning of the second century, after the year 216, when Caracalla turned Edessa into a Roman colony. But this date would not suit these Acts for a different reason: Abgar the Eighth who ruled thirty-five years, from A.D. 179 to 214, was no doubt a firm ally of the Romans, but inasmuch as he was a Christian the apprehension and torture of Thalelæus can hardly have fallen in his period.

The Greek Acts published in the Acta Sanctorum are briefer than the Armenian form, and give quite a different set of miracles. The story of the magistrate's throne sticking to his hinder parts is peculiarly grotesque, and is absent from the Armenian. The incident of the executioner hanging up a bare tree occurs in both forms, and is very curious and wears a Docetic air. The introduction of wizards to contend against the martyr in magic is a not unusual motive in ancient Acts.

Anazarbos or Anazarba is called the metropolis in these Acts. According to Smith's *Dict. of Geography*, it acquired this title from the time of Caracalla on, and was the chief town of Cilicia Secunda. W. M. Ramsay gives some clues about the place, *Geog. Asia Minor*, p. 387. Lightfoot has a note on it in his *Apost. Fathers*, iii. p. 138. From A.D. 117-138 Cilicia, including Tracheia, was an imperial province under a Prætorian Legatus Augusti (W. M. Ramsay, *Geog. Asia Minor*, p. 376). Under the reign of Hadrian Aigai took the title of Hadriana in honour of a visit which that emperor paid it.

There are two Armenian MSS. of these Acts in Venice, which supplement one another, the one containing the first half, the other the last half of the text. They overlap for about two pages in the middle and give slightly different texts. The latter part of the Acts, including the list of the names of the fellow-martyrs of Thalelæus and the subscription of Tanebus his slave is wanting in the Greek. If the notice of Tanebus be part of the original Acts, then the final words beginning, "Who truly," etc., must be a later interpolation added probably by the same editor of the late third century who, at the beginning of these Acts, introduced the name of Numerian. This editor must have made his recension before the year 310, otherwise on the same principle on which he ascribes the martyrdom to Numerian, he would have ascribed it to Diocletian.

Armenian MSS. of these Acts.

MARTYRDOM OF S. THALELÆUS.

In the reign of Numerius,[1] and when Theodorus was judge, in the city of Ægæ, nine days before the kalends, in the month Hori, which was the twenty-third day of the month, the judge[2] took his seat in the Temple of Hadrian in the city of Ægæ, and said: "Summon hither the violator of religion." The guards say: "Behold, here he stands, we pray thee." Theodorus the judge said to them: "Where did ye take him, for I see that his beard just begins to shoot, and that he is resplendent with the bloom of youth?" Denesius,[3] the chief executioner, said: "As we were coming to the metropolis Anazarb,[4] and were still distant by fifty[5] stades, we saw him running in an easterly direction;[6] and when he saw us, he hid himself in the middle of a grove of trees. But we knew he was a Christian, so we invoked the gods and halted in the grove for forty days and forty

---

[1] ἐν ὑπατείᾳ τοῦ Νουμεριανοῦ τοῦ βασιλέως ἡγεμονεύοντος Θεοδώρου τῶν Αἰγαίων πόλεως, τῇ πρὸ ἐννέα καλανδῶν Σεπτεμβρίου, μηνὸς ὑπερβερεταίου εἰκάδι τρίτῃ. But the month Hyperberetæus began Aug. 24 in each year.
[2] The text here has Thallos.
Judge: ἡγεμών may = Consul. The Greek adds that this officer had apprehended many because of Christ, whom he had scourged, drowned, sawn asunder, beheaded or otherwise slain.
[3] The Gk. omits Denesius and simply has ἡ τάξις.
[4] Ἐν τῇ Ἀναζάρβῳ πόλει. Arm. may mean "*from* the city of A."
[5] φ' = 500.   [6] ἀπὸ ἀνατολῶν.

243

nights,[1] till we found him hidden in an olive-tree; and when we took him in order to bind him he began to fight with us, but we beat him with bludgeons and broke his bones, and then we put manacles on his hands and feet,[2] and have brought him to thee."

Theodorus the judge said to him: "Of what religion art thou, or of what rank, or of what city, and what is thy name?" Thalelæus said: "If thou wilt learn of what religion I am, I am named a Christian; but if thou wilt learn how men name me,[3] I am called Thalelæus, and I am from Lebanon,[4] and I have believed in the Galilean, and I am a friend of those of Jerusalem. My mother is Romaniana, and my father Becosianus; and I am by profession a physician, and have become a deacon of John the Bishop. And when there were persecutions of the Christians, they all fled,[5] and they took me alone and brought me before Tiberianus[6] the judge of Edessa. And he subjected me to cruel tortures,[7] and three times he had me scourged publicly and without mercy, thinking that he would turn my mind and make me deny God;[7] but I called upon the Father, and

---

[1] The Gk. om. words "we knew" down to "gods," and for "forty days and forty nights" have merely ἡμέρας ἱκανάς.
[2] The Gk. omits these details.   [3] τὸ κοινὸν ὄνομα.
[4] The Gk. runs: I am from the Lebanon, and as to my parents, my father was called Berekkokius and my mother Rombyliana, and my brother John. But he is also an underdeacon (ὑποδιάκονος), and I learned the physician's art, having been handed over to Macarius the arch-physician.
[5] Gk. omits "they all fled."   [6] Tiberius in Gk.
[7] Gk. omits from "three times" to "God."

Acts of S. Thalelæus.

the Son, and the Holy Spirit,[1] and He saved me from his lawless hands; and now I have come and am brought before thy court, by which it is allotted to me to die for the name of my God. Do with me what thou wilt, for Christ is near who helps me."[2]

The judge said: "Out upon thee, thou runaway; think not that thou art able to escape from my hands." Thalelæus said: "I believe in God, that is Ruler of all, that He putteth not to shame those who trust in Him in Christ, and those who for His name, come to bear this testimony." The judge said: With an awl do ye bore[3] through his ancles and pass cords through them, and drag him over the city; since he is a runaway, and lest he escape from the emperors."

And they began to do so, but they wearied and were not able to. Then came the chief Lictor and said: "We pray thee, O Lord, from dawn until now[4] have we laboured, but have been able to do nothing." The judge said: "Begin to work afresh, to see if ye can bore them through." And Asterius the carpenter came, and said: "As thou didst command, we have bored through his ancles, and have fastened them with thongs." Theodorus the judge said: "Bring hither the runaway."[5] And they brought him in. Then said

---

[1] Gk. adds "the true God, the unerring, the creative, the good."
[2] Gk.="For 'tis right to die for Christ, whom I have to help me, the heavenly God."
[3] τρῆσον ἐν τρυπάνῃ.
[4] Gk.=from the third hour to the sixth.
[5] The Greek omits from "Bring hither" as far as "my God."

he to him: "Come and sacrifice to the gods according to the command of the emperors, that thou mayest be saved from the tortures that await thee." Thalelæus said: "I am a Christian, and I do not worship idols, lest I should lose the rewards promised me by God." The judge said: "Come, hang him head downwards, like one of the mad knaves." But the servants of Satan hung up the mere tree; and the disciple of Thalelæus, Timotheus,[1] said: "See what the ministers of Satan do." Thalelæus said: "Hush, brother, for it is Christ who helpeth us, and maketh their labour in vain." The judge said: "O wretch, what is it? did I not command you to hang yonder man, and you have hung up and tortured a mere tree,[2] and turned to ridicule the royal commands." Asterius the carpenter said: "He liveth, the Lord God of yonder believing man. I do not transgress nor turn to ridicule your commands; but I too acknowledge Christ as king of heaven and earth, in whom he also has his hope and belief."

But Alexander the chief Lictor said: "Truly we have seen a great glory by reason of this blessed man, and we are not able to lay hands upon him, because we too have believed in Christ and are Christians, by whom receiving the knowledge of the truth, we will become fellow-sufferers of the holy Thalelæus." But when the judge saw this he was very wroth with them, and

---

[1] Gk. has Theotimus. [2] ξύλον ἐκρεμάσατε simply.

Acts of S. Thalelæus. 247

he roared like a lion and gnashed his teeth upon them. But Asterius and Alexander fell to praying, and said : "Lord God of the Christians, suffer not that Satan should take captive and snatch away the souls of Thy servants, who make their confession to Thee." And when they had said this, they fled from the presence of the judge. But a certain Midos, from the court, came upon them and slew them; and then he came and told the judge, saying : " O Lord Judge, I came upon them in the mountains, and took and slew them with the sword, and cast forth their bodies on the mountain, and the multitude saw all."[1]

The judge said : " Which dost thou prefer, O Thalelæus, to sacrifice to the gods and be saved, or to die a miserable death ?" Thalelæus said : "Thou canst not persuade the servants of God to sacrifice to vain demons and to their images ; and I have no fear of thy tortures, for Christ is near to me, who is my hope, and He will snatch me from thy tortures."[2] Then the judge was wroth, and rose of himself to torture the blessed one; but his hands were withered. Then the ruler prayed and said : " I beseech thee, servant

---

[1] This episode is much shorter in the Gk., which has Medius. It however adds that the mountain where Asterius and Alexander were captured was fifty stades from the city and was the same on which Thalelæus had been taken. Asterius and Alexander are called speculatores.

[2] Here the Gk. adds a miracle and relates that the judge rose up to bore through the saints' ankles (as if that had not already been done), but his throne stuck to his hinder parts and only fell off because of the saint's intercession. Undeterred, the judge again rose up in wrath to bore through the saints' ankles, and then his hands 'ἐξηράνθησαν.

of the true God, pray for me that my hands may be healed." And when Thalelæus prayed, his hands were healed; and all wondered and began to say: "Great is the God of the Christians." The judge said: "Let a ship-captain be called." And when he came, he said: "Cast yonder man into the ship and carry him to the city of Siprus,[1] and there let him die, but let him not die by my hands." Thalelæus said: "Thou didst make a beginning, and from thee I receive my consummation"; but they took him and threw him into the ship. And as they were going on their way and rowing, Thalelæus said: "Christ is able to turn back the ship to the place where Theodorus smote me." And as they went on their course, there was a violent wind against them in the middle of the sea; and it turned back all the ships along with that one in which was the holy Thalelæus. And when they came near to where there was the tribunal, Thalelæus cried out to the judge and said: "Where then are thy gods, or where is thy boasting? Behold, Christ hath turned against thee and conquered thee, and hath blunted the sting of Satan thy father."[2]

The judge said: "Behold, how that he hath bewitched us and caused the ships to flee."[3] And

---

[1] The Gk. does not name any city. According to it the judge simply orders the saint to be taken out to sea and thrown in, "that he may not die by my hands" (εἰς τὰς χειράς μου).

[2] Acc. to the Gk. the δήμιοι, or executioners, took Thalelæus out to sea as far as the judge ordered and then threw him in and returned. But the saint shortly after presented himself before the judge, clad in a white robe.

[3] τὰ πελάγη ἐμάγευσεν καὶ ἡμᾶς λοιδορεῖ.

Acts of S. Thalelæus. 249

he ordered wizards[1] to be brought before him; and when they were brought in, Theodorus the judge said: "What are we to do with him, for he hath vanquished us with his wizardry? Urbicus, the wizard, answered: "This race of Christians is full of sedition, and worthy of an evil death. But do thou do that which I tell thee, and quickly wilt thou destroy him. Make boards and set sharp nails around as with a compass, and nail the boards against the hair of his head; and then let him be dragged through the midst of the city into the arena, and in that way the force of his wizardry is broken. And thereafter let them throw him to the wild beasts, that they may tear his flesh." And then the judge in haste ordered them to make a machine of nails and boards; and when they had made it they brought in the holy Thalelæus.[2] And having spread out his hands, he stood in prayer, and said: "O Lord God, draw nigh to Thy servant, and vanquish the evil designs of Satan, that Thy name may be glorified in me, and that they may know the impiety of their wickedness, and that it is no wizardry, but the ineffable might of Thy Godhead." And when he had said this, they threw him upon the tables and nailed them, and having bound him, they dragged him through the middle of the city to the arena. And the judge took his

---

[1] Μάγους.
[2] The Gk. omits all mention of the machine of torture. Urbicus merely advises that Thalelæus be thrown to the wild beasts.

seat in the Arena,[1] and said: "Let it be proclaimed, that this is he who hath joined the evil cult of the Christians." The guards say: "But we think that he is dead." The judge said: "Warm a brand and make it like fire, and pierce his side, for fear that he trick us." But the blessed Thalelæus made upon himself the sign of the holy cross of Christ, and moved himself and leaped up, and broke all the bonds with which he was fastened to the nails; and he stood up amidst them, and spoke to the tyrant and said: "Blessed is God, who has raised me from the dead and hath put to shame the worshippers of the idols."

Then the judge commanded that they let loose upon him wild beasts; and a lioness came, but did him no harm. And next he let loose upon him a leopard, but the wild beasts came and lay at his feet and fawned upon him.[2] And the holy Thalelæus with a loud voice said: "Blessed are they who believe in Christ; blessed are they who without looking back shall offer themselves to make confession of Him. Blessed are they who shall

---

[1] The Gk. uses the Latin word Arena. It says nothing about Thalelæus arriving at the arena dead. On the contrary, the moment he arrives there he is brought before the judge, who says: "Wilt thou now sacrifice, or shall I give thy flesh to the wild beasts?" The saint in reply quotes the psalms of David.

[2] At this point, according to the Gk., the judge rises and declares that Thalelæus has bewitched the wild beasts, but the audience rise and cry: "Great is the God of the Christians," and demand that Urbicus be thrown to the wild beasts, which is promptly done. Then the saint goes to εἰς τόπον ἐπίσημον ὀνόματι "Ἔδεσσαν ἥτις ἐστὶ τῶν Αἰγαίων πόλεως; on arriving there, he falls to praying, an earthquake supervenes, the multitude rush to be baptized, and the saint dies. Of what follows in the Arm. text the shorter Greek Acts contain nothing.

give themselves to the torture for Christ's sake, because they vanquish Satan." And when the judge heard this, he said: "How hath he bewitched the wild beasts, by calling upon the name of Christ." And he ordered them to bear him to the wall of the arena, that all the population of the town should stone him.

Then Thalelæus cried out and said: "Almighty Father of our Lord Jesus Christ, turn away from me the threats of men, that they may know that Thou alone art God, and that, besides Thee, there is no other, and that I am Thy servant." And when he had said this and prayed, the stones were turned back, and wounded many of the impious; but the saint was not wounded, for he was overshadowed by the grace of Christ. And the judge ordered him to be taken down, and said to him: "Offer now sacrifice to the gods, for by them art thou helped; wherefore I also have been patient with thee: but if thou wilt not, then I swear by Asclepius,[1] I will order thee to be put to still more bitter torments." Thalelæus said: "I am a Christian, and to demons I cannot sacrifice; do as thou wilt, I have no fear of thy torments, since it is Christ who helpeth me."

Then the judge said: "Mix bitumen and rosin and sulphur, and put it into an iron caldron, and when it is boiling hot, then pour it over his head." Thalelæus said: "I believe in my Lord Jesus, who has helped me and will help me; and

---

[1] Note that there was a temple of Asclepius in Aigai.

He it is who vanquishes thee through me; but thou art lawless, and blinded by impiety, so that thou dost not see the help which Christ renders me." Then they brought the caldron while it was still boiling, and poured it over his head; but it was like cold water, and did not subdue him. The judge said: "By thy exceeding wizardry thou dost conquer all men, and I have fears lest thou shouldst bewitch us also, or persuade us." And he bade them call Urbicus the wizard, and through him he contended against the saint with all manner of charms. But when Urbicus was vanquished in all, the judge said: "Summon hither the enchanters,[1] Ilithopus and Karticur." And when they were come before him, the judge said, "What shall we do with this Christian, for he will boast that he has conquered us? Throw him therefore among the wild beasts." But they said: "Whole days the wild beasts are here and have not tasted him." Then said the judge: "Spare him not, but cast him to the wild beasts that they may destroy him." When they had cast him into the pit, the wild beasts ran and fell at his feet, and licked his feet and did him no harm. And there were in the pit vipers and basilisks and horned snakes. And the saint remained in the pit for three days and for three nights and was ever glorifying God. Then after three days the judge called the enchanters and asked them if the wild beasts had

---

[1] Another MS. has Lydus. At this point a second MS. used for the last half of the Armenian printed text begins. It varies a little in its text from the MS. from which the first part of the Acts is printed.

Acts of S. Thalelæus.

destroyed that wizard. But the enchanters said: "We pray thee, according to thy command, we cast him into the pit, and he has lain among the wild beasts for three days and three nights, but they have not touched him. And meanwhile he, without ceasing, day and night, continued to praise the name of the Lord his God."

Then the judge wondered, and ordered him to be brought in; and when he came in before him, the judge began to try to catch him by words, and said: "Come hither, good man, sacrifice to the gods, acknowledge Hadrian, the autocrat, and I dismiss thee." Thalelæus said: "Even before I told thee, and now I tell thee again, I am a Christian, and I deny not my God, and I sacrifice not to stone idols that are senseless and to foul demons. And as to Hadrian, an impious man, why dost thou constrain me; because I acknow- him not, but that I say which I know, that he is a lawless, and impious, and unholy and crafty man." Theodorus the judge said: "Thou dost not escape from my hands, till I have exacted from thee vengeance for the gods whom thou hast blasphemed and insulted, contemning our judg- ments." Then he ordered a furnace to be heated, and they heated it to excess. And there came one Claudianus[1] from the court and said to the judge: "The oven hath been heated until it glows with the white radiance of fire." Then the judge ordered them to cast Thalelæus into the furnace

---

[1] The other MS. here omits the name Claudianus.

together with his seven companions who bore the name of Christians, and whose names are the following: Narcissus,[1] Thetius, Acastasia, Philadus, Macarias, Theodula, and Anastasia. And the executioners took Thalelæus and his companions who had suffered many tortures for the name of the Lord, and threw them into the furnace; but they continued to praise and glorify God, who made them worthy thus to die and attain to the heavenly crown. And they embraced one another, man with man, and woman with woman, and they cried out and said: "O Thou who wast the Protector of the three children in the furnace, preserve us that we remain scatheless in this fire, and receive our spirits, O Thou that art holy and true; and set us in the ranks of Thy saints in the tents of light, in order that we may without ceasing glorify Father and Son and Thy Holy Spirit, now and for ever, Amen." And having said all this, they gave up their souls into the hand of the Lord. And on a sudden there was a sound of thunder and lightnings and heavy rains, and the fire was extinguished. But the judge fainted from fear, and called out, saying: "Woe to me, a sinner, because I have offended God, and done ill to His saints." And in a few days He was removed from life; and many believed on the Lord.

I, Tanebus, the slave of the Holy Thalelæus, took the bodies of the saints, and I laid them in a

---

[1] The other MS. gives Macarius, Thestus, Astênus, Phillidus, Macaria, Theodula, and Acastis. The MS. ends here from which the first part of these Acts is printed.

tomb at the head of the circus, near to the Temple of Hadrian. Whereby God is continually glorified in the sufferings of His holy martyrs, and bestows healing upon spirit and flesh, to them that build up the memorials of the saints, who truly glorify the Lordship of the Three Persons and the single Godhead, now and for ever and ever. Amen.

ACTS OF S. HIZTIBOUZIT.

INTRODUCTION.

THE following piece is in the main historical and preserves an interesting picture of the condition of the province of Ararat during the last years of Chosrow. The martyrdom of the saint fell in the forty-third year of Chosrow, son of Kavat, or Kobad, as Gibbon spells the name. This king reigned A.D. 531–579, so the saint's death fell in the last part of the reign, about A.D. 574. **Date of these Acts.**

The opening statement, that during this reign the confession of Christ was more than ever persecuted, is not altogether borne out by the subsequent course of the narrative. The two fellow-prisoners of the martyr answer the judge that they were Christians by birth and upbringing, as if that were a sufficient defence. We do not hear of their death, so we may almost conclude that they were liberated after a further short term of incarceration. The two men crucified with the saint are declared to have been malefactors, and therefore did not suffer as Christians. Indeed one is a Jew, whose offer, when about to be crucified, to embrace Magism, is no indication that the Persian authorities were putting him to death because he refused to become a fire-worshipper. If the touch be anything more than a bit of spite against the Jews on the part of the Christian narrator, it simply proves this, that conversion to Magism earned for a Jew, condemned for some other offence, a title to clemency. It is not clear from the narrative why the executioners did not understand him. Probably it was because he did not speak their tongue. The whole incident is likely enough, for the Persian realm was full of Jews. **Condition of Christians under Chosrow the First.**

It is clear that the triple crucifixion of the three condemned men on a hill, with their faces to the sun, was by way of a sacrifice to the god of light and warmth.

Significance of the triple crucifixion. There was, it is true, a tendency on the part of old writers of martyrdoms to make a saint's death resemble as much as possible the crucifixion of Jesus of Nazareth. This tendency has been noticed by Lightfoot in his book on the *Apostolical Fathers* as at work in the narrative of Polycarp's death. In the story of the death of S. Theodore the Soldier the same tendency has clearly led to the addition of some fabulous details. But we need not therefore reckon as fabulous the triple crucifixion of these Acts, for it was quite in accordance with the old Persian custom of human sacrifice. Thus in Ctesias (frag. 36) we read that the Egyptian usurper Inarus was crucified by Artaxerxes the First between two thieves. Similarly Masabates (Plutarch, Artaxerxes) the Eunuch, who cut off the head and right hand of the usurper Cyrus, was by order of the latter's mother crucified on three crosses. The number three was specially efficacious in human sacrifices. Thus the Athenians before the battle of Salamis sacrificed to Dionysus three Persian prisoners of royal blood.[1] And in the legend of S. Pancrazio of Taormina, the demon Falco whom the saint expels, has had offered up to him by the city three spotless children every year for 260 years. The Acts before us prove that such triple human sacrifices were in vogue among the Persian fire-worshippers as late as the end of Khosrow's reign. In stating therefore that the martyr was offered up as a sacrifice the narrative probably states no more than the truth. It is even possible that this martyrdom was a survival of the festival of Sakæa, of which we read in Arrian and Dio Chrysostom and

---

[1] I owe these parallels to my friend Mr. W. R. Paton who has suggested with much probability that the crucifixion of Jesus was intended by the Syrian soldiers, who performed it, as an expiatory sacrifice to a triple god. His arrayal in a royal robe and diadem makes this almost certain, for such was the regular ritual of oriental human sacrifice then and earlier, as we know from Strabo, Arrian and Dio Chrysostom.

Acts of S. Hiztibouzit.

Strabo, at which it was usual to select some prisoner who had been condemned to death, to surround him for a short time with the insignia of royalty, setting a crown on his head and arraying him in purple. When the hour of death came he was deprived of his royal vesture, was scourged and buffeted and crucified. It was very natural to select as a piacular offering to the God a priest of the fire-worship who had apostatised to Christianity. Perhaps even the vision of the saint in prison, wherein some smote the saint on the head with a rod till the blood flowed down over his eyes, while others, three in number and radiant with light, set a crown of jewels on his head, is a reminiscence of some similar ritual procedure having been followed in regard to this saint. Perhaps however this is to force a narrative which has the air of being faithful and trustworthy in all respects. The city of Twin or Dwin lay in the basin of the Araxes, not far from the present monastery of Edschmiadzin. In the sixth century it was the chief religious centre of the Armenians, and the seat of their Patriarchate. We gather from this narrative that they there enjoyed complete freedom of worship. It was however an arch offence for a priest of the sacred fire to become a Christian.

Ritual of human sacrifice in Persia.

The details of the fire-ritual are very correctly given in these Acts, as will be seen by a comparison of it with the following description which I quote freely from the work of Madame Zenaide A. Ragozin on Media: "The âthravan or fire-priest stood in flowing white robes, the lower part of his face veiled with the paitidâna or penom, to keep his breath from polluting the sacred fire. He stood before the âtesh-gâh or fire-altar, which was a metal vessel placed on a low stone platform and filled with ashes, on the top of which burned the fire of dry and fragrant wood-chips. . . . In one hand he carried the khrafstraghna, an instrument of unknown form for killing snakes, frogs, and ants; in the other the baresma, a bundle of twigs, uneven in number—five, seven, or nine—probably divining rods, without which the priest never appeared

Persian Fire-worship in the 6th century.

in public." These rods were originally from the tamarind or pomegranate tree; and the modern Parsee priest has prosaically substituted for them a bundle of rods of brass wire. The offering made to the fire was a little wine, along with a few bits of meat, and at the present day a little milk is offered in a cup with cakes and fruit. The offering which the priests were making in these Acts must have consisted of butter, probably of ghee or clarified butter;[1] otherwise the flames could hardly have leapt up to the roof of the room in which they were celebrating their ritual. The picture of the fire-worship preserved in these Acts is all the more interesting on account of the scarcity of contemporary Persian records of the cult. The name which the Parsee assumes upon conversion is Persian, and Hizti the first syllable is the same as the familiar Yezid, the Persian for God.

---

[1] I owe this suggestion to the Rev. Dr. Mills, of Oxford.

MARTYRDOM OF SAINT HIZTIBOUZIT.

DURING the reign of Khosrow, son of Kavat, the King of Persia, the confession of Christ was more than ever persecuted; and not a few were martyred in Persia and at the royal court. At that time there was a certain man Makhosh, a Magus of that same land, from the region which is called Bershapouh, from a village of the name of Kounarastan, whose parents were ministers of the fire-worship, and who was himself from childhood trained in Magism. And he was strong in counsel and learned in all the lore and wisdom of the fire-worshippers. He by a certain chance came to the camp of the king, and witnessed the sufferings of a certain holy martyr, whose name was Gregorius; and he marvelled at the boldness of the champion of faith, and was emulous thereof, and said, in his heart: "O Lord God of the Christians, look upon me and shew me a path on which to set my feet, and open to me the door of pity along with Thy champion; in order that I may become worthy of Thy kingdom, who art Lord of heaven and earth." But on the same night a wondrous vision appeared to him; for he was as it were in a holy church, and a certain man robed in white appeared to him and said: " Blessed art thou, that thou hast become worthy of the light-giving church; for thou shalt believe, henceforth in God the Creator of heaven and earth, and in His Son of like power with Him, and in the Spirit who shares His works, and thou shalt learn thereof from the tradition of the holy gospel." And he marvelled and understood the dream, and believed with whole heart and said: "The God of the Christians is a true God"; and thenceforth he repented of his magism.

He went thence into the land of Siuni, devoting himself to the hearing of the holy scriptures; and after being there a few months he came to Armenia; and having come into the region of Ararat, he dwelt in the chief town of the Armenians in Dvin, accompanying a certain Armenian who believed with[1] the Magi and whose name was Khosrow Peroz. But he (the saint) treated his Magism with contempt and neglected it. And it was in the winter time, in Mehekan,[2] at the beginning of the Persian month, and according to their custom, they were offering fatty sacrifices to the fire in the palace of their co-religionist. And the blessed Makhosh was standing with them at the spectacle, with his mouth closed with a mask. But the flame leaped up from the fat and reached the roof of the house and blazed up. Then the Magi gathered up the

---

[1] I have so rendered the word "hamakar." But I am not sure that I have given the true sense of this sentence. Khosrow Peroz may have been a convert to Magism from Christianity. His wife was anyhow a Christian.

[2] Mehekan was the seventh month in the Armenian calendar.

sacrifice, and tried to extinguish the fire, but could not; and then they ran out and told what had happened. But he that was governor of the Armenians, when he heard the sound of the tumult, came in haste to the door of the church, and began to urge the officiating priests to take the Holy Cross and bear it to the palace, if, peradventure, the fire might be driven back; for he in his straits believed against his will. Then the ministrants took the symbols of the holy cross and came quickly to the spot; and when the cross was come opposite the palace, the flame had spread and was dying out everywhere. This great sign was wrought by the precious holy cross in the land of Armenia, to the joy of the true worshippers and confusion of idolatry. Now the wife of the co-religionist, when she beheld, sent a great thankoffering to the attendants of the wonder-working holy cross. But the blessed Makhosh took to heart such wonders and broke the rod[1] wherewith he divined and cast it away, likewise, also, the mask for his mouth; and he took and placed his censer in the hands of the deacon and scattered incense before the holy cross, so making manifest the faith which he had in Christ. And he followed the attendants of the cross and said: "Pray to God for me, because I too am a Christian." But when the Magi saw this, they said to him, "Why hast thou dared to do this?" The blessed one said: "For a long

---

[1] The Armenian signifies a bough or bundle o ftwigs.

time I have confessed to the Christians, and was, with reluctance, a Magus; but now I openly preach the faith which is in Christ; and I will not any longer minister to fire, now that I have seen all those wonders."

The next day at dawn the Magi came before the governor of the Armenians, who was called Nikhorakan, and accused the saint. And when he was brought before him, the judge said: "Woe to thee, wretch, why dost thou forsake the Magism of thy forefathers to become a madman and a breaker of vows?" The blessed one made answer and said: "I tell thee truly, O judge, concerning myself, that during twenty-five years I have professed a vain heresy; but now I have come to learn of the true God, and have put away the polytheism of my forefathers. Wherefore, henceforth, the deceits of life shall not part me from this faith, for I am ready to bear the appointed[1] tortures." Then the governor was angry and ordered the blessed saint to be scourged twelve times over; and he shaved off his beard and hair and wrote out his sentence,[2] and, binding him hands and feet, he cast him into prison. But in the prison the saint found a sharer of his plight in one whose name was Nerses, who had been bound for a long time in the prison because of God. And from him the blessed one learned the holy faith and twenty psalms; and thus he worshipped without ceasing and prayed to God.

---

[1] Apostasy from the fire-cult was therefore a recognised offence.
[2] The Arm.="question," but I have given what must be the sense.

Acts of S. Hiztibouzit. 265

After a little time one named Nakhapet[1] succeeded to Nikhorakan; and when he had taken his seat in the court of judgment, they brought Makhosh before him. Said the Nakhapet: " How hast thou dared to abandon the god of thy fathers and to put thy faith in the unknown Christ?" The blessed one replied: " There is one Creator of all, who hath regard to all doers of good works; Who saw that my soul was weary of the ceremonies of polytheism, and guided me to a knowledge of the true God." Then the Nakhapet was wroth and ordered him to be violently scourged, and they bound him with iron fetters and cast him into prison. And he remained in prison for another three years, and he besought the priest that he might receive of him the seal of the Lord (*i.e.* baptism), and that he might be named Hiztibouzit, which is, when translated, Given by God: that is to say, saved by God, which name the Holy Spirit pictured to them. By the which Spirit also he was strengthened in prison, and he took and gave his garments to the poor, and himself wore goatskin and coarse sandals. And thus he continued to watch with prayer and fasting, singing without ceasing the psalms of his fair religion. But after the lapse of another three years, the Nakhapet was succeeded by one whom they called Knaric. A certain scribe of his came to the prison and tried to ensnare the blessed one, and said to him: " For thee alone the land of the

---
[1] Nakhapet is old Armenian for "prince." It is here less a proper name perhaps than an official designation.

Arians was not sufficient, that thou hast gone astray from Magism, driving thyself a captive from the whole land, and straying from thy religion." The saint gave answer and said: "All who lack knowledge by nature wait upon the craftsmen who have it, and the animals are the slaves of their owners. Even so men ought to serve God alone, their Maker. Wherefore I, also, in my negligence have been the servant of vanity; but when God took pity on me, He took my thoughts and enchained them with the love of His commandments, and bathed them in the hope of His grace, which the temptations of life will not avail to change." But when the scribe of the court heard this, he leapt to his feet with rage, and began to beat him mercilessly with a club. And he inflicted many other tortures of various kinds upon the saint, that he might persuade him to keep his Magism.

At that time the king heard of the much violence and sufferings which his officers inflicted upon the land of the Armenians, and he sent three rulers, trusty men, to inspect the country; the name of one was Nati, which is called Drowandacan, and of the second Peroz, who was chief Magus of the district Rêi, and of the third Choyap, who was a royal minister; and these came into Armenia and worked many reforms. But on a certain day they held a public assembly, and were sitting in the court of justice about the edict of the king. At that same time some impious men gave information to the rulers, saying: " There are three

Acts of S. Hiztibouzit. 267

men in prison who have abandoned our religion and have embraced Christianity; one Nerses, a Rajik, and one Sahak, from Atropatacan, and Hiztibouzit, a Persian." And they commanded that they bring them before them. The chief Magus said to Nerses : " Why hast thou become a Christian?" The saint answered : " My mother was a Christian, and from my childhood I was brought up in the Christian faith ; I know not your religion at all." Then they put the question to Sahak, and he said : " From my childhood I had become a Christian." But the blessed Hiztibouzit stood behind, and in a weak voice he was singing the sixth Psalm : "O Lord rebuke me not in Thy anger, neither chasten me in Thy hot displeasure." And the judge separated them, and said to Hiztibouzit : " Woe to thee, wretch, why hast thou abandoned the religion of light and believed in the dark and obscure faith of Christianity, and that after thou hadst zealously sacrificed to fire?" The saint replied : " Aye, after sacrificing, and I know Magism better than thyself; and if thou command me to speak and make it clear, thou shalt learn how much better is Christianity than all the ceremonies which I have explored and clearly comprehended. Christianity alone has the power to save from the terrible death." And when the chief Magus heard this, he ordered his servants to rend the saint's tunic and to tear off his cowl ; and they beat the head of the blessed one and tore out his beard by the roots. And once more they ordered that the three blessed ones be kept safe for three days ;

and after that they brought them up, but could not persuade them. Then they confined them in a single house without food ; and the chief Magus gave orders to send up smoke all the night.[1] The saints, in their torment, cried out and said : "O God, look upon us to help us, and, O Lord, hasten to assist us." And thus they continued to sing hymns until the dawn. And they remained in the prison ten days ; but on a certain night, on the Lord's day, on the which Hiztibouzit was to suffer martyrdom, a vision appeared to him. A certain man had in his hand a rod, and touched him on the head therewith ; and the blood flowed down between his eyes. And then there appeared three radiant men, who drove away the man who struck him, and bringing a crown of choice pearls set it on his head. But he was overjoyed and told his companions ; and they knew that his hour was come. And at early morn there came trusty men to take the saints to the prison, and the chief executioner came to the prison to lead him away, and he bade farewell to his brethren and departed. But as he went he continued to sing the fourth Psalm, beginning it as he left the prison, and going on till he came to the place where was the court : "When I cried out Thou didst hear me according to Thy righteousness, from my tribulation didst Thou give me peace." And having finished the psalm he came to the place of the

---

[1] Whether by way of torturing the confined saints or simply as a religious function is not clear, nor is it clear who sent up the smoke. Presumably the Magi with their censers.

Acts of S. Hiztibouzit. 269

court. And when the Christians heard, they all ran together to behold the combat and victory of the saint. But the holy Hiztibouzit stood up before the four judges. And they prepared three crosses for those condemned to death. And when these were brought forward, the chief Magus said to the saint: " Dost thou behold yon trees, upon which thou art about to die? Have pity on thyself, neither persist in thy obstinacy." The saint made answer: " Nay, all the more am I set firm in Christ, who is my hope; but do thou fulfil that which is commanded thee concerning me." And he ordered him to be crucified; and the saint with ready heart and joyful mind went to the cross, and they took from him and deprived him of what poor raiments he had. The blessed one said: " This is as it should be, for my Lord's Son, the only-born Saviour, when by His own will He was crucified, was nailed naked upon the Cross, in order that He might put on the nakedness of our first father, who will give me also strength to overcome in my body the deceits of Satan." And having stretched himself out upon the tree he began to say the forty-third Psalm: " Arise, O Lord, and help us and save us because of Thy name; we were numbered as sheep for slaughter." But when the cross was set up the chief of the Magi sent to him, in the hope that he might be converted. But the saint spurned his message and gave no answer; and remained tied to the cross in the crowded court, and they pierced his side with arrows (or javelins).

It chanced upon the same day that they crucified two men condemned to death, and these they crucified along with him. One of them was of the tribe of Khoújik; and he when he was brought to the cross kissed the feet of the holy martyr, and taking up the clay mixed with the blood which trickled from the martyr, he plunged it in his bosom. But the chief executioner struck him on the head with his fist, and they crucified him on the right hand of the martyr, and into him they drove the javelin[1] and so he yielded up his spirit. But the other one was a Jew, who when they brought him to the cross, cried out to the judges: "Destroy me not, I embrace Magism." But the judges did not understand him, and they hung him on the tree to the left of the saint. And the blessed one was thus offered up as a sacrifice between two malefactors on a hill top, opposite the sun and before all the multitude.

And therein lay a wonderful mystery; for there was remembered unto him the word of the Lord, according to the true promise which says that: " He who believeth in Me, the work which I do, he also shall do, and still greater things than that." And the apostle says: " Whom Thou foreknewest, Thou didst predestine to be sharers of the likeness of the image of Thine own Son." And thus the holy Hiztibouzit bravely suffered martyrdom in the forty-third year of King Khosrow, on the second day of the month Kalotz, on the Lord's

---

[1] *Cp.* Jno. Ev., 19, 34, and the Introduction, p. 258.

day, at the third hour. And it was ordered that they should keep the body of the blessed one upon the tree. But the faithful, by the help of God, took the body of the saint and wrapped it in precious raiment and deposited it in a resting-place with brilliant honours, celebrating as a festival with great joy the day on which the light thus shone and rejoiced the souls of orthodox believers; inasmuch as it is meet to render to the Saviour of all, Jesus Christ our Lord, together with the one Almighty Father and Holy Spirit, glory and honour now and for ever.

ACTS OF S. CALLISTRATUS.

INTRODUCTION.

THE following martyrdom has hitherto been known through the text of the metaphrast alone; of which the Latin form published in the Acta Sanctorum under Sept. 26th (Sept. vii. 190) is no more than a translation. From a comparison of the Armenian text with that of the metaphrast we are able to learn how much of its local colour and freshness, as well as of the actual history and doctrine which it contained, might disappear from an earlier document, when it was revised and cut down by the tenth-century editor. The metaphrast's recension moreover seems to have effectually supplanted all earlier texts; for an early eleventh century codex in the Bodleian library (Cod. Gr. Baroc. 230) merely gives the metaphrast's form just as it is printed in the Migne's *Patrologia Græca*. Nor is there any trace of an early Latin form, though the Armenian text states that it was originally written in that language.

<small>These Acts much curtailed by the metaphrast.</small>

There is a homily of Basil the Great (Migne, *Patrol. Gr.* xxxi., p. 149) entitled : εἰς τοὺς ἁγίους τεσσαράκοντα μάρτυρας, which some have referred to Callistratus and his companions. But Callistratus and his fellow-martyrs were fifty and not forty in number, nor is there a single feature in common between the very vague and rhetorical account of Basil and these Acts. Basil does not mention a single name, and all that we can gather from his homily is that forty soldiers were, under some emperor who is not named and in some city which is not specified, marched out naked on a cold winter's night across a frozen lake, were exposed to the tortures of cold

<small>Not known to Basil the Great.</small>

and then marched back and burned alive; the mother of one of them urging her son, who shrank back, to share the fate of his comrades. It is clear that Basil's forty martyrs were not those to whom our Acts refer.

There are many points of interest in this piece to which we will now briefly allude. There is first the curious story of the martyr's ancestor, Neocoros as the Greek calls him, or Ocorus according to the Armenian, who had been at Jerusalem an eyewitness of the death and resurrection of Jesus, and then returning to his city had bequeathed his testimony and teaching to his descendants. Though we may rightly put aside as fable such a story, yet it seems to indicate that in many regions, down to even late in the third century, the Christian tenets were passed on from father to son not through books, but by oral tradition.[1] Had this not been the case, such a story as the above could not have found its way into our narrative; for the idea of private oral tradition as opposed to the written gospel must have been familiar to the minds of the readers to whom these Acts were addressed. Nor are there wanting signs of the late promulgation in some parts of the ancient world of our present gospels. In Africa, for example, we have the admission of Cyprian that the apostolical teaching of the use of wine by Jesus in the last Supper was not known in the diocese of Carthage until his own generation. This implies that the synoptic gospels were not known in Africa before the third century. Callistratus refers to the Gospel of John, but not to the synoptics. In the Acts of Indus and Domna we hear that the Acts of the Apostles and of the fourteen Epistles of Paul were in the hands of the martyrs in question, but not it seems

Allusion to Tradition as opposed to books.

Evidence of early Acts proves the general diffusion of Canonical Gospels to have been late.

---

[1] Clem. Alex., *Strom.*, lib. i. p. 275, ed. Paris. Ἀλλ' οἱ μὲν τὴν ἀληθῆ τῆς μακαρίας σώζοντες διδασκαλίας παράδοσιν, εὐθὺς ἀπὸ Πέτρου τε καὶ Ἰακώβου, Ἰωάννου τε καὶ Παύλου, τῶν ἁγίων ἀποστόλων, παῖς παρὰ πατρὸς ἐκδεχόμενος (ὀλίγοι δὲ οἱ πατράσιν ὅμοιοι), ἧκον δὴ σὺν θεῷ καὶ εἰς ἡμᾶς τὰ προγονικὰ ἐκεῖνα καὶ ἀποστολικὰ καταθησόμενοι σπέρματα.

any written gospel. And it may be remarked that these two saints celebrated their Eucharist with water, as did the Carthaginian churches, until Cyprian promulgated among them the "apostolical" teaching as to the use of bread and wine. The hero of the Acts before us, Callistratus, seems in the same way to have used water in his Eucharist; so we may infer from the passage on p. 292. All the passages relating to the diffusion of the N. T. Scriptures which are contained in trustworthy martyrdoms need to be carefully collected and the results tabulated; so as to gain an idea of what writings were diffused and where. It would seem as if the martyrs often had the apocryphal gospels. For example, Callistratus certainly had the Descent into Hell and the Gospel of the Infancy, preserved to us in Arabic and Armenian. S. Polyeuctes of Melitene similarly must have had the Acts of Pilate or some such Scripture, which he called "the history of Christ." S. Eugenia at Alexandria about 200 A.D. had a gospel, but her citation does not agree with our existing gospels. And to speak generally, it must strike every reader of the older martyrdoms that the writings best known to the saints were not the canonical gospels, but the Epistles of Paul and the Psalms. Of the canonical gospels, that of John seems to have been diffused before the others.

The statement met with in chap. III. (p. 293) of these Acts as to the language in which they were first written presents difficulty. The Latin words in which the captain addresses Callistratus are transliterated . **Were these** in the Armenian, and the fellow-soldiers of **Acts originally written** Callistratus answer the question of the officer **in Latin?** as to who is the delinquent also in Latin: "bonus miles." Then the narrative continues: "which is translated Callistratus. And the captain commanded him to be brought before him, and said to him in the Roman tongue, for the captain could not understand Greek, because the Romans cannot at once speak Greek on account of the richness of the tongue. And he said to him: Quid dicunt socii propter te, celerius dic. Which is translated: What do thy companions say about thee, quickly say. This history," the

Acts proceed, "was written in the Roman tongue, et cet." From the whole passage we learn—

1. That the captain only spoke Latin and did not understand Greek.
2. The rank and file could answer the captain in Latin.
3. These Acts were originally written in Latin.

But we are left in doubt as regards the following points :—

1. Did the rank and file talk Greek among themselves, only answering their officer in Latin?
2. Was the language into which the Acts were "learnedly" translated Greek?
3. Who are the "we" for whom the Acts were translated and who, on receiving them, disseminated them, retaining however the Latin words which still appear even in the Armenian?

Question (2) must certainly receive an affirmative answer. Question (1) is not so easy of answer. The use of the singular verb: "for the captain *did not understand* Greek," perhaps implies that the common soldiers did understand Greek and were Greeks. Their names given in chap. VIII. are for the most part Greek names. It is supposed by the Bollandist editor that they came from the Greek city Chalcedon, opposite Constantinople, and that the city of Rome where the martyrdom took place is Constantinople. The Arm. reads Chalcedon.

On the other hand, if so, why were the original Acts written in Latin? The statement that they were so, points rather to Carthage as the region whence these recruits had been levied against their will, and to Rome in Italy as the scene of the martyrdom. The metaphrast reads Καρχηδων.

Was Callistratus a Carthaginian?

Nor are we helped to a decision by the notice near the end of the Acts to the effect that "a scribe of the court listened to the words of Callistratus during the night, and wrote them down on paper in shorthand and gave them to *us* and we arranged truly the history of the meditation (? = ἐπιτηδεύματος)." Is this "*we*" the same as the former "*we*"? Probably not. Rather it must be the author of the Latin Acts who "arranged the history"; and the former "*we*" must refer

Acts of S. Callistratus. 277

to the persons who got these translated into Greek and disseminated them among the faithful.

I am inclined on the whole to think that the Carchedon of these Acts was Carthage in Africa, and that the martyrdom was in Rome. If the original Acts were in Latin, then Callistratus must have spoken in Latin, and the shorthand writer who took him down must have taken him down in Latin. But this is unlikely to have been the case in Constantinople. It is true that Callistratus in chap. v. is cast into the sea, and that this could have occurred at Constantinople, but not in Rome. But firstly, **The Scene of Martyrdom Rome or Constantinople?** this entire incident is so mixed up with fable, that we are probably entitled to regard it as an interpolation absent from the original Latin text; and, secondly, the forty-nine fellow-sufferers of the saint are thrown into a lake, columbethra or piece of artificial water, which was called Oceanus. There is nothing to prevent there having been such a columbethra in Rome, though I can find no trace of it in the works of archæologists. Could one identify this detail either in Rome or Constantinople the whole question would be settled.

There is one statement which favours the view that Constantinople was the scene of the martyrdom, namely that "*we* built in Rome in the name of the Holy Callistratus a place of expiation for sinners and a meeting-house of union for angels and men." For we hear of no Church of Callistratus in Rome, but we do hear of one in Constantinople.

The above discussion has a bearing on the date at which these Acts had assumed the form in which the Armenian presents them. If Constantinople was the scene of martyrdom, then as Constantine did not invent the title of New Rome till A.D. 325, these Acts must be subsequent to **Date of these Acts A.D., 300-350.** that date. On the other hand if the old Rome was the scene, then they may have been composed a little earlier. The extreme importance attached to a right understanding of the dogma of the Trinity indicates that they were composed between A.D. 300 and 350. But one does not know whether or not to attribute the whole of these lengthy dogmatic disquisitions to the martyr about to die. They impress me personally as the genuine discourse delivered by him, merely arranged and touched up by a second hand.

However this may be, these Acts still retain their value as a picture of the mind and character of an early fourth-century saint. Of peculiar interest is the admixture in his creed of elements drawn from apocryphal gospels with those taken from the canonical gospels, especially that of S. John's. Of still higher interest is the early representation we here get of a purgatory of souls. The Mechitarist editor prefixes thereto a note to the effect that it is not orthodox, and that he only adds it because it is part of his old literature. It seems indeed to be akin to Origen's beliefs, and it makes room for the conversion after death of infidels by the grace of God acting in response to the tears and prayers of their Christian kinsfolk. I do not know of any other similar sketch of the same age of the condition of the souls of the departed. Even if it was not actually delivered by Callistratus, it yet has a lasting value for the history of Christian opinion. We may indeed say of these Acts as a whole what a great teacher, who has lately passed from our midst, says of the Phædo of Plato: "How far the words attributed to Socrates were actually uttered by him we forbear to ask; for no answer can be given to this question. And it is better to resign ourselves to the feeling of a great work, than to linger among critical uncertainties."[1]

Early doctrine of Purgatory in these Acts.

For these Acts are, like the Phædo, "a great work," and express for us the genius of fourth-century faith as the Phædo expresses the genius of Athenian speculation in an age earlier by seven centuries. In spite of the wide difference in time there is much in common between the two works. The scene is laid in both within the walls of a prison, and

Their resemblances to Plato's Phædo.

---

[1] See *Dialogues of Plato*, translated by Jowett, 2nd edition, vol. i. p. 428.

the shadow and awe of impending, but undeserved, death invests with a solemn earnestness the discourse in which each teacher hastens to impart to a band of eager disciples his last thoughts concerning the soul and the mysteries of the life after death. The irony of Socrates has its counterpart in the humility of the Christian Saint, in his distrust of his own power to adequately set forth his saving truths. Neither is the substance and net result of their teaching so very different in the two cases, if we make abstraction of certain intellectual peculiarities due to the diversity of their ages. Yet there is one great difference.

In Socrates we listen to the voice of a fellow-explorer, to the voice of one who speaks to us not with an air of authority, but with arguments, in order to persuade us and win our rational assent. His appeal lies to our private judgment, as does the appeal of every real thinker ancient or modern. But in Callistratus' addresses we seem to listen to the voice of a church that is willing to enlighten us, but not to argue with us; that has truth to impart, but only in a dogmatic fashion; that demands our assent, but only as a despotism demands obedience from its subjects. *Contrast in spirit between Greek Philosophers and Christian Church.*

For the appeal of a fourth-century theologian lay not to the free reason and judgment of men, but to their submissive faith. And if it be borne in mind that the pagan cults of the third and fourth century were, as theories of the universe and as moral systems, far inferior to Christianity, that they were losing their hold on the best minds and were everywhere crumbling to decay, it will be seen that the authoritative and infallible air and attitude assumed by the Catholic Church was not only warranted by the intrinsic superiority of its moral and theoretic teachings, but was better calculated than any other to lead to success and conquest of the world. Men in doubt, who felt the insufficiency of their inherited paganism, drifted naturally towards a church which allowed of no doubts, and which by professing to be divine *Secret of the success of the early Church.*

and always the same, still seems to offer a ποῦ στῶ to all who wish to act and must act; but who do not think, either because the cares of life press on them and leave no leisure, or because they are too timid to face the problems of the Infinite.

In conclusion, a few words may be allowed in regard to the tortures inflicted on martyrs. The punishment of laying a man down on his back and pouring water down his throat through a funnel, which we hear of in these Acts, was rare. At least I have not met with it in any other Acts. The whole question of the *rationale* of the punishments and tortures to which the Christian confessors were subjected is an obscure one and has not been fairly worked out, mainly owing to the assumption made by nearly all writers, that Christians were treated in an exceptional manner and not merely as other criminals. The ancient Greeks, who were more humane than the Romans in these matters, never tortured free citizens. Even the Thirty Tyrants at Athens, who were in a subsequent age notorious for cruelty and usurpation, were restrained either by their own humanity or the public feeling of Athens from inflicting any other penalty on their most hated opponent Socrates, than painless extinction by a cup of hemlock. Had Socrates suffered as a Christian martyr at the hands either of the Roman Government or of any of the so-called orthodox Christian Churches of a later day, he would probably have been first subjected to the most revolting tortures and at the last burned alive. None but slaves could be tortured in ancient Greece, and they under restrictions which must have mitigated their treatment. For example, the party claiming to torture a slave had to make good to his owners any harm done to him.

Now the end aimed at in torture was to make a slave give the evidence wanted by one or the other of the parties in a lawsuit. It was purely judicial and it was only applied to slaves who might be called on to give evidence in a law

Acts of S. Callistratus. 281

court. They were tortured just as we have istered to us, and their evidence was not supposed to be of any value unless given under torture of some kind. It was usually first applied in a private chamber, before the slave was produced in the open court. It is proof of the extraordinary hold which this belief had on the mind of the best of the ancients, that Aristotle and Cicero held it firmly.

Oaths administered.

End of torture was to extort evidence from witnesses.

During the republican epoch of Rome and under the early emperors free citizens were never subjected to torture; but under the worse emperors who succeeded, their exemption ceased, at least in the case of those accused of majestas or high-treason. But the torture was only for the purpose of extracting evidence from them. The idea of torturing men by way of punishing them for their religious opinions was alien to the Roman mind. It was the Christian Church that first instituted religious persecution in the true sense of the phrase, *i.e.*, as punishment of purely speculative tenets.

It was at first confined to slaves.

Now there can hardly be a doubt that Christians were tortured for the same reason that slaves were tortured, namely in order to extract evidence required of them, and to force from them certain admissions. That this is so is clear from Pliny's letter (96) to Trajan asking for guidance in regard to "cognitiones de Christianis." He writes thus: "Interim in iis qui ad me tanquam Christiani deferebantur hunc sum secutus modum. Interrogavi ipsos an essent Christiani. Confitentes iterum ac tertio interrogavi, supplicium minatus: perseverantes duci iussi. Neque enim dubitabam, qualecunque esset quod faterentur, pertinaciam certe et inflexibilem obstinationem debere puniri." Later in the same letter he writes: "Quo magis necessarium credidi ex duabus ancillis, quæ ministræ dicebantur, quid esset veri et per tormenta quærere. Nihil aliud inveni quam superstitionem pravam immodicam." Trajan answers that the Christians "puniendi sunt, ita tamen ut qui negaverit se Christianum esse idque

Torture of early Christians purely judicial.

re ipsa manifestum fecerit, id est supplicando dis nostris, quamvis suspectus in præteritum, veniam ex pænitentia impetret." Hence it is clear that the torture applied by Pliny was simply judicial, in order to extract a statement from the accused adverse to Christianity, a denial of their faith, or else to get at the truth about so obscure a religion. These Christians therefore suffered as witnesses in the strict sense. The design of the judge was to make them say what they were wanted to say. They were not tortured as Christians, but as witnesses called on to give evidence in a law-court. It was an easy and natural mental transition from the conception of a Christian suffering as a judicial witness to that of him as witnessing by his suffering to the truth of the faith.

It is not easy to say when the word μάρτυρ acquired the new sense of a Christian confessor, who had shed his blood for the faith. It seems to bear this sense in Acts xxii. 20; Rev. xvii. 6, and perhaps Ep. to Heb. xii. 1. In Rev. iii. 14 μάρτυς bears the same sense. Perhaps the Acts and Revelation and Hebrews were not written till the end of the first century, and that is why this use occurs in them when it occurs nowhere else in the N.T. The apostles are witnesses of the resurrection (Acts ii. 32), and Jesus is Himself the witness to God. And the latter use seems already to have been so long and so generally recognised as the sense κατ' ἐξοχὴν of the word that the martyrs of Vienne, in Euseb. 5. 2. 1, in their humility disclaimed the title.

The word martyr got its distinctive sense about A.D. 100.

The tortures inflicted on martyrs were in the main those of which we hear in earlier times as inflicted on witnesses, especially on slaves. In Cicero we hear of the *candentes laminæ* or red hot plates, which we often read of in the martyrdoms. The *eculeus* or horse-rack was also used to martyrs. The magistrates as a rule threatened their Christian victims before applying torture, and the prisoner could always escape the penalty by conforming to the pagan rites, by sacrificing to the statue either of the emperor or of the gods. In all cases the objection of the Christians to do what was demanded of them seems to have been dictated by their monotheism. The Jews all over the empire would have had the same scruples and would certainly have died rather than violate them. Hence it is clear that the persecution of the Christians had nothing to do with their monotheistic rejection of the cult of the emperor and of pagan rites in general, and the command to sacrifice and swear by the emperor's genius was chosen by the authorities as an easy and convenient test of the sincerity of their convictions. If their refusal to sacrifice and to conform to the state religion had been the real gravamen against them, then the Jews would have been equally liable to prosecution and martyrdom.

The command to sacrifice a mere test of Christian opinion.

In what then did the offence of the Christians lie, if not in their haughty rejection of popular cults? What was it about the new religion which made even the profession of the name of Christian a capital offence? Here is a question which seems never to have been answered quite satisfactorily. Jewish monotheism was from the first recognised and tolerated by the Romans as a respectable cult. "Judæorum sola et misera gentilitas unum et ipsi deum, sed palam, sed templis, aris, uictimis cœrimoniisque coluerunt," says the opponent of Christianity in the Apology of Minucius Felix (ch. 10, 4).

For their offence lay not in their monotheism,

I believe that the original prejudice against Christianity was purely social and popular and well-merited. It sprang from the *flagitia* of the Christians, and these consisted of the many actions and abstentions from action by which they were felt to menace the whole structure and permanence of society and of recognised social institutions. Let us enumerate some of them.

But in their anti-social tendencies;

1. There was first that rejection of family ties and relationships which accompanied the belief that the world was speedily and any day coming to an end. Young men and maidens were taught not to marry, husbands and wives not to cohabit and beget any more children. Eunuchism, because of

the kingdom of heaven, was even tolerated by the very founder of the religion. And all this just at a time when the most thoughtful and patriotic of the Romans were deploring the decay of population all over the empire, and were even making laws against celibacy and holding out rewards to married men with families.

<small>e.g. their rejection of family ties,</small>

2. There was the interference with family relations. The first duty of the convert was to the body of ecstatic religionists with whom he had been induced to ally himself. All the most sacred duties of the old world were to yield to the necessities of that body: "Another of the disciples said unto Him, Lord, suffer me first to go and bury my father. But Jesus saith unto him, Follow Me; and leave the dead to bury their own dead." That is to say, none but those who believed in His Messiahship and in the immediate inauguration by Him of the kingdom of heaven, were really alive. The rest of mankind were dead and the convert had no duties towards them. "Think not that I came to send peace on the earth: I came not to send peace but a sword: For I came to set a man at variance against his father, and the daughter against her mother, and the daughter-in-law against her mother-in-law: and a man's foes shall be they of his own household. He that loveth father and mother more than Me is not worthy of Me; and he that loveth son or daughter more than Me is not worthy of Me."

<small>in their interference with family relations,</small>

Even if this open trampling on the oldest and most sacred of human instincts and affections was not actually inculcated by Jesus of Nazareth, it was certainly urged by the millenarist society which He founded, or it would not be so prominent in all the gospels. It must have excited sorrow and indignation in thousands of hitherto happy and united households. Unfortunately the Church has destroyed the works of profane observers like Celsus, from whom we could have formed an idea of the havoc wrought. In the story of Thekla, who in response to the new teaching throws over her betrothed lover, abandons her sorrowing family and unsexes herself by leaving her home disguised in male attire, we have recorded what must have been a typical case.

3. Nor did the Christian nihilism destroy the ties of sentiment and affection alone. The early Church was a communistic society, and those who joined it handed over into the control of its officers whatever private means they possessed. We to-day are not slow to resent the action of brothers or sisters who joining some religious society, with whose methods and creeds we have no sympathy, make over to it property which in the natural course of things would have benefited ourselves and our children. Parallel cases there must have been by tens of thousands between the years 50 and 150 A.D. <small>in their Communism,</small>

4. Along with the rejection of family ties and affections there went a refusal to fulfil the leading duties of citizenship. The converts to Christianity refused to bear arms and defend civilization from its external enemies. Their refusal to take oaths in itself prevented them from serving as soldiers; for the armies took the sacramentum afresh with the accession of each new emperor. It also prevented them from entering the public courts of law either as judges or parties to a suit.

5. A modern divine has said that a modern state which should attempt to regulate its external policy purely according to the precepts of the gospel, that should turn the other cheek to the smiter and resist not evil, could not endure even for a short time. Justice and morality however is not of one kind for a state and of another for the individual; and if we have to-day achieved a level of prosperity and comfort for all classes, far short, it is true, of what is desirable, yet much above anything the world has yet witnessed, it has certainly not been achieved by a following of the gospel precepts to take no thought for the morrow and to imitate the lilies of the field, which toil not neither do they spin. On the contrary, the latter phrase is applied nowadays by democratic leaders in reproof of an indolent aristocracy. The early Christians dreamed that the morrow <small>in their elevation of improvidence and poverty into virtues,</small>

would bring the millennium; there was therefore no need to take thought for it, no necessity to lay up riches on earth. Such teaching must quickly lead to misery and destitution among those who literally practise it, and the saints of Jerusalem, who perhaps strove to do so longer than did other congregations, soon became a burthen on the Christians of other regions.

6. Repudiation and ridicule of other religious cults was of course no less characteristic of the Jews than of the Christians. But then in the Jews it was not part of a general moral and social nihilism. The Jewish monotheistic progaganda moreover could not make way like the Christian, because it imposed circumcision on the proselyte; for which reason, as Renan has pointed out, it spread more among the women than among the men. This explains how it was that the Jews, hated as they were by the populace, were yet never the objects of penal legislation. Their religion was never put under ban and a systematic attempt made to extirpate it. They were dreaded less, because their propaganda was slower, and still more because its missionaries did not preach that the end of the world was at hand, and persuade people to behave as if it were really so. The Jewish religion moreover was more open and public, and in its sacrificial system resembled other cults. The Christians on the other hand wrapped up their rites in mystery. They met by night and were pledged not to reveal the secrets of their religion. A long catechumenate was necessary in order to baptism, and one who was not initiated could no more witness their rites or join in their worship than an Englishman can at the present day enter a Hindoo temple. As late as the middle of the third century Babylas, bishop of Antioch, endured martyrdom rather than allow the Emperor Decius to enter the church when the congregation was met therein.

<small>in their more wide-spread propaganda,</small>

<small>in the secrecy of their rites.</small>

The teaching of early Christianity was thus altogether subversive of ancient society. So it would be of modern society, and any one set of people who should literally carry it out in their conduct would very soon come into conflict with established law and morality, and would certainly descend sooner or later into beggary and destitution. A system of ethics inspired by the belief that the existing order of things is shortly to succumb and by an abrupt peripety give way to a kingdom of heaven, in which angels and superhuman agencies will supersede the slow and arduous methods and industry of this earth,—such a system will not much avail us until the promise is fulfilled; we shall be fortunate if it does not put us into much useless conflict with the old and permanent constitution of things. Into such conflict the early Christians fell. They were regarded, and rightly, as enemies of the human race. If it is possible to endorse any judgment of the past we may endorse this one of the authorities of the Roman empire.

<small>Early Christianity was subversive of society.</small>

The Christians waited and waited for the heavenly bridegroom who was to come like a thief in the night. Gradually the form of their enthusiasm changed, when the world continued its course undisturbed as before and yet no signs of the second advent. And then they began to compromise with the world which was after all so stable, and they laid up their old millenarist system of faith and morality " like a pattern in the skies." They recognised it to be an ideal too good for the earth, and "the virgins began to marry,"[1] and the men to accumulate riches, and to serve in the armies of the Empire, and in time they forgot all about the precept "Swear not at all," and frequented the law courts like other people, and left to posterity the entire Corpus iuris ciuilis.[1]

<small>It was soon forced to compromise with the world,</small>

But the early period of Christianity had lasted long enough for it to become the fixed and justifiable belief of ancient society that a Christian was a perverse being who believed the

---

[1] In this connection we may note how the phrase "to leave the world (κόσμον)," which in an earlier age simply meant to become a Christian, came in the third or fourth century to denote the monastic life.

end of all things to be imminent, and was therefore ready to subvert and sweep away every institution, social and political. Dynamite and explosions apart, the Christians of this first age resembled the most extreme of the Russian nihilists, and it cannot be denied that the Roman government had as good grounds for trying to eradicate them as the Russian has for trying to make an end of nihilists. Of the history of Christianity between A.D. 40 and 120 we have few direct monuments, because people who thought the end of the world was at hand did not want to write history.[1] They did not look forward to posterity; indeed they did not believe in it. All their care was to get themselves ready for the imminent crisis. When a conviction is once ingrained in a society and in a conservative bureaucracy that a particular set of people are dangerous, it is difficult to remove it. The Christians little by little parted with their early dreams, and began to compromise with the world and live like sober citizens. But it needed generations to pass away before the belief died out for which they had at first given ground that they were enemies of the human race.

yet not before it had established a reputation for Flagitia.

---

[1] Another reason why so little of the earliest Christian literature has survived is, that it was too impregnated with wild Chiliastic dreams to suit post-Nicene readers, who therefore took no trouble to make copies of it. Even Papias on this account seemed to Eusebius to be σφόδρα σμικρὸς τὸν νοῦν. The Greek Irenæus has vanished for a similar reason. Paul's letters and the gospels have remained, because they were saner than other writings of the first age.

THE MARTYRDOM OF THE HOLY CALLISTRATUS, AND THE FORTY AND NINE MARTYRS THAT WERE WITH HIM.

I. IN the times when Diocletian was emperor, there was much fury on the part of the heathen; and not only did they, because they knew not God, work destruction to their own selves, but they tried to seduce all men to conform to their unholy cult. And those who did so conform, especially those who were in high places, not only received honours from the Emperor, but also made much parade of themselves in the great army. But those who avowed their faith in Almighty God, and in His word, and in the Holy Spirit, were subjected to interrogatories, and to torture, and so received the speedy crown and the honour of the glory; but, humanly speaking, their flesh was consumed with evil and cruel tortures.

II. In that time, first and alone, the brave athlete of Christ, whose name was Callistratus, in the city of Rome, took unto himself the crown of victory; and in solemn and sturdy combat he raised the standard of victory for them who had believed in the Lord. For this Callistratus was a soldier of the band which was called Chalcedon; because these came after the band of the

Acombiti,[1] which was in Chalcedon, men whom they brought against their will to Rome, according to the law of conscripts. But Callistratus was of the district of Chalcedon, of free family, and of one that was benevolent and was filled with divine wisdom ; and his great-grandfather, Okorus,[2] had been in Jerusalem in the days of our Lord Jesus Christ, under Pilate the judge. This Okorus had

---

[1] Acombiti is a barbarism for Accubiti.
The metaphrast reads here :—

Καλλίστρατος, ὃς τῆς Καρχηδονίων μὲν ὥρμητο, σπείρᾳ τῇ τῶν Χαλινδῶν λεγομένῃ κατειλεγέντος, ἐν 'Ρώμῃ, γενόμενος δὲ σὺν ὅλῳ τῷ τάγματι, κομιδῇ νεόλεκτος ὤν.

Under the Earlier empire every Roman citizen was liable to military service and could be forced to serve, unless he found a substitute or vicarius (Trajan ep. to Pliny, 30). There was thus no special law making every man liable to service. From the age of Diocletian onwards, there was a growing tendency to substitute a money payment for the levy of recruits which a province had to supply, and to take as soldiers only such men as desired to serve. So Mommsen (*Hermes*, vol. 24. art. : " Die römische Militärwesen seit Diocletian ") remarks, that the words of Ammianus, 21. 6. 6 : Supplementa legionibus scripta sunt indictis per provincias tirociniis were true under the old system ; under which, however, professors and doctors were exempted (Modestians, Dig. 27, 1, 6, 8 : μὴ εἰς στρατείαν καταλέγεσθαι ἄκοντας). The reference to the law of conscripts may thus, in these Acts, be retrospective and glance at a system of compulsory military service which was gradually falling into disuse, as in the fourth century it actually did. In the inscriptions of an earlier period (second century) there are references to several Cohortes Chalcidenorum (see Mommsen, *Observ. Epigr.*, Berlin, 1884, pp. 193, 194). But there is only one inscription (*C. I. L.* 2, 2,103) which mentions a Cohors Chalcedonen. In it Mommsen would change the reading to Chalcidensis. These Acts confirm the inscription in question. Of a Cohors Carthaginensis after the metaphrast's reading nothing is known. In what sense this Cohors "came after" the Accubiti I do not understand. I presume that the Accubiti were a cohort privileged to attend on the person of the emperor, a bed-chamber force, as the term implies. The word occurs in the inscription of Diocletian regulating prices. Bread and bacon were the regular rations of a Roman soldier in that, as in earlier epochs. The reading Χαλινδῶν or Χαλανδῶν for Accubiti I do not understand.   [2] Νεωκόρος in the metaphrast.

Acts of S. Callistratus.

seen the Saviour on the cross, had witnessed His death and burial in the tomb, and His resurrection from the dead, and He believed and was baptized on the day of the holy Pentecost, at the descent of the Holy Spirit on the holy Apostles, and He had believed with the Galileans; and he had come to his city and there taught his children and his grandchildren to put their hope in the Lord Jesus Christ; and they learned one from the other and kept up the lore[1] in which their great-grandfather instructed them, right on to the blessed Callistratus. He alone was a Christian in his band; and at every hour he would glorify the Lord by means of the words of the Holy Spirit.

III. Now on a certain night Callistratus arose and offered prayers to God; but certain of his fellow-soldiers noticed this, and began to say to him: "It is not fitting that thou alone shouldst be childish among us all; be persuaded therefore, and come to the image of Zeus, and take frankincense and blood, and sprinkle them upon it, and become along with us dear to the gods. But if thou wilt not, then blame us not, because we must needs inform our captain of all that thou doest." But the holy Callistratus made answer and said: "My brethren, why hath Satan filled your minds? I have not harmed any one of you, nor have I oppressed any one of you; in war I am along with you; in the register of names I am perhaps classed before you, but on parade I do not

---

[1] ἐμπορεύματος.

separate myself from you, nor in the squadron do I pass you by. What reason then have ye now to speak evil of me, this I know not; but this I know that ye have not power to cut me off from the unspeakable benevolence of Jesus my Saviour and from His orthodox worship; not only have ye no power to do so, but not even many more like unto you can do so. Let Christ who bore witness before Pontius Pilate, and of whom my great-grandfather Okorus was an eye-witness, testify unto this for me."

When they heard this, they rose at dawn and informed Presentinus the captain, saying: "One of the number of thy soldiers who are under thy control, rebels against the worship of the gods, and calls a certain one who is named Christ His King and God, and he acknowledges Him crucified; but he also takes upon himself to pray and fast, and all his rations of pork and of good bread he gives to them that need it, and he himself once a day eats dry bread, dipping it in water; but lest he should inspire many of thy soldiers to revolt with him, therefore we have laid information before thy serene Majesty." But Presentinus said: "Who is he, and what is his name?" And they said: "Bonus Miles," which is, being translated, Callistratus. And the captain ordered them to bring him before them; and he said to him in the Roman tongue, for the captain did not talk Greek, for the Romans cannot at once talk Greek, because of the richness of the tongue. And he said to him: "Quid dicunt socii tui, propter te, celerius dic." Which, being translated, is: "What do thy comrades say concerning thee, quickly tell us." This history was written in the Roman tongue, and thus it is that they pronounced the words, who knew the language and translated them, and gave them to us; and we, without altering them, sent them on to all places, which have Christ before their eyes in faith and holiness.

Callistratus made answer and said: Let them say, O my Lord, what more they have to say concerning me; for I know of nothing wrong to impute to myself." Presentinus said to the slanderers: "What do ye know concerning Callistratus, boni militis?". But they said: "Nay, rather let your serene Majesty command him to sacrifice to the great god Zeus, and thou shalt know then his perverse disposition." So the captain said: "Sacrifice, O Callistratus, to the god Zeus." Callistratus said: "I offer the sacrifice of praise to the great God who made heaven and earth and everything in His wisdom; who fashioned man out of dust, and fixed his destiny eternal and inviolable; for I know not the gods made by hand, but I walk as I have learned. For it is written:[1] 'All the idols of the heathens are demons, but the Lord made the heavens;' and this also:[2] 'The idols of the heathens are gold and silver made by the hands of the sons of men.' I therefore, O lord Count, do not worship or pay homage to the work of men's

---

[1] Ps. xcv. 5.   [2] Ps. cxiii. 4.

hands; but since I am thy enlisted soldier, and am under thy hand, I have obeyed thee in war and in drill and in all service; surely thou hast not authority over my soul also, that it should serve thee? God forbid!" IV. Presentinus said: "Here, O Callistratus, there is no need for rhetoric, but we have to talk about obedience; wherefore comply and sacrifice, that thou mayst not compel me to destroy thee in a cruel manner. But I think that thou too knowest, that when I arrest any man by force, before torturing him, I consume him with my roarings." Callistratus said: "Thy roaring and thy threatening is but transient; but the wailing and the gnashing of teeth is eternal.[1] For if I deny my Lord Jesus Christ before men, He will shut me out, He the Master of the house, and there shall be weeping of eyes and gnashing of teeth."

Then the captain ordered that he should be pinioned and beaten with clubs, until eight men had taken their turn at it. And as they beat him, the holy Callistratus said: "I have sworn and have resolved to keep the judgments of thy righteousness, O Lord.[2] We were very faint, but do thou revive me, according to Thy word,[3] nor suffer the destroyer and the many-headed beast to rejoice over me; but strengthen me, Christ, and be unto me a tongue, in order that I may answer, and a physician, in order that my wounds may be healed;

---

[1] Matt. viii. 12.   [2] Psal. cxviii. 106.
[3] Psal. cxviii. 107.

for many pangs have I in my flesh because of these torments."

But when the captain saw his blood gushing out in rivulets upon the earth, he ordered them to cease from beating him; and he said to him: "Sacrifice, O Callistratus, to the gods, in order that thou mayest be saved from instant tortures; for I swear by Artemis, crowned with rays, and by all the company of the gods, unless thou obeyest me, I will cut thee into bits, and the dogs shall devour thy flesh and the lions lick up thy blood." Callistratus said: "I hope in the King of Heaven, in God, that He will bring me out of the mouth of the lions, and save my helplessness from the hands of the dogs, in order that not I alone of this thy band may praise Him; for I have expectation that by opposing Him, and going out against Him, I shall raise the standard of victory over the Devil, who incites thee against me. V. Then the captain ordered them to pound up potsherds and to scatter them beneath him, and to stretch the saint on his back, so that the potsherds might lacerate his back and his wounds. And they placed a funnel in his mouth, and he ordered them to pour water with a jug into his mouth. But the brave champion of Christ suffered these tortures with courage. And when he had risen up, he said: "O God of Abraham, Isaac and Jacob, give me strength to meet the artifices of the devil; and save me from him, lest he destroy me, and lest he find a vantage-ground against me."

The captain said: " Sacrifice, O Callistratus, to

the gods; otherwise I will take away thy life, that others of this band be not also lost through thee." The holy Callistratus said: "Unworthy man, and shameless, thou art eager to do combat for the flock of Satan, thy master, not knowing that this flock belongs to my Christ. But I hope in the King of Heaven, in my Lord Jesus Christ, that however much thou mayest struggle in behalf of the Devil, yet I shall take him captive, and shall snatch them from the number of thy forces, and illuminate them, and establish the Church of Christ in the middle of this city." But the captain said: "Out on thee, unholy one, and thrice miserable; behold my command is urgent before thine eyes. This instant my government orders me to cast thee into a sack, and to seal up its mouth, and to take and throw thee into the middle of the sea. How then canst thou establish the Church of Christ, or when wilt thou illuminate any of the number of the bands of my soldiers?" And he ordered them to bring a linen sack, and to throw him into it, and he sealed the mouth of the sack with lead, and he gave it into the hands of the crew, and the crew bore it into the middle of the sea, about forty furlongs, and threw it into the sea. And the captain stood on the shore of the sea, until the sailors came. But the sack went down and was caught in a hollow of the rocks; and even while he was under the sea Callistratus offered up prayers, saying: "O God, invisible and unsearchable, unattainable and unutterable, whose throne of glory cannot be declared, before whom all things tremble and quail, whose threats consume the mountains, and whose name and title cleaves asunder the abysses, before whom the sea shrinks abashed along with the rivers and the whales, who didst search out the heart of Jonas and didst receive his prayers when he came forth on the land, even though he was imprisoned as it were in everlasting bonds, and didst rescue his life from destruction; now also receive the prayers of me, who am a sinner, and in distress, and let my prayers come to the temple of thy holy glory; save me from this present oppression, for thou hast known my works even from my childhood. Thou knowest, O Lord, that I desired to establish Thy Church in the midst of this city; be my fellowworker for good, because Holy is Thy name forever."

And after he had offered his prayer, the sack chanced upon a narrow passage between rocks, and was torn asunder, and a certain fish[1] of the dolphin tribe took him and bore him upwards from the depths to the shore of the sea, and laid him down upon the sands, and then it turned round and fled back into the sea. But when the soldiers and their captain beheld him, they were much dismayed. But Callistratus began to sing a psalm and said, "I descended into the depths of the sea, and the cataracts engulphed me;[2] but I was not disquieted, and cried out,[3] for Thou hast heard the voice of my prayer; Thou hast

---

[1] According to the metaphrast *two* dolphins.
[2] Ps. lxviii. 3, 4. [3] Ps. xxx. 23.

torn asunder my sack, and hast established me in gladness."[1] VI. Then forty and nine of the soldiers fell down before the blessed Callistratus, saying: " We pray thee, servant of God on High, save us from the vanity of this world, for we also are Christians; for great indeed is the God of the Christians, who hath brought thee out of such an abyss; He is able also to help in battle whomsoever He will, for He alone is God." The holy Callistratus said: " My Lord Jesus Christ shall deliver you, and henceforth ye shall see the king of Heaven."

And he prayed thus: " Lord, who hast Thy dwelling for ever in unapproachable light, look upon this Thy flock which is in Thee, and preserve them, because Thou art merciful, continually, and for ever." VII. But Presentinus said, "I swear by the sun, by the Emperor, this fellow is full of exceeding wizardry, for he hath cloven asunder the sea, and hath tricked these men." And he said to him : " I will oppose this wizardry of thine; grant me a little while, and thou shalt know who is Presentinus, and who is the God whom thou servest." And he sat down upon his judgment-seat, and ordered them to bring rods, and he caused the forty and nine men to be scourged one after the other. But they said, " Lord Jesus, this torture we endure for Thy sake; help us, O God, the Saviour, and give us strength to bear it; preserve also our shepherd,

---

[1] Ps. xxix. 2.

Acts of S. Callistratus. 299

Callistratus, in order that he may teach us perfectly, for we are as it were dumb animals, and have not the knowledge of Thy will. Look graciously upon our salvation, for blessed is Thy name for ever."

VIII. But thereupon the unholy captain ordered them to be put in prison, in order that he might think about them : for he was very grieved at having lost fifty men out of the number of his soldiers. And when they came into the prison, the holy Callistratus began to establish with prayer the forty and nine men, whose names are the following:[1] Acacius, Domnasius, Bibianus, Basiliscus, Bemarchus, Dorotheus, Gerontes, Alpius, Anthimus, Aragseos, Anictus, Bitalius, Grigorius, Georgius, Gigandius, Genadius, Domninus, Dulcimius, Dometianus, Dedalius, Dalmatius, Eusebius, Evagrius, Elsiidius, Eutolius, Evarestus, Evagrius, Tharasimides, Theodorus, Therasius, Lysimachus, Lambliricus, Liminus, Constantinus, Canditianus, Heliages, Hysicus, Heliodorus, Memnus, Milinus, Madrinus, Marcianus, Nicatius, Nicolaius, Olombrius, Utripeus, Olipeus, Xanthius. All these fell down before the holy Callistratus, and sought of him the knowledge of Christ. But the holy martyr of Christ spread out his hands to heaven, and spoke thus : " O God, who hast made everything, who art the all-wise Lord of all, who art praised by the numberless hosts of angels, who art perfect Creator ; O God of our

---

[1] The metaphrast omits the names. I give the Arm. spelling.

fathers, look down upon this Thy flock; come unto us, and be among us; fulfil, O Lord, Thy faithful promise, that where two or three are gathered together in My Name, I am there in the midst of them.[1] Hear us, O King of eternity, scatter, O Lord, the flame of the devil. Remove, O Lord, the furnace of fire, that it may not rise higher than forty and nine cubits;[2] in order that all the heathens may see Thy glory, and may glorify Thee, O King of eternity. Vouchsafe unto me, O Lord, wisdom and knowledge, in order that I may cause Thy servants to believe, and bring them before Thee; for blessed is Thy Name for ever."

And they all with one accord uttered the Amen; and one of them, whose name was Dalmatius, arose, and said to the holy Callistratus: "I pray thee, my lord Callistratus, make us Christians, and teach us the word of God, that we may not be ever in doubt. Show us our hope and our future help. Recount to us all the wisdom of God, in order that we too may, by the grace of Christ, be glorifiers of Him along with Thee. For our fathers did not ever teach us the paths of righteousness." Then said unto them the holy Callistratus, "Children mine, and dear brothers, may the Lord give you grace and pity, and may my God bring to light your desire. May the God of

---

[1] Matt. xviii. 20.
[2] In the descent of Christ into hell (see Tischendorf, *Evang. Apoc.*), the Saviour causes the flames to retreat. The passage in the text may refer to some such legendary belief.

heaven and earth fill you with all goodness; for I know that ye have an exceeding desire to hear the commandment of God. Now, therefore, since ye are athirst for righteousness, may the Lord fill you and intoxicate you and satiate you with the all-good and sufficing grace of the Holy Spirit, and with all the hope which ye have in the Lord Christ. But yet, my friends, I am unworthy and weak to tell of the unapproachable depths of the thoughts of God, but let each of you ask what he will, and make prayer for me; because I hope in the Lord Jesus Christ that, through your prayers, the Lord may give me speech to open my mouth boldly, and to speak clearly as an interpreter the plan of the economy of Christ." Then Bemarchus fell down before him and asked him, and said: " I pray thee, sir, tell me, how God is understood and known, and in what way He begot Christ, or for what reason and why the Jews crucified Him and slew Him."

IX. The holy Callistratus said, " God is light without shadow, invisible and unapproachable; He hath neither beginning nor end; life without term, eternity without change, this is He. He has neither limits nor place, but in all things He is everywhere, and there is nowhere a place in which He is not. No one is before Him, nor after Him, nor yet beside Him. He is an unknowable, an unintelligible nature. But for our weakness He is called light and life, reality, immortality, eternity, might, wisdom, mind, and whatsoever other names are heard in the holy books. Father and Son, spotless birth and unsearchable; the Word from the heart of the Father, and indivisible from the Father, Offspring inseparable, as is the light from the sun; Son, but not created, nor yet fashioned, and not in a lower degree, nor subservient, but sharer in reality and in being, and sharing in His quality of being without beginning. For ever in the bosom of the Father, according to the holy John, the evangelist, who saith, ' From the beginning was the Word, and the Word was God; He was from the beginning with God. Everything was through Him, and without Him was nothing which has been made. Through Him was life, and the life was light unto men, and the light was ashine there in the darkness, and the darkness apprehended Him not.' And again, ' God hath no one seen at any time, except the Only Born, who is in the bosom of the Father,' and the Holy Spirit, who emanated and proceeded from the Father; though not born, as is the Word, but an emanation and an effulgence of the eternal light; not made, nor yet lower than Father and Son, but coequal with them, and sharing their substance and partaking equally with the Father and Son. All substance of the Father is of the Son, except that He is not begetter, but begotten; and all substance of the Son is of the Holy Spirit; except that this is not begotten, but emanation; yet not that which sends forth the emanation, but that which has emanated; and through unity, by reason of His Godhead, He is equal in honour

Acts of S. Callistratus. 303

with Father and with Son, and there is one glory and one Godhead of the Trinity, one beginningless eternity of Father and Son and Holy Spirit; three Persons in their completeness, one self-hood and rule, one will and one counsel. It is wholly vision, it is wholly light, it is wholly hearing, wholly life, all this and whatsoever name and title else, by which we who are made of clay, call Him according to our weak understanding. One they are and equal, and on a level; except that there is Father, and there is His Offspring, the Word, and the emanation likewise of Him, the Holy Spirit, in three perfect persons.

"Therefore the holy and co-equal Trinity willed and established everything. The Father, by means of the Word, through the Holy Spirit, made heaven and earth, and divided the heavens with fire and the earth with water; He made also the light, according to which He also created the heavenly host; and parted waters from waters, and shot out the foam-flakes of His firmament. And the earth He adorned with things which blossom and grow, and the firmament with the sun and moon and stars; the earth, too, with four-footed animals and creeping things and with fishes did he fill, and the air with birds, according to the command which He gave to earth and waters to bring forth the breath of life.

"And when He had established all things by the power of His awful Godhead, which hung the heavens from nothing, and laid the earth upon nothing, and made all the elements real out of nothing; then at last He fashioned man out of dust, according to the image of His own Immortality, and gave Him free will to rule withal over all creatures which are below heaven. And He gave him a dwelling in the sinlessness of the garden of delight, and promised to advance him to yet greater glory, if he would be obedient to His law in a little thing. But Satan was an angel formed first, and created in the heavens; and because he was full of pride, and rose up in spiritual revolt against the Omnipotent God, therefore he fell from his glory. And he was jealous of man, and in his guile he sowed polytheism by making him taste of a fruit; and because man desired to be equal to God, God deprived him of his glory, and cast him out of the paradise where he was cherished by God. But forasmuch as he was the image of immortal God, Satan was not able nor had strength to efface him, and utterly destroy him; but, by reason of his free will and of his craft, he fought against the race of men, and polluted them with all kinds of evils, with murder of their brothers, and with lawless unions. And the first race who did not obey the preaching of the just Noah, were therefore destroyed by a flood; and there only remained Noah and his children, eight souls. After that, by reason of their building the tower, their tongues were separated one from the other, and race by race, so that they were seventy and two races in number over the whole earth. And after that, Satan prompted them to worship idols, and to pollute themselves with the worship of everything, as you now behold—worship which the Lord will remove and destroy from among us. And thus he sowed the first seeds, and made the beginning of polytheism, when he said to Eve, 'Ye shall be gods'; so leading men to vain worship; and the whole earth was in great sin.

"And the great God was moved to pity them, and He chose the patriarchs Abraham, Isaac and Jacob; and their seed He took to Himself as His chosen people. And them He brought out of Egypt by the hand of Moses, and gave them laws, which laws also Satan destroyed, for they made a calf in the desert, and polluted themselves with abominations. And the second time in pity He gave them priests and prophets; but they believed not in them either, because of the promptings of Satan; neither were they schooled or corrected by tribulation or slavery, or invocation by name of the angels;[1] and the whole earth with one accord was perverted, and followed after Satan, seeking from him the fulfilment of their evil wishes. But God, in His noble pity, had compassion on the race of men, and sent His only-begotten Word into the world, who hallowed the virgin Miriam, and dwelt in her, and (she) conceived inviolate without the seed of man, and without concupiscence, of herself fashioned an incorruptible body, according to the leader of the

---

[1] = ἐπικλήσει ἀγγέλων. The Essenes bound themselves by oath not to reveal to unbelievers the names of the angels. Comp. Paul, Ep. to Eph. i. 21.

angels, Gabriel, who said, 'The Holy Spirit shall come upon thee, and the power of the Most High shall overshadow thee; for that which shall be born of thee is holy, and a Son of God; and they shall call His name Jesus, because He shall save His people from their sins.' And He was conceived incorruptible, and was born incorruptible, yet was wrapped in swaddling clothes, and was laid in the manger of the brutes as if He were man; by the magi He was honoured with sacramental gifts, by the shepherds He was glorified, who sang with the angels; 'Glory in the highest to God, and on earth peace, good will to men.' He was circumcised as man, He was presented in the temple as man, but the aged Simeon besought[1] Him as from God. He was driven by persecution into Egypt, and there He turned the city of idol-worshippers to a knowledge of God.[2] Thence He returned, and dwelt in Galilee in the city of Nazareth.[3]

---

[1] Probably the original reading here meant "regarded him."

[2] This incident is related in the apocryphal Gospel of the Infancy.

[3] This entire chapter IX. is by the metaphrast compressed into a single page. The Incarnation is also set forth rather differently. God sends His only-born Son, and arranges that He should become man like ourselves, without, however, giving up His essential divinity (αὐτὸ τὸ εἶναι θεός); in order that He might by the screen of flesh and human form deceive the devil who had deceived us, and that the latter, supposing that He was only attacking man, might be drawn into a conflict with God. (ἵνα τῷ τῆς σαρκὸς προβλήματι καὶ τῇ ἀνθρωπίνῃ μορφῇ τὸν ἡμᾶς ἀπατήσαντα δελεάσῃ, καὶ ἀνθρώπῳ οἰόμενος προσβαλεῖν, θεῷ περιπέσῃ. ὃ δὴ καὶ γέγονε.) This explanation of the Incarnation as a divine ruse to catch the devil was very common. We meet with it again in the Acts of Eustratius (Migne, *Patrol. Gr.*, 116, p. 493). There the Divine Word ἐτέχθη ἐκ τῆς ἁγίας παρθένου μὴ τραπεὶς τῇ θειότητι, ἀλλὰ φορέσας τὴν τοῦ προβάτου δορὰν διὰ τὴν τοῦ λύκου πρόοδον, *i.e.*, He dons the sheepskin to lure the devil on.

Acts of S. Callistratus. 307

" But let not one of you stumble and say that Christ took His origin from the Virgin ; for, according to the flesh, He appeared from the Virgin, but according to His Godhead, He is equal. to the Father, as I said above. And let not one of you say that He brought His flesh and body from heaven, for He derived it from the Virgin. Nor let any one of you say that He was merely God or merely man, but rather that He is God and man, God in the flesh, and man in His Godhead, not confounded nor changed. For He says in the Proverbs :[1] 'The Lord acquired Me the beginning of all paths in His works, before that the abysses were, before the fountains of the waters, before all the hills He hath begotten Me ; when He made ready His throne, I was with Him. I it was with whom He was rejoicing.' But with regard to the flesh, He says that the mystery of the incarnation of Christ was, before the world came into being. However, He was fashioned incorruptible from the Virgin. This same only-begotten Word of the Father, who was incarnate by the holy Virgin, was silent for thirty years ; but after that He was baptized by John in the river Jordan. And as He went up out of the water, the heaven was opened to Him, and the

---

"For if," continues Eustratius, "God had simply struck down the devil with His heavenly might, as He might have done, but as I cannot, then He would have enabled the devil to explain his defeat by saying, 'I conquered man, and was conquered by God.'" καὶ εὐαπολόγητος ἂν ὑπῆρχεν. The devil is assumed to be too stupid to penetrate the divine disguise.

[1] Prov. viii. 22 seq.

Holy Spirit descended in the visible form of a dove upon Him; and the Father from on high bore witness to His body that could be seen, saying: 'He is My beloved Son, in whom I am well pleased.' This John saw and marvelled, and hesitated to baptize Him; but the Lord said to him: 'Grant this now, for thus it is meet that we should fulfil all righteousness.' As the sinless John, son of the high priest Zachariah, bore witness to Christ, and said: 'Behold, Christ, the Lamb of God, who taketh away the sins of the world.' For He was named Jesus from His birth, whom the angel heralded to Mary, but Christ from the anointing of the Holy Spirit, which came down into the Jordan in the likeness of a dove. And after this, He was tempted by Satan, but vanquished the tempter in a threefold manner; for He was for forty days without food, and the God who was united and joined in Him with man, enabled the man to triumph over vain glory and pride, and avarice and love of wealth. He walked among us yet another three years, and preached the good tidings of the kingdom of heaven. On the blind He bestowed sight, the lame He made to walk, the lepers He cleansed, demons He cast out, the legion He gave to the deep sea, the dead He raised, and healed all other pains and diseases; and many other works of power and greatness He wrought. But they did not receive Him, neither did they believe in Him, as saith the holy evangelist John, namely: 'He came to His own, but His own received

Him not,' and in all ways mankind went out after nothing and found nothing.

"But our Lord Jesus Christ for this reason came to suffer, in order that He might break the power of Satan. Sitting upon a young ass, He entered into Jerusalem, after He had summoned from the grave, where he had lain for four days, His loved Lazarus. He preached beforehand the destruction of hell, and therefore also the young men of the Jews went before Him with branches of palm and sang: 'Hosanna in the highest, blessing to the son of David, peace upon earth and glory in the highest." And He, even before this, had upon Mount Tabor, given a foretype of the mystery of His resurrection, with the testimony of Moses and Elias. And He came to Jerusalem on the great day of the Passover, an old and lawful festival, and on that day He also washed the feet of the disciples, and made them sharers of the holy mystery, and dispensed to His disciples His body and His blood. And having come to the cross, He was nailed upon it by the lawless Jews, and confirmed the word of the prophets who foretold concerning Him in their preachings. But at His crucifixion the sun was darkened and the rocks were riven, the earth was shaken, and the veil of the temple rent in twain. And at the same hour in which Adam went forth from the garden, in that same hour He gave the robber entrance into the garden, saying to him: 'This day shalt thou be with Me in the garden.' He went down into hell alone, but went forth thence with a great multitude; He loosed them that were bound by Satan, but him He bound in darkness with bonds that shall never be loosed, and He brought to light the treasures of darkness. He rose from the dead on the third day. With the same incorruptible body He ascended into heaven, and with the same body He sat down on the right hand of the Father; and He cometh with the same body to judge all creatures.[1]

"But then, O my brethren, those who were taken in madness were miserable; but now, by means of the cross of Christ, they have been raised to ineffable glory. But he who shall deny Him before men, is given over into the hands of hell. But think ye not that they are few who believe in Christ, but many those who worship the work of men's hands; for I hope in our Lord Jesus Christ that this faith of ours will be so multiplied, that it will be rather spread abundantly

---

[1] All the extra-canonical details in the above are omitted by the metaphrast.

For the binding of Satan cp. the Descensus Christi, pars II. ch. viii. (xxiv.) : Et Ecce dominus Iesus Christus . . . catenam suis deportans manibus Satan cum collo ligauit, et iterum a tergo ei religans manus resupinum eum elisit in Tartarum et cet.

I cannot find in any apocryph the detail that the crucified thief entered Paradise at the very hour in which Adam left Paradise. The entry of the thief into Paradise is described in the Descensus Christi. These legends are all to be found in the Testaments of the Patriarchs (Test. Levi, ιη'): καίγε αὐτὸς ἀνοίξει τὰς θύρας τοῦ παραδείσου, καὶ στήσει τὴν ἀπειλοῦσαν ῥομφαίαν κατὰ τοῦ Ἀδάμ, καὶ δώσει τοῖς ἁγίοις φαγεῖν ἐκ τοῦ ξύλου τῆς ζωῆς, καὶ πνεῦμα ἁγιωσύνης ἔσται ἐπ' αὐτοῖς. Καὶ ὁ Βελίαρ δεθήσεται ὑπ' αὐτοῦ, καὶ δώσει ἐξουσίαν τοῖς τέκνοις αὐτοῦ τοῦ πατεῖν ἐπὶ τὰ πονηρὰ πνεύματα.

Acts of S. Callistratus. 311

over the face of the whole earth. But do ye, my friends, stand strong in this faith, which I have taught unto you, with candid heart, as to genuine brethren."

X. And when the saint had finished the summary of his argument, Heladorus[1] rose and asked him and said: " I pray thee, my lord Callistratus, when a man dies, what becomes of his soul, where does it go, or what does it do, or where does it dwell, whether in torment or in repose?" The holy Callistratus said: "As Christ rose from the dead, so also must we rise and stand before His judgment-seat; and each of us will have to give answer according to his works, according as they are good or bad, in the day of reckoning. But the garden is made ready for them that are worthy of Him. Now when his last day comes upon a man, angels come to him; and when they see the soul of the man, if he is just, they rejoice, and they take it with psalms and hymns, and carry it eastwards,[2] and they carry it past six

---

[1] Heliodorus in the Greek.
[2] For the belief that the soul went eastwards cp. Eusebius, *H. E.*, 430. 19, where a martyr puzzles the judge Firmilianus by saying that he was going to the heavenly Jerusalem, the country of the pious (πατρίδα τῶν εὐσεβῶν) and that this κεῖσθαι πρὸς αὐταῖς ἀνατολαῖς καὶ πρὸς ἀνίσχοντι ἡλίῳ.

For the belief in the seven heavens consult the Testamentum Levi, chs. β' and γ' and the Vision or Ascension of Isaiah, passim. In Origen, *de Principiis*, 83, we read: Denique etiam Baruch Prophetæ librum in assertionis huius testimonium vocant, quod ibi de septem mundis vel cœlis evidentius indicatur.

Origen also seems to have believed in an intermediate stage of existence or purgatory, as an interval between death and day of judgment such as Callistratus taught. In it the soul is not yet rejoined with the body, and

spheres (or circles), past the storehouse of hail and snow, past the streams of rain, and past all the regions of storehouses, and past the spirits of wickedness which there are in the air; and they carry it in to the seventh circle, and set it down full opposite the glory of God, and he adores God in the seventh circle below the firmament; according to the preacher, who saith, that the flesh shall return to the dust whence it was created, but the spirit shall return to God who gave it. And the spirit, having returned by means of the providence of the angels of God, beholds the garden and the reward apportioned to its good works, and is glad with the hope of what is to come. However, without the body the spirit cannot receive its reward; but remains there and glorifies God in silence. But the places of their abode are below the firmament, above the sun. For when Christ died and descended into hell, He veiled His Godhead with His spirit; for His Godhead remained inseparable and undivided of body and of soul. But when He had robbed hell, and liberated the spirits which were in prison, and given them over into the hands of the Father, then He gave them a dwelling-place in the air, below the firmament, in a place which was put

---

is escorted by angels who "leád the soul" (ψυχαγωγοῖς). Cp. Origen, *de Princ.*, 105 : Ut etiamsi quis ex hac vita minus eruditus abierit, probabilia tamen opera detulerit, instrui poterit in illa Jerusalem sanctorum civitate, id est, edoceri et informari, et effici lapis vivus. See E. R. Redepenning's note on the above passage, and for the transition to this class of belief from the earlier millenarism cp. Martineau's *Seat of Authority in Religion*, p. 570.

high and lifted out of reach of the power of Satan, and of the wickedness of the air. For the evil powers of the air fight for our spirits, and for that reason our spirits are transmitted by means of angels and issue forth into regions high above the dwelling-place of the devil and of his host. But just as a good spirit is conveyed by means of good angels, so also an evil spirit is conveyed by means of bad angels; not that angels are bad, for the devil alone is bad, and the demons who comply with his bad wishes; but because men are evil doers and because of their impure courses, their angels also are in name called bad. Thus let us understand it: one soldier is sent by the king, to praise and do honour to the good and virtuous, but to slay and torment the evil-doers. Now in one and the same way, the angels of some men are good and of others bad, because of their respective actions. Thus the angels are good and fond of man, and minister to the complete fulfilment of the will of the benevolent God, being holy and pure. When therefore the sinner dies, the angel takes this spirit, and bears it away in sorrow and grief, being ashamed of its works. Then at once there come upon him the demons of the air dancing, and they raise a war, and they name him as their own, and they clap their hands and leap. But the angel drives them back and murmurs fiercely against them, and so passes by them, and brings the spirit up to the seventh circle, underneath the water-borne firmament, and stations it there full opposite the glory of God, and then does homage in reverence before God. As it is written also in the psalm: 'All the races which Thou hast made shall come and prostrate themselves before Thee, they shall make Thy name glorious for ever.' And by means of the angel the spirit beholds the place of judgment and the reward of his works, and he is grieved and perpetually laments the destruction of his soul. For when the spirit is separated from the body, it comprehends and beholds the future more clearly than if it were before its eyes. But until the judgment comes, the spirits receive not their rewards nor their torments; however, they know from their own deeds what they are going to receive, and apart by themselves they rejoice or sorrow, and with still voice they praise God in security. But the just are filled with desire to see the day of requital; but the sinners look at the deeds they have done, and they sorrow and lament, knowing full well what torments they are going to suffer in the day of judgment. But by the Divine goodness, patience and rest is bestowed on both sides until the day of reckoning. But to the Christians there is great hope even after death; for if there are anywhere parents or brothers, or children, or relatives, or anyone at all who is a Christian and who is compassionate, and who offers up prayers or consecrates oblations and alms, so gaining the intercession of the saints, they can thus consign to this great place of rest him who looked forward to torments. For God is propitiated and remits the sins of them who have fallen asleep by means of the offering of Christ, which is sacrificed upon the holy table for the salvation and for the life and for the pardon of the living and the dead. But, my brethren, deceive yourselves not in your hearts, nor suppose that at the time of death the just man has received the rewards of his righteousness, or the sinner the sentence of his requital. For how can this be? For our bodies remain here, but the soul passes alone and by itself into the afore-mentioned place. For if there be no resurrection, and if our bodies do not rise from the tombs and stand before the awful tribunal, and receive each according to its works, how would it be possible for the sinful flesh to be destroyed, and the soul alone judged. Perhaps a man might string together reasons, putting upon the body the harm of a man's sins. The just therefore cannot receive their reward, nor the sinners their torments, until the coming of that day, concerning which Paul saith: 'The trumpet sounds and the dead shall arise in the twinkling of an eye.' For, as Christ died, so He also arose with the same incorruptible body; not that it became incorruptible after His resurrection, God forbid! for rather He put on Himself incorruptible from the Virgin, the sinful body of Adam, and absorbed and sunk its corruptibility in His Godhead, and with the same body thus made Divine, He died and rose. Even as my great-grandfather Okorus accurately heard and learnt in Jerusalem from the holy apostles, who, with their own eyes, saw Him upon the Cross, saw Him laid in the sepulchre, saw Him risen from the sepulchre; and when He came to His disciples in the upper chamber, wherein He made good the deficiencies in faith of Thomas, my great-grandfather Okorus saw him; and when the Holy Spirit descended on the day of Pentecost he believed and was baptized by the holy apostles. I therefore learnt this from his tradition, and from the holy evangelists, and from the apostles, and from the prophets before them. But that which I teach you I say truly in Christ, and lie not, that as Christ rose, so we shall rise with the same body incorruptible, and shall stand before the tribunal of Christ, and shall enjoy the fruits of our respective works, according to the just and impartial award of Christ.

"But this also I teach you, brethren, that when they rise from the dead, after that there is not any expiation or remission of their sins, nor any intercession, for the door of the kingdom is shut to them who have not entered here in the body. As therefore ye henceforth know all this, my brethren, be ye zealous in good works, and hasten to enter before the door be shut."[1]

XI. Domitianus made answer and said: "What dost thou say, my lord Callistratus? Surely, then, those who sin are not judged at all in this world, and receive not here their requital, but for

---

[1] The entire § X is in the metaphrast compressed into a section of twenty lines.

all the day of judgment is reserved to the other world?" The holy Callistratus replied : "God is long-suffering and very compassionate, He desires not the death of a sinner who repents of his sins, and who is conscious of his transgressions, and acknowledges them, and falls down in prayer before God, lamenting, and saying from the bottom of his heart : "O God, expiate my sins," and who thenceforth does righteousness. Though his sins be many, he is able to wipe them out by means of prayer, and fasting, and almsgiving ; to him God remits them, God who is benign and not revengeful, and who desires that every man should live, and come to a knowledge of the truth. But if any one pollute himself for a long time in many sins, and blaspheme God, if he shall rob and stint the orphans, and oppress the widows, swearing falsely, and ridiculing them, adding extortion to extortion, and usury to usury, and if he grow rich out of his injustice, and treasure up his own damnation ; if, in addition to all this, he also should soil himself with adultery, and with the abomination of all kinds of fornication, then the benevolent God looks upon him to see if he lingers and tarries over his evildoings, and after that He will apportion unto him in remembrance of his evil deeds, when he can no more be turned away from evil. And the life of such a one shall be destroyed, and his goods shall be plundered, and his body shall be destroyed, and taking with him his evil deeds alone, he shall pass miserably out of life, unburied in his own land ; his orphans shall be plundered, and his life shall leave no trace of itself. This is the portion of them that are puffed up by their riches which they have gained by injustice, and who have not walked according to the commandments of God. But if a man be poor, and walk in the like evil path, he is troubled with miserable woes, being full of sin during his life, and the might of God is in no way a help to him; for God hates evil-doers, who return not from their evil paths. And such a one is found to have lost his riches, and to have forfeited all the good things of life, and even his bare wants of the body are not supplied to him. And if his life be prolonged, it is still more pitiable; and unless he devote himself to prayer, and do righteousness, he is miserable beyond all men. For straightway there come upon him tribulations and afflictions from which there is no escape, anguish that is intolerable, and all the means of life fail him. And frenzy, and care, and many other troubles befall him, and consume his flesh like a viper, and like a basilisk suck his blood; and he is the prey of detestable woes, leprosy and scurvy, and he shall desire only his daily fare, and shall not find it, and he shall be hateful and despicable to all, a laughing-stock, and source of scoffing, an eyesore, and a butt to all beholders; ambushes shall come on him whence he knows not, and he shall be smitten with unforeseen accidents. Yea, and many such take their own lives, and mercilessly massacre themselves on account of the woes that they cannot endure, and their memory is miserably effaced from their life. So is it for the poor man who soils himself with many sins, and regards not the commandments of God. But there is also another fate which may befall both classes, both those who live in evil doing and are rich, and also those who are poor. For God is merciful, and may grant them on earth long spell of health, and to suit His ends, even bestows unbroken prosperity in all directions; bodily health, fruitfulness of lands, fecundity of animals, respect and honour from great and little alike, life altogether without care, and long and glorious, an old age of pomp and honour, glory and praise, and a blessed death, and a great and famous funeral. And yet one who lives such a life as this, and does not walk in the commandments of God, which are light, and give light to the eyes; who rather contaminates himself all his time with savagery and cruel actions, and does not thank God nor glorify Him with good actions, nor recognise Him as the Giver of good things, fearing Him as is right and lawful to do, but who is ungrateful to God, and when he has good things vouchsafed to him by God's grace, reckons it to his own merit; let not such a one have any rejoicing, for all the more will he be tortured in Gehenna, like the rich man who heard Abraham say, 'Thou hast received thy good things in thy lifetime, and a great gulf is between me and thee.' But David also says, 'Requite to my neighbours sevenfold into their bosoms their insults with which they have insulted Thee, O Lord;' and again, 'I saw the impious man growing up and overtopping, all like the cedars of Lebanon; I passed, and he was not; I sought, and his place was not found;' for their end is seen in the bottom of the pit, according to Him who talks in parables. This is the lot of every sinful man, whether he be rich or poor, who enjoys the good things of God, but doeth not His will. And, moreover, because of them there is tribulation upon the earth, either the onset of enemies, or sudden death, or famine, or hail, or any other of the afflictions on account of sin which befall all men at once, like the flood or the fire which consumed Sodom. For when a sinner inflames the wrath of his Creator, then the Divine anger descends upon him, like an involuntary repentance of sin.

"And now, since ye are new in the faith, and have not read the holy books; for it is written in the Book of Kings about Achab and Jezebel, because they inflamed the wrath of God, the Creator of all, by their idolatry, and extortions, and robbery; they slew His prophets, they destroyed His altars; one prophet alone was left, Elias by name, who was consumed with the zeal of the Almighty God, and he, by his prayers, curbed the clouds that they should not give rain, and hindered the dew from heaven, that no shoot might rise from earth according to its nature; for the word went forth from Elias, and shut up and closed the boundaries of the eternal, so that for three years and six months there was no rain, neither did the fountains play and spring up, because they were dried up. All creeping things also dwindled, the four-footed animals and the birds, for the Lord was wroth; and all blossoms and plants which were upon the earth were dried up. All the beauty of the earth was consumed, the earth was rent asunder to its depths by the drought, and all the kings and mighty ones of the earth staggered. The heavens rang like brass, and the earth roared like a heifer, and all living things repented against their wills because of the exceeding famine. But the word of a single prophet had command over all this, who built an altar to God, and brought down water from heaven, and cut off the false prophets of Baal, eight hundred and fifty men, and so appeased God's wrath, that after that the door of His pity was opened upon the earth. Such were the afflictions which happened because of the sins of men; for they are chastised, even though they do not understand; for God acquits not the impious, because He is just and powerful. But He does not destroy them at once, because He is pitiful and long-suffering, and He is indulgent to the wickedness of men, in the hope that they will return to repentance. But if they continue in their sins without turning, He destroys them utterly, as He did Rehoboam and Bassa and Achab, the princes of Israel, who with their families were effaced with dishonour. But those who turn from their wickedness and repent, to them He vouchsafes remission of their sins, as He did to Manasses, King of Judea, and to Nebuchadnezzar, ruler of Babylon. But him who insults God, God destroys; as He did Senecherim and Antiochus, the kings of Assyria. Thus, then, it is that God chastises some of us here, and some of us in the future. Therefore, my brethren, let us follow after virtue, in order that we may be glorified with Christ, both here and in the future."

Then Evarestos made answer, and said: "My lord Callistratus, is it according to the number of days that God terminates the world, or is it according to chance? Otherwise, how is it that men die unexpectedly, either by hunger or thirst, or on the sea, or in rivers, or in the fire, or by any other of the accidents which may bring about dissolution of the lives of men; or it may be that one comrade slays another, or a man dies by the agency of a demon, or suddenly? But when a man dies either in his youth or in old age, is the tale of his days fulfilled? And so, too, with those who fall in war, for, behold, many of our host fell in the war with the Persians?" The holy Callistratus said: "Learn ye also concerning this, my brethren; for at the beginning God said to Adam, 'Dust thou wast, and to dust shalt thou return.' And at the same time the edict of death went forth upon men from their birth, even to their old age. And not only is death ordained unerringly by nature, like other things that are weighed and calculated; but the knowledge thereof is in the hands of God alone, who is the Lord of life and death. Not that it is ordained that all should reach to old age; for many a time a father has

Acts of S. Callistratus. 323

died in his youth, but his sons have reached an extreme old age; and the sons have died in youth before their fathers, as happened in the very beginning, for Adam lived nine hundred and thirty years, and Seth, his son, nine hundred and twelve, but his other son had not yet arrived at even a hundred years when he was slain by Cain his brother. But death is appointed for all; not but what there are some who are given a long life because of their just works, while to others God shortens life because of the excess of their sins; and in the case of some He pities their tears, and adds to their life, as in the case of Hezekiah, and for others He lengthens life because of the prayers of widows and orphans, and sometimes parents because of the tears of children, and children because of their parent's tears, have been brought back from death. And there are many requirements[1] of the world, on account of which He adds to the life of men, both adds and takes away. But the blow of death also falls upon men because of their sins, sometimes by the sword, sometimes by fire, sometimes by water, or in some other way of those in which the blow can fall. But a man may contend against us in argument, and say that he will not die because his day has not yet come, and for that reason he will boldly venture to go upon the sea when it is stormy, or into a river that is in flood, or on a snowy mountain, or

---

[1] There is something wrong here with the Arm. text, of which I make sense as I can.

on a scorched plain, or among wild beasts, or he will take harmful food ; in such cases death comes not as a surprise and ambush, nor is it accidental, but it is a wilful dissolution of life, and they who so act are reckoned with those who die by their own sin. But there are also other forms of death, from the temperament of the body, from cold, or bile, or blood, or some other of the accidents by which life is dissolved. But as I said before, death is appointed to that life in man which he shares with the plants, and therefore, the Lord said, ' Pray that ye be not led into temptation,' for ye must at all times pray diligently, and say, ' Lead us not into temptation, but deliver us from the Evil One.' For many are the snares which are set by the Evil One ; for throughout our lives he lays deadly ambushes in rivers, in fields, in mountains, on the plains, in the fire, at the hands of a wicked man, by a man's own act in strangling himself through his irascibility, as in the case of Judas and Achitophel ; and in many other ways he lays deadly snares, and death is fated for him that is caught. But we must pray to God continually to preserve us from evil accidents, and in His grace bestow upon us a good end. There are also other forms of death, as when a stone should fall from a wall through ignorance, or the branch of a tree may fall upon us, or we may be butted by an ox, or thrown from a horse, or we may tread upon a sword, or meet a wild beast, or be bitten by a viper ; all these are evil accidents, and they occur because man is puffed up with his strength, so that God remits His aid, and then man becomes ridiculous, and falls into all kinds of deadly snares; wherefore it is necessary that ye should be watchful, and pray to God, for he who prays to God with all his heart, to him the very snares become a source of good, as Paul said:[1] 'He will with the temptation also make the way of escape, in order that we may be able to suffer it.' But there is not allotted to Satan any foreknowledge, but he knows very little of the time of man's death. However, he abides continually in the evil man, and if the pity of God did not prevent him in the case of each man, he would destroy all men together. And on account of this the Lord says, 'Be careful, lest your hearts be weighed down with dissoluteness, or drunkenness, or worldly cares, and that day come suddenly upon you, as an ambush is sprung upon all men who dwell over the whole face of the earth. Be watchful, and for ever make prayers, that ye be accounted worthy to escape from all that which is to come, and to stand before the Son of man;' but death in war is open and not secret, for every one who takes a sword in his hand and goes into war, either slays another or himself dies; but if he survives and is left whole, the providence of God has intervened. All the time of man's life, therefore, is destined, but all sorts of snares beset him during his life. But if a man humble himself, and prostrate himself before God, he is delivered from

---

[1] 1 Cor. x. 13.

them ; for although even his body be exacted of him, yet his spirit goes rejoicing to its Creator, in the way in which I before described.

"But let us, brethren, stand firm, for I trust in Christ, that by His hope we shall all overcome the machinations of the devil, and receive the emblem of victory. Listen to me, my brethren, in case it befall me to die before you. Forasmuch as ye are intimate with me, I would have you know that many a time Satan fought with me in my youth ; but I hope in my Lord that now he will be worsted by me ; for much alms have I given, and was proud as if I had won the whole realm. For when a man gives alms, he saith not, 'I have proffered but of that which God gave me,' but rather, is puffed up, as if he had given what was his own, and declareth that he hath done something great. Nay, rather have we received the command to minister to the poor, and we ought so to give, that what our left hand doeth our right should not know. That is to say, let not the devil on the left hand steal away the grace that the better hand wrought. But do ye, my dear friends, be on your guard, because all this is of the devil, for he opposeth everything that is good. For many a time hath he been able to filch away my mind, when he saw that I was praying with tears to God my Helper. At such times he would distract my mind, and would agitate all kinds of earthly cares, and intrude them on my soul, and would prompt me to gape and yawn. But I spurned him, and thus the adversary was not able to steal me away. For God takes account, not only of those who sing hymns and pray in the churches, but also of the very steps and foot-prints of those who, with sincere faith, enter into the temple of God. And whatsoever a man wishes to ask he knows beforehand, and vouchsafes the prayers which are according to His will ; and wheresoever there is a man who bends the knee, and prays with his whole heart, unto him God hearkens, and will give all that he needs with free grace. For if thou sayest, 'Have pity upon me, O God,' He knows thy meaning, and understands that which thy words represent. Therefore, dear friends, it profits the adversary nothing when he desires to snatch away our understanding, and intrudes all sorts of thoughts among our prayers. But who is there of men who knows not this : that man is prompt to sin, and wearies not therefrom, and is eager to transgress ; but in prayer he is weak and idle, and remiss, and is faint and drowsy, and thinks that all this is a natural affection, instead of being an invention of the devil ? But understand this, my brethren, that all these things are inspirations of the evil one, from which we must flee, and with faithful diligence, glorify God, who made the heavens and earth, the sea, and all that is in them."

Lysimachus made answer, and said : "My lord Callistratus, did God really make the heavens and earth, the sea, the moon, and the stars ? "

The holy Callistratus said : "Did I not tell you that, even while ye learn or pray, ye slumber ? Did ye not apprehend what I said before, in answer to the question of our brother Bemarchus? But come, do you tell me, then; How did you learn about them from your fathers? or how did ye reverence those things made with hands which ye used to call God?" They made answer all at once, and said: "We learnt thus, that the heavens came into being of themselves, and so also the earth, and that the sun is the god of gods, because he gives light, and that the stars are images of the gods."

The holy Callistratus replied, "Learn also concerning this, my brethren, lest Satan trip you up. All this world which is visible is the creation of the heavenly and single and beginningless and increate Holy Trinity, and of the single Godhead. For it founded heaven and earth. It drew the heavens across like a tent, and stretched them out like curtains, and by its word, fixed and made sure the watery firmament, and vaulted it, so that it was round like a ball; and established the earth above the waters, and the waters upon nothing at all. And the earth trembles and is afraid at His presence; for He made rifts in the firmament and above the illimitable expanse of the torrents of ocean, which has under itself all the elements, the upper and the nether ones. Likewise He made also the stars, and set them in the vault-like firmament to illumine the darkness. But the sun, by a law which never ceases, runs his courses; for he goes forth from the region of the portals of the east, and he travels along the south, revolving like a wheel, till he comes home to the west, and there he enters the portals of the west ; and then forthwith darkness covers all things as the night is drawn over them.

"But when he has entered, and sunk below the vast prison bars of the south, in the nether firmament, he runs in the direction of the right hand, until he reaches once more the portals of the East, and masks the darkness with his light. So, also, the moon fulfils her courses according to the same law, waxing and waning as she approaches the sun, or goes away therefrom in her period of thirty days. And how can your teaching be true that the sun is God? If he were God, how would he obey the law, and be enslaved by it? How could he suffer, and be subject to affections, as when he is sometimes covered with clouds, and sometimes darkened? In the same way, also, the moon and the stars likewise fulfil their courses according to command. In one and the same manner, they all leap up from the east, and they travel to the setting of the sun, and they return to the right of the north without entering the gates of heaven ; but they revolve themselves in the firmament, and fulfil their entire courses by day according to the order of each of them, until they reach the east by way of the south, wherein are seen by us the vestiges of their paths. But many concoct fables, and say that the heavens revolve, whose words are vain ; for the firmament is immovable. But many of the stars run in a circular path, and some of them are fixed, and have the rest of the stars to turn round themselves ; as is the case with the northern stars, which are, by some, called Arcturus, but by some Hephtasagiron; but by the farmers, it is called the Wain, and by sailors Bazmojth, for these stars do not alter from their path, but revolve where they are. But other stars have a period of their own, in which they fulfil their courses, as, for example, Aruseak (Venus) and Mazarôth, and the Alôsounk (? the Pleiades), and Haik (Orion). Each of these obeys its period, according as it was appointed to do; as it was also written: 'The moon and the stars which Thou hast established.' But the prophet, in speaking of the firmament, does not mean that it is immovable, and in that sense speak of its immovability; but he alludes to its strength, because they are subservient to an invincible and unerring command before their God. And now, my brethren, cast away the vain preaching; for God made all creation, but He honoured man alone with His image, and made everything subservient under his feet. And it is meet for man to know Him, because, for his sake, all creation was established out of nothing; for his sake the sun fulfils his unerring command, and the moon her course, according to her command; for his sake all the most ancient stars were set in order, which men of vain understanding called gods, giving them the names of animals, as for example, of the Ram and the Bull, of Capricorn, and the Virgin, and the Yoke, and so forth. And they go on thence to conduct researches of a kind, and profess to derive from them seasons of plenty and famines; and they also declare that the fortunes and the terms of men's lives are ordered by them, in order that they may deceive men with empty words. But these constellations are appointed to make clear to us the various seasons, and to indicate to sailors their path over the sea. For man's sake were made the rivers and the mountains, and every blade of grass, and every plant. By the word were they manifested upon the earth; but man alone, on the earth, was honoured with the image of the immortal and benevolent God who made him. But he yielded to deceit, and fell into sin, and became mortal, and was ensnared by the outward appearance of the evil one, and by his false and empty flattery. And now, brethren, it is a great task all over this earth for man to save his soul. But let us labour to receive the token of victory in war, wherever there is contention with the devil, and let us boldly defy the evil warrior, and let us be found to have conquered his lawless pride, and he shall be worsted by us, and fall, never to rise again; but we, having escaped from the delusions of life, shall receive the crown of undying glory from our Lord and Saviour Jesus Christ, to whom is glory for ever and ever, Amen."[1]

XII. And when he had said this, he was silent for a while, for it was late even-tide; and the whole night long he remained in prayer until the dawn. But there was a certain scribe of the

---

[1] The metaphrast abridges § XI. into 40 lines.

law-court, who was near to the prison, and he listened to the discourse of the holy Callistratus, and wrote it down in shorthand on paper, and gave it to us; and we set in order with all accuracy the record and outline of his thought.[1] But at dawn the captain Presentinus took his seat upon the throne of judgment, and commanded them to be brought before him. And they brought them into the great court in which were set up many images of idols. There were mustered together not only the captains of the force, but the whole number of the soldiers. The captain said: "How is it, O Callistratus, hast thou schooled thyself and those of the king's soldiers that were inveigled by thee? Hast thou instructed them to sacrifice to the gods, and save themselves from the torture?" The holy Callistratus said: "As to myself, I have given this answer and adhere to it, that nothing shall persuade me to forsake Christ my hope; but as to them, they are themselves grown up, and of full age, so ask them." The captain said: "What do ye say, who have been deceived, and have assented to this babbler?" They made answer and said: "O unworthy man, and shameless, if thou wilt still keep us on the list of thy band, we shall not resist; but as to our worship and religion, we believe in the King of heaven and earth, in the God of all, and in His Offspring Jesus Christ, and in the Holy Spirit, for He is

---

[1] The metaphrast omits these details and says nothing of the scribe.

God in three persons, a Trinity, but one Godhead, and one power; without flaw is He, and full of wisdom, which is and was and abides for ever, as our teacher Callistratus taught us." XIII. But the captain commanded that they should be scourged with green switches; and after the scourging he ordered them to be bound hand and foot and dragged all of them to the edge of a lake,[1] and said to them: "Sacrifice to the gods, for if not, ye shall be drowned in the waters." But they said: "We believe in the true God, do thou what thou wilt." But when they were about to be thrown into the great lake, which was called Oceanus, the holy Callistratus fell to praying and said: "God eternal, who art unapproachable and all-powerful, who didst establish the heavens by Thy might to be Thy throne immoveable for ever, and the earth to be Thy footstool; look upon this Thy flock, and be among us and save us from destruction, and grant that these waters be unto these men for the baptism of regeneration. Make them worthy to be washed with the eternal and pure baptism, unto the casting away of the vanity of the old man, and unto their participation with those who labour for Thy cross. Grant us, O Lord, to come unto Thy treasuries, by means of this washing, in order that we may be fellow-workers with Thy Holy Spirit in these waters. For glorious is the name of Father, Son, and Holy Spirit, for ever and ever. Amen."

---

[1] Gk. has: κολυμβήθραν ὠκεανὸν οὕτω καλούμενον.

But when they had said with one accord Amen, they threw them bound into the water; and in the same moment the bonds of the saints were loosed, and they came to the top of the water and passed on to dry land, resplendent with the grace of the Holy Spirit. And as they came out of the water, there went forth a voice from Heaven saying: "Be of good cheer, My loved ones, for I am with you; be ye glad, for, behold, I have made ready for you a place in My kingdom. Rejoice, for I have written your names in My record in the Book of Life." And there was terrible thunder and a great earthquake, so that the images of the idols fell down and were broken. But when we saw[1] the light which shot forth over the heads of the saints, and heard the blissful voice along with the earthquake and the breaking of the idols, we believed,—we, the soldiers, a hundred and five of us. Then the lawless Presentinus was taken with great fear, and he ordered them to be led into prison. And when they had entered into prison, the holy Callistratus again taught them, and said: "Men and brothers, behold the Lord hath summoned us to Himself. For I received baptism from my very youth, but now He has called you also; arise, therefore, and let us pray." So they raised their hands and he began to say: "Lord, Lord, how wonderful is Thy name for ever, who, before all things didst with Thy infinite word establish all things; who

---

[1] The metaphrast has "They saw," depriving this part of the narrative of its personal character.

Acts of S. Callistratus. 335

art the Lord of indestructible and invisible and flawless treasures ; preserve this Thy flock, and deliver it from the mouth of the lion, and lead it into eternal salvation. And make us worthy to die in Thy confession. Save us spotless and pure from the sin-loving life. Bring us in at the narrow gate into the royal temple, that we may praise with holy and unresting voices the all-blessed name of Father, Son, and Holy Spirit, now and for ever."

XIV. But the lawless and impious captain, Presentinus, took counsel with a vir ducenarius,[1] and sent into prison and beheaded them, for the soldiers of Christ were fifty in number. And the saints died in the month Hori,[2] on the twenty-seventh day thereof. But we soldiers who believed when we saw the vision of the wonders, and were baptized in the name of Father, Son, and Holy Spirit, we came privily in the night, and we took up the relics of the saints, and laid them in a proper place.[3] Wherefore the Lord

---

[1] The metaph. has Ὑίρῳ Δουκιναρίῳ *i.e.* Uiro Ducenario. Ducange (*Glossarium*) explains Ducenarius thus : Dicitur qui duobus militum centuriis præerat, sicut uni centurio. The Armenian has "vir pholarius" which I cannot explain. I have therefore followed the Greek text.

[2] The metaph. has September.

[3] The conclusion runs thus in the metaphrast : "And they raised a temple to them, with which few can compete in splendour ; and it stands in the middle of Rome, the most queenly of cities. But they also found a paper (χάρτην) in the prison, on which the teaching and forthshadowings of the martyr Callistratus were written down. And after his death Marinus also was martyred, a man of great eminence and fame and culture. He shewed the most manly fortitude to the end, to the glory of our Lord Jesus' Christ, whom befits all glory, praise and worship, now and ever, world without end. Amen."

made us worthy to establish His church in Rome in the name of the saints, and we built in the name of the holy Callistratus a place of expiation for sinners, and a meeting-house of union for angels and men ; for the glory and worship of the All-holy Trinity, Father, Son and Holy Spirit.

ACTS OF S. DEMETRIUS.

INTRODUCTION.

I HAVE chosen this piece as the last of my collection, rather on account of the interesting letter of the Bishop of Thessalonica which accompanies it in the Armenian text, than for its own merits. Not that it is without a certain interest of its own; for it **Local colour in these Acts.** has a good deal of local colour, and the outline of the teaching of Demetrius which it contains has about it a noble simplicity and directness which reminds us of the Apology of Apollonius. The date of the saint's martyrdom cannot be earlier than 305 A.D.; and it is therefore a matter for surprise that the Acts contain no reference to the doctrine of the Trinity, as is usual in martyrdoms of this date. Still more remarkable is it, that in the brief outline of the saint's dogmatic teaching, Christ is merely said to have been born in an ineffable manner without reference being made to the **Primitive character of their Christian teaching.** Virgin Mother. Such a silence is rare except in Acts of the second century. The combat in the arena between the stripling Nestorius and the giant gladiator Lyæos may have been modelled on the legend of David and Goliath; and the prophecy ascribed to Demetrius is sufficiently quaint, as coming from the lips of a saint. The story is perhaps an allegory destined to convey to the reader the disgust with which the gladiatorial games inspired the Christians, one of the first-fruits of whose triumph under Constantine was the abolition of these degrading spectacles. The learned Tillemont, however, was so shocked at the idea of a saint inciting his pupil to do combat with a gladiator, that (*Monument. Eccles.*, p. 639) he argues the incident to be an invention later than the ninth century. The Bollandist editor (*Acta SS.*, ad diem 8 Octobris Tom iv.) admits it to be an invention, but points out that a history of the saint at least as old as the eighth century and probably of the seventh already contains it.

There is a slight historical error in the appended letter of the Bishop of Thessalonica, in which the Emperor Justinian is spoken of as the father of the Emperor Maurice. For the latter was no kinsman of Justinian, and only began to reign in 582, seventeen years after Justinian's death. The phrase however may be honorific only, and mean nothing more than "your majesty's predecessor." It is in any case not enough to discredit the authenticity of the letter. In an age which set so much store by the relics of saints, no one would have invented so dignified a rebuke to a relic-mongering emperor; much less have inserted it in the history of a martyred saint. We do not know who is the writer who thus inserts the letter of Eusebius in his narrative; nor can we be certain that the Acts of the martyr Demetrius which precede his narrative are from the same pen.

Their condemnation of relic-mongering.

In the Armenian martyrology the narrative of the miracles wrought through the dead saint is continued through two more chapters, which I have not thought it necessary to translate. These two chapters which I give do not recount anything later than the reign of the Emperor Maurice. It is therefore probable that the writer of the narratives lived either in his reign, which terminated in the year 612, or soon after, and that the entire narrative which is in the form of an address to the faithful, was composed early in the seventh century for delivery on the feast day of the saint. What is remarkable about it is the admission, that at that early date the true place of interment of any one of the many martyrs who had suffered under Diocletian in Thessalonica was unknown to any one, and the memory of them lost, with the sole exception of the saint Mamrinus.

Their date about 610 A.D.

Acts of S. Demetrius.

In Migne's *Patrologia Græca* (vol. 116) much space is allotted to the Acts of this saint, and the lengthy dissertation of Byæus is reprinted from the *Acta SS.* The Acts are found in two forms, namely, that of the metaphrast of the tenth century, and in an earlier recension by some anonymous writer, to whom in my notes I refer as Gk. Anon. The relations of the three forms of the Acts, viz., the Armenian, the Gk. Anon., and the metaphrast, are worth examining, for they present in a very striking way the power of growth inherent in a hagiological writing. Thus the Gk. Anon and the metaphrast contain the following miracles absent from the the Armenian :—

Genealogy of the texts of these Acts.

1. That of the scorpion (see note on § VI.).
2. The cure of Leontius (see note 3 on § XVI.).
3. The miraculous passage of Leontius over the Danube in the §§ added in the Greek forms.
4. Lupus and the royal ring. The Armenian quite ignores Lupus (see note 6 on § XIII).

Byæus thought that the Gk. Anon. made his recension in the seventh century, and that the metaphrast's form is a simple amplification of the same. This is certainly the case as regard nine-tenths of the metaphrast text ; but it is not the case all through, and in one passage (see note 2 on § XV.) it is the metaphrast and not the Gk. Anon. who retains the text which we find in the Armenian. A diligent comparison of the three texts reveals the same phenomenon elsewhere, but less markedly. We are thus precluded from supposing that the metaphrast used the Gk. Anon. and that alone as the basis of his form. He must have had a document which closely resembled it, and like it contained the miracles which the Armenian omits ; yet in some few points truer to the original document than is the Gk. Anon. The following diagram therefore brings before the eye the genealogical relations of the three forms :—

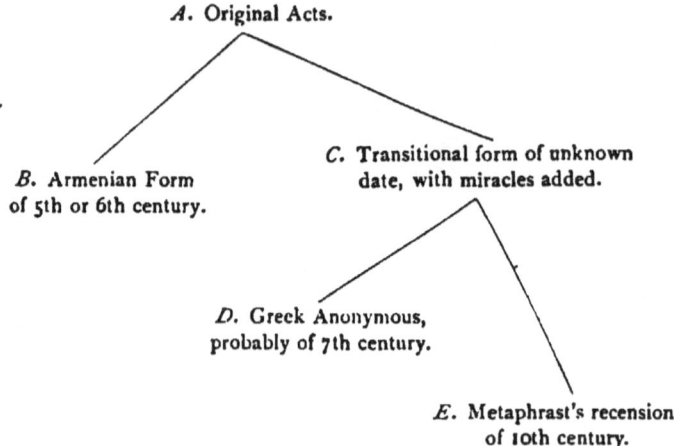

Of these *B* is by far the simplest and nearest to *A*. *C* is a hypothetical form necessary to explain the existence of *D* and *E*. I have not put *B* in the direct line of transmission because it omits some very probable details, such as that Lyæus was a Vandal by birth, which we find in *D* and *E*. The Armenian translator may easily have omitted such a point, as also certain topographical details which are contained in *D* and *E*, because they were not of a kind to interest or edify his countrymen.

S. DEMETRIUS.

I. At this time there was much wickedness in high places, and Maximianus the emperor, the enemy of God, was in the city of Thessalonica, where the ministers of religion were subjected to every kind of torture. For he was sunk in the depths of idolatry; so that he made strict search and enquiry after those who had embraced the religion of God, and imprisoned and tortured them. But of the Christians who were in the city, some took the advice of the wise Paul, and bowed their heads before the storm, and hid themselves for a season; but others were more courageous, and publicly avowed their faith in the middle of the crowded city. II. Of the latter, there was one whose name was Demetrius,[1] a brave and virtuous man, who had no fear of the death allotted by nature to us. He spurned the terrible threats of the Emperor, and openly avowed himself to be a Christian; and in and out of season with the greatest boldness he taught the saving Name, which he upheld in his own soul, to all who came near him, in accordance with apostolic com-

---

[1] According to the Gk. Anon. and metaphrast, Demetrius was ἐκ γένους τῶν περιδόξων, καὶ τῆς συγκλήτου βουλῆς ὑπάρχων, ἐσκέπτωρ τὸ πρῶτον στρατευσάμενος καὶ ἀνθύπατος γεγονὼς τῆς Ἑλλάδος, καὶ ὑπάτου ὡραίωνα ἔλαβεν ὑπὸ τοῦ βασιλέως Μαξιμιανοῦ.

mands. Now this saint was very learned in the divine scriptures; and would expound before all the life-giving mysteries which were hidden in them, and this, too, was part of his teaching— that it was his disobedience which caused the first man to go astray from the truth; wherefore also we became liable to death, and idolatry entered into the world. For this cause, also, the allwise Word, God, born in ineffable wise of God the Father, came into the world, having put on flesh;[1] and He shone forth as the light of the world, He lifted up the fallen, and raised up the sunken, and found the lost, and made us pure from all the filth of sin. And not only did he do these good works, but he also taught unto all who received his word, the righteousness of holiness, gentleness and tranquillity, love and peace, to despise what is transitory, and, in the hope of what is to come, to welcome the earnest of life that is eternal, and passes not away. III. With such language the saint would comfort all who came to him; and in consequence many came to him because his fame was spread abroad in many places. At that time

---

[1] ἡ πάνσοφος τοῦ θεοῦ Λόγου κατὰ σάρκα παρουσία. The outline of the saint's teaching, as given in the Armenian, is almost identical with that of the Gk. Anon.; the metaphrast garbles it, introducing more pronounced dogmatic, and omitting the moral elements, *e.g.* ζωῆς ἄρτον.... τῷ πατρὶ συνάναρχος λόγος, οὔτε τῆς θεότητος ἀποστὰς καὶ σάρκα λαβὼν ἐκ παρθένου.... καὶ ἡ φήμη πανταχοῦ τὸν ἄνδρα παρέπεμπε κηρύττοντα τὴν τριάδα.

The Gk. Anon. adds that Demetrius taught ἐν τῇ ἐκεῖσε (*i.e.* in Thessalonica) χαλκευτικῇ λεγομένῃ στοᾷ, ἔνθα καὶ εἴωθει τὰς συνόδους ποιεῖσθαι ὑπὸ τὰς τοῦ ἐγγὺς δημοσίου λουτροῦ ὑπογαίους καμάρας. Such details evince an early and close knowledge of the city.

Acts of S. Demetrius. 343

then, the officers of the Emperor went about in search of the Christians; and having taken the blessed Demetrius, they brought him before Maximianus the enemy of God, as if they had taken some great quarry. IV. Now it happened that the Emperor just then was going forth to take his seat in the arena of the city, in order to witness the gladiators, who were going to exhibit in the sight of all the common people; and the place of the arena was fitted up with scaffolding, and was itself built of cut stone, in order to contain those who came and sat therein.[1] And there was there a man by name Leos, strong of limb, and powerful as a giant.[2] V. He was the terror of all when he fought in the shows; but in his life he was reckless and murderous, and was therefore a special favourite in the eyes of Maximianus, who reckoned him among his foremost champions, because in that land there was none found like him. When therefore the Emperor entered the circus, the executioners set Demetrius before him. VI. And the Emperor, after asking him if he were a Christian, commanded that they should take him close up to the portico of the baths, where a red-hot fire was kindled; for the baths were close to the Court of Justice.[3] VII. Then he bade them

---

[1] Gk. Anon. and metaphrast say nothing of the cut stone, but the former has as follows: ἐκεῖ γὰρ αὐτῷ παρεσκεύαστο διά τινων σανίδων περιπεφραγμένος κύκλῳ ἐν ὕψει κρεμάμενος, ὁ δέχεσθαι μέλλων τοὺς ἐν αὐτῷ εἰσιόντας. The metaphrast gives similar particulars later on.

[2] The Gk. Anon. spells the name Λυαῖος, and says he was a Vandal, who in the *ludi* had slain many both in Rome and Sirmium.

[3] Here the Gk. Anon. and the metaphrast, add a miracle. As the

bring Leos into his presence, and a herald made a public proclamation, asking who was willing to engage in combat with him, and promising great rewards. Then there rose up in the middle of the court a young man, whose name was Nestor, a Christian, who had formerly gone to the blessed Demetrius, to ask him to pray for him; and he had blessed him, and prophesied: " By the name of our Lord Jesus Christ thou shalt conquer Leos, and by reason of Him art thou martyred."[1] VIII. The young man laid aside his garments, and binding round himself a single loin-cloth, he leaped into the level of the arena, full opposite Maximianus, and championed Leos to do combat with him.

But when the Emperor saw his tender age, he wondered, and called Nestor to himself, and began to give him good advice, saying: " I know, little son, that because you would fain be rich and because of your poverty, you are so eager to lose your life at the hands of Leos, a man mighty and strong of limb. But I am sorry for the comeliness of your youth, which is graced with all beauty; and therefore I give you much wealth; only give up this desire of yours to do battle with

---

saint sits confined under the portico (καμάρα) of the baths, he sees a scorpion about to sting him. He makes the sign of a cross over it, and it instantly dies. Then an angel appears and crowns the martyr with a crown, saying: " Peace to thee, athlete of Christ, be strong and of good courage."

[1] The Gk. Anon. and the metaphrast have: καὶ τὸν Λυαῖον νικήσεις, καὶ ὑπὲρ Χριστοῦ μαρτυρήσεις. The metaphrast elaborates this incident. The Anon. agrees better with the Armenian.

one who is powerful as a giant, and who conquers all; and depart rejoicing in your own fair looks."[1] IX. Then the stripling, Nestor, was in no wise deceived by the promises of the Emperor, nor in any way took his advice, nor had any fear because of the praise bestowed upon Leos. For he trusted alone in the prophecy of Demetrius, and he drew his strength from the might of Christ, and he therefore answered the Emperor thus: " I, O Emperor, am not come hither for the sake of wealth, or of the life that passes, but that I may prove myself a choicer man than Leos, and because I shall attain to the better life." And when the Emperor and all his great men of state around him heard this, they were filled with anger, and considered that the words of Nestor were mere braggadocio; so they incited Leos to fight with him, and to give him a death blow, so that he might die at once. X. And then when they met one another face to face, the stripling Nestor, made strong in spirit,[2] hurled himself at Leos, dashed him to the ground, and in a moment slew him.[3] XI. But the Emperor, seeing this, was very wroth, especially when he ascertained that Nestor

---

[1] The Gk. Anon. and metaphrast have : καὶ λαβὼν ἄπιθι μετὰ τοῦ ζῆν ἀπολαύων καὶ τῶν χρημάτων.

[2] The Gk. Anon. has : ποιήσας τὸν ζωοποιὸν σταυρὸν ἐν τῇ καρδίᾳ. The metaphrast omits.

[3] The Greek § is much longer, for a prayer is put into Nestor's mouth: "O God of Demetrius Thy servant, and Thy loved Son Jesus Christ, who didst subject Goliath the alien to the faithful David, do Thou Thyself cast down the boasting of Lyaius and of the tyrant Maximianus." The metaphrast gives a similar prayer, but does not mention Demetrius.

was also a Christian; and instead of bestowing upon him the rewards which by proclamation he had beforehand promised to any one who would fight in the arena with Leos, he ordered the youth to be beheaded as a Christian.[1] Thus the Emperor was very vexed at what had taken place, for he was sorry for the death of both;[2] and he accordingly rose from his throne with a sad countenance, resolved to go to his palace. XII. Then some evil speakers came and maligned Demetrius to him, saying that he was the origin of it all; whereat the Emperor was so incensed, that he became like a wild animal, and commanded the saint to be transfixed with a javelin, there in the very Court of Justice.[3] And thus died the saint, making a goodly confession of Christ, on the 26th day of the month of October.[4] XIII. But Maximianus the enemy of God, ordered his holy body to be thrown out to feed the wild beasts and birds; and then some brethren, who were reverent, and loved the martyrs, came in the

---

[1] In the Gk. Anon. the Emperor accuses Nestor of γοητεία. Nestor replies that an angel really wielded his sword. He is then beheaded, ἐν τοῖς δυτικοῖς τῆς πόλεως μέρεσιν ἐν τῇ ἐπονομαζομένῃ χρυσέᾳ πύλῃ, by the hand of Menutianus, a protector (προτέκτορος), and so receives the crown of martyrdom. The metaphrast gives a similar, but more elaborate, account of Nestor's death; omitting, however, the topographical details supplied by the Anon.

[2] The Gk. Anon. omits this touch, which being favourable to Maximian's character, may be genuine.

[3] The Gk. Anon. and metaph. say in the *vaults of the baths*.

[4] The Greek omits the date, but adds a § about Lupus, the saint's servant, who took τὸ ὀράριον of the saint and caught his blood in it; also dipt in the blood a royal ring, which then wrought cures. Lupus also is martyred. Similarly the metaphrast.

night and stole his body, and bore it away,¹ and buried it in a certain house in the city, there to wait for a while until the Lord should visit and reveal the relics of His saints. But after a little while great signs and acts of power began to occur unto those who called upon the holy martyr to help them ; and thus the cures which were wrought in the name of the saint came to be known far and wide. XIV. Then a certain Leontius,² a God-fearing man, who belonged to the land of Illyria, a bishop, came to Thessalonica ; and he acquired the house in which were the relics of the saint ;³ and finding it narrow

---

¹ The Gk. Anon. says they buried the body deep down under the rubbish heap on which it had been cast. The metaph. that they buried it on the very spot where the saint was executed.

² According to the Gk. Anon. and metaphrast Leontius was τις ἀνὴρ τοὺς ἐπαρχικοὺς τῶν 'Ιλλυρίων κατακοσμῶν θρόνους.

³ According to the Gk. Anon. Leontius, being miraculously cured of his disease. threw down the porticoes or vaults (καμάρας) of the furnaces (τῶν καμίνων), as also of the hot baths : and cleared away the public entrances and shops (δημοσίων ἐμβόλων καὶ προπινῶν), and raised a solemn house (πάνσεπτον οἶκον) to the martyr. It is in the metaphrast that we here find the original of the Armenian : καὶ τὸν μικρὸν οἰκίσκον ὃς τὸ ἱερὸν εἶχε τοῦ μάρτυρος σῶμα ἐπὶ βραχέος κομιδῆ καὶ στενοῦ τοῦ σχήματος ὄντα, τοῖς περιβόλοις τε τοῦ λουτροῦ καὶ τῷ σταδίῳ ἀπειλημμένον, καταστρέψας αὐτός, εἰς ναὸν αὐτῷ τῷ ἄστει Θεσσαλονίκης ἐξ αὐτῶν ἐδείματο τῶν κρηπίδων ὃς καὶ νῦν ὁρᾶται. The metaphrast in the 10th century could not have seen the original church, which was burned down in the 7th century.

The Greek forms add two §§ relating how Leontius took a garment (χλαμύδα) drenched in the saint's blood, and returned homewards to Dacia. But he could not cross the Danube because of the wintry weather. Then he had a vision of the saint, after which he mounted his chariot and drove across the Danube, dryshod, to Sirmium, where he deposited the relic in the church of Demetrius, near the shrine of Anastasia.

In the above the geography is confused, for, though Dacia was across the Danube, Sirmium was not. Vehicles can cross the Danube when it is frozen, but Leontius possessed the car of Neptune.

and confined, he threw it down, and enlarged the place, and sanctified it, and built a magnificent temple in honour of the saint's name, wherein great acts of healing were wrought, to the glory and praise of the All Holy Trinity, and of the consubstantial nature of the Father, and Son, and Holy Spirit, now and for ever and ever. Amen.

II. A history of the wonders which took place through the holy Demetrius; how that after a long time, in the days of Justinian and Maurice, emperors of the Greeks, search was made for his relics.

Let us now, dear brethren, glide over a long period of time, and relate the miracles which took place through the God-clad martyr Demetrius. In order that a little attention to a few details may give you an understanding of many ineffable works wrought by the almighty power of Christ through His saints. Now on every occasion when the saints died, the Christians, who loved the martyrs, were careful to take their bodies and inter them in a secret spot, in order that the foul smoke of the sacrifices of the heathen might not come nigh them to pollute them. And for this reason their tombs are sometimes certainly known, but sometimes not so; even though we see beautifully decorated shrines erected in their memory by certain pious people. So it is in Thessalonica, where although a great many martyrs lie hidden and although their shrines are shown, and among the rest that of the blessed Demetrius, celebrated

Acts of S. Demetrius. 349

for its miracles; yet their real tombs, and the spots consecrated by the relics of these same saints, are not anywhere to be found, with the sole exception of the holy virgin Mamrinus. But in the time of the pious emperor Maurice, by his reverent and devout wishes, search was made for many saints who had died in Thessalonica, and especially for the holy Demetrius, because of the great fame of his miracles; and a letter was written to the blessed Eusebius, who was at that time Bishop of Thessalonica, asking him to send to the Emperor some part of the relics of the blessed saint Demetrius. On which occasion Eusebius wrote the following letter in answer to the Emperor: "We know full well, O Emperor, that your request is dictated by the true faith which you have in the holy martyrs of Christ. But while informing your reverence of the faith of the Thessalonicæans, and of the miracles wrought among them, I must yet in respect of this request of yours, say that the faith of this city is not of such a kind, as that the people desire to worship God and to honour His saints by means of anything sensible. For they have received the faith from the Lord's holy testimonies, to the effect that God is a spirit, and that those who worship Him must worship Him in spirit and in truth. And for this cause there are hidden in this city all the bodies of the saints, so as to be altogether out of the ken of man. And this is what your pious father, Justinian, who was filled with the same devout zeal as yourself, found to be the case by actual trial. For he in martyr-loving mood wrote a letter to my predecessor in the bishopric of the city, such as your worship has written to us, asking for some part of the relics of the holy martyr Demetrius, which it was his pious and royal desire to enshrine. So they went and dug into the shrine of the holy martyr, and dug into the floor of the church, where they thought had been laid the remains of the saint. And the bishop entrusted such a work to God-fearing priests, of whose merits he was well assured. But when they had made the hole deep enough, and others stood round with psalms and hymns, and lighted tapers, and fragrant incense, they wanted to dig still further, when suddenly a fire issued from within and filled all the hole they had dug, and enveloped without burning them; and they heard a voice which said: 'Cease henceforth from any more tempting the power of Christ, which is united with the bones of the saints.' But they were filled with fear and trembling, and took clay from the hollow, and sent it to the Emperor, and acquainted him in writing with the wonders which had happened.

"This then, O Emperor, took place in the reign of the pious Justinian, your father. And we in the same way have sent to your devout majesty a portion of the same blessed clay, which was laid in the chest in this church with a view to the healing of the sick. This we pray your majesty also to welcome gratefully, and to receive it without misgiving; as if therein you had with you the entire martyr, as beseems your faith. And by trial of it, you will learn its wonderful properties, and will not deem us to have been disregardful of your pious majesty. Glory be to Christ for ever and ever. Amen."

ADDENDA.

Note to page 30.—In the *Neue Kirchliche Zeitschrift*, vi. Jahrgang, 10 Heft, October, 1893, Professor R. Seeberg has republished the Apology of Apollonius, using the German translation made by M. Burchardi for Prof. Harnack. His notes contain much useful matter.

Page 36, *line* 1.—Prof. Seeberg remarks that the predecessor of Perennis was named Tarruntenus, and that a reminiscence of this may underlie the Armenian reading "Terentius." It is noticeable in this connection that the metaphrast's text of the Acts of Eugenia in the same way gives the name Terentius as that of the successor of Philip the Martyr, in the eparchate of Egypt, where the Armenian and old Latin have Perennius, the Greek form of Perennis (see page 180). Tarruntenus shared with Perennis the office of Prefect until the year 183. He occupied a position so subordinate to that of Perennis, that he is not so likely as the latter to have tried Apollonius. But if he did, Apollonius must have died two years earlier than is usually supposed.

Prof. Seeberg's conjecture that Terentios is a mistake for Tarruntenus, who was prefect under Commodus, A.D. 182-3, is confirmed by an uncial Armenian Codex of the XIth. century, No. 88, of the Bibliothèque Nationale at Paris, in which the name is transliterated Tarrintinos. Apollonius must therefore have suffered at the very beginning of the reign of Commodus.

Page 40, § 13. In regard to the edict of the senate, referred to in this section, and again in § 23, it is to be noticed that in the Acts of Codratius (page 198) there is a similar reference to " the edict of the Emperors and of the Great Senate, that not a single one of the Christians shall live." On § 23 of the Acts of Apollonius, Harnack and Seeberg, compare Tertull., Apol. 4: "definitis dicendo: *non licet esse nos*, et hoc sine ullo retractu humaniore praescribitis."

Page 41, § 18. Prof. Seeberg explains the references in this § from Pausanias 1, 24, 2: Κεῖνται δὲ ἐξῆς ἄλλαι τε εἰκόνες καὶ 'Ηρακλέους. . . . 'Αθηνᾶ τε ἐστιν ἀνιοῦσα ἐκ τῆς κεφαλῆς τοῦ Διός. ἔστι δὲ καὶ ταῦρος ἀνάθημα τῆς βουλῆς τῆς ἐν 'Αρείῳ πάγῳ ἐφ' ὅτῳ δὲ ἀνέθηκεν ἡ βουλή, πολλὰ ἄν τις ἐθέλων εἰκάζοι.

Page 76. In addition to other references explicatory of the nature of Alexander's crown, I owe the following to Mr. Rushforth, viz. Suetonius Vita Domitiani, ch. 4: "Instituit et quinquennale certamen capitolino Iovi triplex, musicum equestre gymnicum, et aliquanto plurium quam nunc coronarum. . . . Certamini praesedit crepidatus purpureaque amictus toga Graecanica, capite gestans coronam auream cum effigie Iovis ac Iunonis Minervaeque; adsidentibus Diali sacerdote et collegio Flavialium pari habitu, nisi quod *illorum coronis inerat et ipsius imago.* Therefore the priests of the worship of the reigning Caesar had his imago or medallion fastened in their wreaths. The offence committed by Thekla becomes quite clear, and the severity of the sentence passed upon her intelligible. It can hardly be denied that the Armenian and Syriac texts in preserving this detail about Alexander's wreath, which the other texts omit, have kept a proof, no less convincing than those which Prof. Ramsay has discovered, of the authenticity of these Acts of Thekla. The more closely they are examined, the more clearly does their value as a contemporary record reveal itself.

Page 146. That the memorial feast of S. Polyeuctes was kept on Dec. 25 is good proof that this homily was delivered before A.D. 400; for after that date Dec. 25 was reserved to the newly instituted festival of the birth of Jesus Christ.

INDEX OF NAMES AND SUBJECTS.

N.B.—Italics signify that the reference is to the introductions; *n.* =notes at foot of page.

Abgar, notary, *217, 219*, 231.
— King of Edessa, *241*.
Acombiti or Accubiti, 290.
Acts of Saints, the Dialogue in, often genuine, *6, 276*; read publicly at their Festivals, 103, *123*; in early times addressed to special Churches, *97*, 103; continually re-edited, 151.
Adam, hour of his leaving the garden, 309.
Africanus, 101, 105 foll.
Aigai, *240* foll., 243.
Alexander, 76 foll.
— Martyr at Aigai, 246.
Allard, P., *155*.
Alexandria, Church in, *149*; Monasteries near, *153*.
Anastasia, M., in Aigai, 254.
Anazarb, *241, 242*, 243.
Angels, Good, 313.
Anicetus Prefect, (or Nicetius), 186.
Apamea, 208.
Apollonius of Tyana, *52*.
— M., his creed, *14*, 46; his Stoicism, *29*; form of his trial, *33*; on Sacrifices, 39; his Acts compared with those of Phocas, 99.
Apparitions of Jesus as Paul, 72, 73 and *n.*; to Polyeuctes, 133, 136, 140, 142, 144; to Hiztibouzit, 268.
Aquilius Consul, *152*, 158.
Ararat, 262.
Arians, Land of, 266.
Aristotle, 108.
Armenian Martyrology, *2*; age of the Arm. texts, *3, 59, 89, 97, 102, 124, 147, 156, 242, 339, 350*.

Armenia, Christianity in, *257* foll., 261 foll.
Arrian, *258*.
Artemis, worship of, in Asia Minor, 228; in Rome, 186, 295.
Asterius, M., at Aigai, 245.
Astrology, condemned, 330.
Athenians, worship ox-head, 41 and *n.*
Atropatacan in Persia, 267.
Aubé, B., his edition of Greek Acts of Polyeuctes, *123* foll.
Augustine, Saint, half a heathen, *11*.
Avitus, his Poems, *148*.
Avitus Consul, son of Philip M., *150*, 157.

Babelon, Ernest, *241*.
Babylas, M., of Antioch, his date, *151*.
Baptism provided escape from Hellfire, *17*; of Thekla, *57*, 82, 86; Thekla demands it of Paul, 75; a fulfilment of the law, *101*, 118; not essential to salvation, *125*, 136 foll.; of companions of Callistratus, 334.
Baresma, *259*, 263.
Baronius, Annals of, *2*.
Basil the Great. Homily on the 40 Martyrs, *273*.
Basil of Seleukia, *53*.
Basilia or Basilla, M., 181 foll.
Becosianus or Berekkokius, 244.
Beliefs, Early, about Paradise, 115, *191, 192*, 311 foll.
Bemarchus, M., 301.
Bernard, S., his miracles, *7*.
Bezæ, Codex, 138 *n.*

355

Bithynian Persecution under Trajan, *90* foll., 105, 111.
Bollandist Acts, *3*; reject Acts of Thekla, *89*.
Bread, Salt, and Water, 75 (*see* Eucharist).
Burchardi's German version of Acts of Apollonius, *see* Addenda.
Burning alive of Thekla, *56*, 73; of Phocas, 120.
Byæus on S. Demetrius, *339*.

Cæsar's genius, to be sworn by, *95*.
Cæsar-shaped crown worn by presidents of Cæsar worship, 76 and *n.*, *see* Addenda.
Cæsareia on the Hellespont, *191*, 209.
Callistratus, *273* foll.; his Church in Rome, 336.
Cananeots, *124*, 145.
Carthage, *276*.
Castelius, pro-consul, *52*.
Catacombs, Roman, *148*.
Catholic Church, the phrase not in Polycarp's Acts, *4*.
Caucasus, ancient gods exiled thither, *12*.
Chalcedon, the Cohort, 289, 290.
Χαλανδῶν, 290.
Chosrow, son of Kavat, *257*, 261, 266.
Choyap, a Persian, 266.
Christian, the name penal, 43 and *n*.
Christians and Ancient Art, *10*; their iconoclasm, *13*, 141, 227; attitude towards sacrifices, 39; hunted down under Trajan, *102*, 105; in Persia, *257* foll., 261; true reasons why they were persecuted, *283* foll.
Chrysostom, Pseudo-, on Thekla, *57*, *60 n*.
Chrysostomus Dio, *258*.
Claudius' Speech on Gallia Comata, *6*; kinsman of Tryphæna, *51*.
Clodia, *157* foll.
Codratius or Quadratus, *191* foll.
Commodus, 37 foll., *149*.
Communism of Early Christians, *285*.
Conscripts, Law of, 290 *n*.
Conybeare and Howson on Thekla, *49*, *50*.

Coptos or Cana in Egypt, *124*.
Corneille's Polyeucte, *125*.
Cornelius, bp. of Rome, 151.
Cornutus and Philo, *9*.
Creed, Early forms of, *14*, 33, 46, *99*, *154*, *337*, 342.
Crossing, Practice of, 119, 344 *n*.
Crucified God, 108, 119.
Crucifixion, Triple, its significance, *258*; its details imitated in Martyrdoms, *258*.
Ctesias, *258*.
Cyprian, 182, 274.
Cyrus, *258*.

Dancing among Early Christians, 129.
Daphne, Grove of, *52*, *53*.
Decius, and Valerian, their edict against Christians, 131, 193.
Demas, 61 foll.
Demetrius, S., his creed, *14*, *337*, 342.
Demons of air, fight for a dead man's soul, 313.
Demosthenes, 110.
Denesius' executioner, 243.
Depositio Martyrum, *155*.
Descensus Averni, Gospel of, 310.
Devil, The, 326, 327.
Dio Chrysostomus, *258*.
Diocletian, 289, *338*.
Domitian, Name Christian became punishable under, 7.
Dove-worship and Holy Ghost, 42 *n*.
Ducenarius, Vir, 333 *n*.
Dwin or Twin, 259.

Earthquakes in Martyrdoms, *96*, 112.
Edessa, *240* foll., 243.
Egypt, Prefects of, *152*; early monasteries in, *153*.
Egyptian Superstition, 42 and *n*.
Elias, 320
Elvira, Synod of, *13*.
Eucharist, Primitive form of, with bread and water and salt, 75 and *n.*, *274*.
Eugenia imitated Thekla, *4*, *59*, *147*, *154*, 161, 176.
Eukhaita, *217*, 222.
Eunuchs as Priests, *155*; as Martyrs, 160.

Index of Names and Subjects. 357

Eunuchism inculcated in Gospel, *24*; by Philo, *24 n.*; by Justin M., *24 n.*
Eusebius, Hist. Eccl., *4*; on Apollonius M., *29*; on Firmilianus M., 311.
— bp. of Thessalonica, 337 foll.
Eutropius, 166.

Faith alone needful to Salvation, 137.
Falconilla, name late, *53, 55*.
Father, Son, and Holy Spirit, formula used, 48, 244, 262.
Felix, Minucius, on Hell, *16*; on Sacrifices, 38 *n.*; his teaching compared with Apollonius, 44 *n.*
— father-in-law of Polyeuctes, 141.
Fire-worship, *259*, 261 foll.

Galatarch, *53*.
Galatia, the Province, *98*.
Galilean, the (*i.e.* Jesus), 244.
Galileans, 291.
Gallienus, Emperor, *150*.
Gallus, Emperor, *150*, 181.
Gladiatorial Games, *337*, 343 foll.
Görres, Dr. Franz, *148*.
Gospel, in what sense anti-social, *19, 283* foll.
Gospels, Apocryphal, 138 and *n.*; early, *155*, 169, *278*, 306, 309, 312; their diffusion in early times, *274, 275*.
Greeks, the ancient, their humanity, *280*.
Greek Art and Early Christianity, *10.* (*See* Iconoclasm.)
Gregory of Tours, *124*.
Guardian Newspaper, *30 n.*

Hadrian, *239* foll., 253; temple of, in Aigai, 243, 253, 255.
Hardy, G. E., *102*.
Harnack, Professor A., *30 n.*, *32*, 75 *n.*
Helenus, bp. of Heliopolis, *152*, 161 foll.
Heliopolis, *152*, 161.
Hell, the Spoiling of, 310.
Hell-fire, Belief in, pre-Christian, *15*; how made use of by Christians, *17*.
Heracleia in Cappadocia, *219*, 225.
Hermogenes, 61 foll.

Hieronymus quoted, *31*.
Hindoos, *13*.
Hippolytus, Com. on Daniel, on Millenarism in Pontus and Syria, *21, 22*; Philosophumena, 155.
Hiztibouzit M., *260*, 265 foll.
Holy Ghost compared to dove in Philo, 42 *n.*
Homer quoted, 196.
Horoscopes, 201, 323.
Human Sacrifice, *258*, 270.
Hyacinthus, *148*, 159 foll.

Iconium, *52*.
Iconoclasm of Early Christians, *13*, 141, 227.
Idols, 41, 114, 159, 200, 226 foll.
Ignatius, his epp. compared with Acts of Phocas, *100*.
Incarnation, a divine ruse, 306 foll.
India, Paganism of Modern, *13*.
Indictions, 146 and *n.*
Indus and Domna, *374*.
Iras or Zareas, a wizard, 163.

Jesus of Nazareth, addressed his teaching to Monotheists only, *7*; represented as a youth, 144; a human sacrifice, *258*.
Jews, Christian spite against, *257*, 270; why not persecuted like the Christians, *286*.
John, the bp., 244.
Josephus on Oaths, 37 *n.*
Justin Martyr, his imperfect monotheism, *9, 11*; on oaths, 37 *n.*; on *name* Christian, 43 *n.*
Justinian orders a search for the relics of S. Demetrius, 349.

Lapsed, Treatment of the, 203.
Latin Acts translated into Greek, *276*, 293.
Latin Version of Acts of Thekla, *59*.
Latin Version of Acts of Eugenia, *156*, 159 foll.
Latina, Via, 188.
Law fulfilled in Baptism, The, *101*, 118.
Lectra, The Name, *53*, *56*.
Leontios, a bishop of Illyria, 347.
Licinius, *217*, 224 foll.
Lightfoot on Bithynian Persecution, 90 foll., *258*.

358 Index of Names and Subjects.

Lioness defends Thekla, 81.
Lipsius, his text of Acts of Thekla criticised, 59.
Lucretius on Hell, 15.
Lyæos or Läus or Leos, a gladiator, 337 foll.
Lystra, 62.

Macarius M., in Aigai, 254.
Magism, 259, 261 foll.
Mahommedans, 13.
Manou, king of Edessa, 241.
Makhosh, M., 261 foll. (see Hiztibouzit).
Mamrinos M., of Thessalonica, 349.
Marcia, 155.
Marriage, repudiated by Jesus, 23; by early Christians, 283; by Paul, 24; in Peter's Acts, 26; Platonic among early Christians, 25.
Martyrs upheld right of private judgment, 1; deprived of their goods, 44, and n., 112; relics of, venerated, 145, 178, 236, 271; nature of tortures inflicted on, 279 foll.; meaning of word, 281.
Martyrdoms, re-edited in each age, 151.
Maxentius, 227.
Maximianus, 341 foll.
Maximus, Consul, 182.
Mary, Virgin, 14, 305 foll.
Maurice, the Emperor, asks for relics of S. Demetrius, 338, 348.
Mehekan, the mouth, 262.
Melani or Melanthia, 171 foll.
Melitene, 145.
Metaphrast, see Simeon.
Military Service refused by Christians, 285.
Millenarism of Gospel, 19 foll., 286; and marriage, 23, 58, 287.
Mills, Dr., 260.
Miracles in Acts often interpolated, 4; how to be regarded in N.T., 5; of St. Bernard, 5.
Miracles of Healing of the Blind (Matt. ix. 28), 139.
Mommsen on Bithynia, 94; on Cohors Chalcedon, 290 n.
Monasteries in Egypt, 153, 162, 168 foll.
Monotheism of Jews, 41 n.; no offence in Roman Empire, 283.

Monotheistic Propaganda of Paul and Philo, 8.
Montanism, 58.
Myra or Merou, 54.
Mysteries, Ancient, Relation of Christianity to, 17.
Myths, Pagan, related of Christian Saints, 18, 297.

Nakhapet, a Persian governor, 265.
Narcissus M. at Aigai, 254.
Nati called Drowandacan, 266.
Nearchus, 129 foll.
Nebuchadnezzar, 117.
Neocorus, 274 (or Ocorus), 290, 315, 316.
Nerses M., 264; a Rajik, 267.
Nestor, bp. of Rome, 150, 182.
Nestorius of Thessalonica, 337 foll.
Nicæus, 201.
Nicomedeia, 193, 218, 224.
Nihilism of early Christians, 284 foll.
Nikhorakan, a Persian governor, 264.
Numerianus, Emperor, 151, 239, 243.

Oaths forbidden, 37 and n., 285.
Oceanus, name of a Columbethra in Rome, 333.
Onesiphorus and Paul, 61.
Oral tradition, 274, 290, 315 (see Neocorus).
Origen on Seven Heavens, 311 n.
Orthodoxy, Standard of, fluctuated in early Church, 3, 14 (see Creed).

Pancrazio, S., 11.
Parable of Vineyard and Labourers, 137.
Paradise, 192, 311 foll.
Paton, W. R., 258.
Paul, addressed his teaching to Polytheists, 8, 9; inculcates virginity, 25, 58, 34, 67; believed in approaching end of world, 58; his personal appearance, 62; his beatitudes, 63; on marriage, 63; on baptism, 63; accused of wizardry, 52, 68; his defence, 69; appears to Thekla as Jesus, 72, 73 n.; his creed, 99; his epistles, early diffusion of, 275.

Index of Names and Subjects. 359

Paulina, 143.
Perennis, prefect, 155, 35 n., 30; (or Perinos eparch of Egypt, 179); (or Perinius consul in Bithynia, 192, 201.
Peroz, a Magus, 266.
Perpetua, S., 128.
Persian Fire-worship, 259, 262 foll.
Peter's First Ep., 97.
Phædo of Plato, 278.
Philadus M. in Aigai, 254.
Philip eparch of Egypt, 149.
Philosophers and Christianity, 45, 106, 108, 202, 279.
Philo as missionary of Monotheism, 8, 9; his Therapeutæ, 20, 76 n. 153; on oaths, 38 n.; compares Holy Spirit to a dove, 42 n.
Phocas, 89 foll.; his prayer, 99; his creed, 99, 110; his Acts addressed to certain Churches, 96 foll., 103.
Pilate, Acts of, 138 n.
Pliny 38 n., 90 foll.; his letter to Trajan unknown to author of Acts of Phocas, 93 foll., 281.
Plutarch on Hell, 15; on crucifixion of Masabates, 258.
Polyeuctes, Acts of, their heterodox tendency, 125, 137 foll.
Polycarp, Acts of, and phrase Catholic Church, 4; resemblance of, with Acts of Apollonius, 33; with Acts of Phocas, 95 foll., 258.
Polytheism and Paul, 8.
Pompeianus (or Pompeius) Consul, 150, 184.
Pontus-Bithynia, 98.
Poseidon, 118, 212.
Prayers for dead, 314.
Prefects of Egypt, 152.
Private Judgment, right to, upheld by martyrs, 1; attitude to it of later Church, 279.
Presentinus, a captain, 292 foll.
Prophecies of Jesus, 47.
Protus M., 148, 160.
Prousa, port of Cæsareia, 191.
Psalms, use of, 159, 265.
ψυχαγωγοί, Angels, 313.
Purgatory, 314 foll.

Ragozin, Zenaide A., 259.

Ramsay, W. M., 50 foll., 98, 191, 240, 242; on position of Eukhaita, 219.
Rajik, 267, see Nerses.
Rêi, a district of Persia, 266.
Relics of Martyrs venerated, 145, 178, 211, 233, 236, 271, 336, 338, 347, 349.
Resurrection of the body, 315.
Rhyndacus, river, 213.
Roads in Asia Minor, 50, 51, see Ramsay.
Roman Empire, stimulated growth of Monotheistic belief, 17.
Rome, "the great city of," 35 n., 157.
Romeliana or Rombyliana, 244.
Rufus, M., 210.
Rushforth, G. McN., 76 n., see Addenda.

Sacraments not essential to Salvation, 136 foll.
Sacrifice, human, 258, 270.
Sakæa, Persian festival, 258.
Satan bound by Jesus, 310.
Saturninus M., 210.
Seal of Christ = baptism, 75, 118.
Seeberg's edition of Acts of Apollonius, see Addenda.
Seleukia, 88.
Senate, Roman, Acts of, 7; Apollonius tried before it, 36; its decree against Christians, 40, 43 and Addenda.
Sergius, 150, 157.
Seven heavens, 311 foll.
Severus, baths of, in Rome, 187.
Simeon, Metaphrast, 147, 217, 273, 339, 340.
Sinope, 101.
Socrates ridicules Athenian religion, 42; compared to Jesus, 47; death of, 278.
Son, relation of, to God the Father suggested by Roman institutions, 18.
Syrlarch, 53, 55, 76 n.

Tacitus, 6.
Talmud, 42 n.
Tanebus, 239, 254.
Temple, Village of the, on the Rhyndacus, 213.
Terentius or Perennis, 35, 180 and Addenda.

Tertullian on Thekla, *4*, *154*.
Testaments of XII. Patriarchs, 310, 311.
Thalelæus, 239 foll.
Thamyris, 64 foll.
Thekla, her Acts, a divine book, *59*, *154*, 159 ; bas relief of her and Paul at Edschmiadzin, *60* ; her rank as an Apostle, *60 n.* ; her Acts, 61 foll.; asks Paul for baptism, 75 ; her modesty, 81 ; baptises herself, 82, 86 ; visits Seleukia, 88 ; dresses as a man, 86 ; her Acts rejected by Bollandists, *89* ; referred to, 128, *154*, 158, 176; her Acts imitated, 168 ; her folly, *284*.
Theodore M., *258*, 216 foll. ; the Tiro, date of his festival, 221.
Theodorus, Hegemon in Aigai, 243.
Theodula M. in Aigai, 254.
Θεοσεβής, *53*.
Thessalonica, Theatre at, 343; the brazen Stoa, 342 *n.* ; the baths, 347 *n.* ; the golden gate, 346 *n.* ; shrine of its saints, 348.
Thief, penitent, 138 and *n.*
Tiberianus or Tiberius, Roman judge in Edessa, *241*, 244.
Tiberian (or Severian) baths in Rome, 187.
Tillemont, *337*.
Timotheus, a Cananeot, 146.
Tiranas, a Church in Alexandria, 180.
Titus and Onesiphorus, 61, 62.
Tombs of Martyrs, lost in the sixth century, 348 foll.
Torture of Martyrs, *280* foll., *294*, *295*.

Tradition, Oral Christian, its transmission, *274*, 291.
Trajan, conflicting views of his attitude towards Christianity, *90* foll. ; his edict that Christians were not to be hunted out, *102*, 105 ; worshipped, 105 ; tries and condemns Phocas, 113 foll. ; his death, 120.
Transubstantiation, origin of belief in, *10*, *11*.
Trebizond, Dia, Apollo and Artemis worshipped there, *12*.
Trinity, a late dogma, *14*, 64 and *n.*, *277*, 302 foll. ; the formula used, 255.
Tryphæna, *50*, *53*, *55*, 77 foll.
Twin or Dwin, in Armenia, *259*.

Urbicus, wizard at Aigai, 249.

Venantius, Fortunatus, *148*.
Vergil on Hell, *15*.
Vicarius Africæ, *150*.
Virgin Mary, *14*, 305 foll., *337*.
Virginity, 25, *see* Paul, 58, 64, 67.

Wizards, 72, 209, 249, 252, 298.
Word of God, made universe, held by Phocas, 109; by Demetrius, 342.
World, approaching end of, belief in. *18* foll., *see* Millenarism.
— Renunciation of, *18* foll., *see* Gospel.
Wright, Prof., his translation of Syriac Acts of Thekla, *59*.

Zacharias, 180.
Zenonia, 61.

www.ingramcontent.com/pod-product-compliance
Lightning Source LLC
Chambersburg PA
CBHW020317240426
43673CB00039B/840